Musical Performance

A Guide to Understanding

This accessible guide for students, teachers and performers at all levels unravels the complexities of musical performance and focuses on key aspects of learning, playing and responding to music. A survey of performance through the ages leads to a presentation of basic historical, analytical and psychological concepts. Four chapters follow on teaching, development, practice and memorisation. The next section considers the 'translation' from score to sound, physical projection, ensemble playing and performance anxiety. The final section addresses the act of listening, the legacy of recordings, music criticism and 'performers on performance'.

John Rink is Professor of Music at Royal Holloway, University of London. His books include *The Practice of Performance: Studies in Musical Interpretation, Chopin: The Piano Concertos* and an annotated catalogue of Chopin's first editions (with Christophe Grabowski). He is one of three Series Editors of *The Complete Chopin – A New Critical Edition,* and he performs regularly as a pianist and lecture-recitalist.

Musical Performance

A Guide to Understanding

EDITED BY

John Rink

Royal Holloway,
University of London

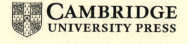

CAMBRIDGE
UNIVERSITY PRESS

PUBLISHED BY THE PRESS SYNDICATE OF THE UNIVERSITY OF CAMBRIDGE
The Pitt Building, Trumpington Street, Cambridge, United Kingdom

CAMBRIDGE UNIVERSITY PRESS
The Edinburgh Building, Cambridge CB2 2RU, UK
40 West 20th Street, New York, NY 10011-4211, USA
477 Williamstown Road, Port Melbourne, VIC 3207, Australia
Ruiz de Alarcón 13, 28014 Madrid, Spain
Dock House, The Waterfront, Cape Town 8001, South Africa

http://www.cambridge.org

First published 2002
Fourth printing 2004

Printed in the United Kingdom at the University Press, Cambridge

Typeface Minion 10.5/14 pt   *System* LATEX 2_ε [TB]

A catalogue record for this book is available from the British Library

ISBN 0 521 78300 3 hardback
ISBN 0 521 78862 5 paperback

Contents

Contributors

Eric Clarke is Professor of Music at the University of Sheffield and has published widely on the psychology of performance, the perception and production of rhythm, and musical meaning and the relationship between language and music. He is co-editor (with Nicholas Cook) of *Empirical Musicology: Aims, Methods, Prospects* and has been active as an improviser in the Lapis String Quartet.

Jane Davidson is Reader in Music at the University of Sheffield. She has published on musical expression, gesture, music practice and the determinants of musical excellence; is co-editor of *The Music Practitioner*; and has edited the journal *Psychology of Music*. She performs regularly as a vocal soloist, has directed and devised music theatre pieces, and has choreographed dance works and operas.

Jonathan Dunsby is Professor of Music at the University of Reading. He has written extensively on music of the last two centuries, and his books include *Performing Music: Shared Concerns*, *Structural Ambiguity in Brahms*, *Schoenberg: Pierrot Lunaire* and (with Arnold Whittall) *Music Analysis in Theory and Practice*. He studied piano with Fanny Waterman, won prizes in various international competitions and has accompanied many distinguished artists.

Elaine Goodman is Lecturer in Music at the University of Hull. She is an accomplished cellist and pianist and performs widely in chamber ensembles and orchestras. Her doctoral dissertation at Royal Holloway, University of London was on ensemble rehearsal and performance, and her research interests include the psychology of performance, music analysis, music education and popular music studies.

Peter Hill is Professor of Music at the University of Sheffield. His publications include *The Messiaen Companion* and a book on Stravinsky's *The Rite of Spring*. As a pianist he has made over 100 programmes for the BBC and has recorded an award-winning Messiaen cycle. Recent CD releases

include a recital of Stravinsky and the complete solo piano works of
Schoenberg, Berg and Webern.

Peter Johnson studied in Cambridge and Oxford and has published on
Webern as well as various aspects of performance studies. His recent
research interests range from the philosophy of performance to its acoustic
analysis, and he has worked extensively as a conductor and a keyboard
player. He is Head of Postgraduate Studies and Director of Research at
Birmingham Conservatoire.

Colin Lawson has an international profile as a period clarinettist,
performing with such orchestras as The Hanover Band, the English
Concert and the Orchestra of the Age of Enlightenment. His recordings
include solo discs for numerous labels, and he has published extensively
with Cambridge University Press, including many edited volumes and
handbooks. He is Pro Vice-Chancellor and Dean of the Faculty of Music,
Media and Creative Technologies at Thames Valley University.

Raymond Monelle has written music criticism for thirty years, his reviews
appearing in *The Independent, The Scotsman, Scotland on Sunday, Opera* and
several other publications. He was formerly a composer, pianist and conductor. His work on music theory and semiotics is internationally known,
and his books include *The Sense of Music.* (Princeton University Press,
2000).

Stefan Reid teaches music at The Forest School in London. He studied at
the University of Oxford, Surrey University and Royal Holloway,
University of London, where his doctoral research was on the art of good
practice. He performs regularly as a pianist and has established a
distinguished reputation as a choral and orchestral conductor.

John Rink is Professor of Music at Royal Holloway, University of London.
His books include *The Practice of Performance: Studies in Musical
Interpretation, Chopin: The Piano Concertos* and (with Jim Samson)
Chopin Studies 2. He is one of three Series Editors of *The Complete Chopin
– A New Critical Edition* and is co-author of an annotated catalogue of
Chopin's first editions with Christophe Grabowski. He performs regularly
as a pianist and lecture-recitalist.

Janet Ritterman has been Director of the Royal College of Music since
1993 and was appointed DBE in 2002. She has worked professionally as a
pianist and an accompanist, and has specialised in the education and
training of gifted performers. Her research interests include the
development of the conservatoire, instrumental pedagogy and historical

performance practice. She has published on nineteenth-century composers and has spoken at many national and international conferences.

Elizabeth Valentine is Reader in Psychology and Director of the Psychology of Music Research Group at Royal Holloway, University of London. Her research interests include the psychology of musical practice and performance, and she has published on such topics as the effect of singing on mood and background music as an aid to autobiographical recall in dementia. She is an amateur keyboard and woodwind player.

Peter Walls is Professor of Music at Victoria University of Wellington in New Zealand. He has published widely on performance practice, and his *Music in the English Courtly Masque 1604–1640* received an 'Outstanding Academic Book' award from *Choice* and the British Academy's Derek Allen Prize. He has performed professionally as a baroque violinist and is an orchestral and operatic conductor.

Aaron Williamon is a research fellow and Head of the Centre for the Study of Music Performance at the Royal College of Music. His doctoral research at Royal Holloway, University of London studied how skilled musicians learn, rehearse and recall information when practising and performing, and he received the SRPMME's Hickman Prize for his work on the evaluation of memorised performances. Other research interests include performance anxiety and techniques of collaboration in learning and rehearsing music.

Preface

Musical performance is a fundamental part of human existence, yet even the most experienced performer, teacher or scholar can fail to appreciate what lies behind it. It is well known that a performance in public usually represents untold hours – indeed many years – of learning and preparation, but how interpretations are put together, on what basis and with what effect may be less widely understood. What makes some performances come across as 'musical'? Should one try to honour the composer's intentions, and if so how can they be ascertained? What is the relation between the score, the musical work and the performances that they give rise to? How can practice sessions and rehearsals be made more effective, and how might performance anxiety best be overcome? Questions like these are often in the back of the performer's mind, not to mention the minds of their teachers, but until now it has been difficult to find compelling answers. For too long musicians have had to resort to tradition and intuition for the solutions, and important as those undeniably are, they are not always enough. The burgeoning academic literature on performance from recent years has offered little in the way of practical assistance: targeted at a highly specialised readership and generally written in somewhat impenetrable language, it has tended to neglect the concerns of performers themselves despite the need for clear and engaging writing on such topics as practice, memorisation, stage fright, analysing music for performance and the modern performer's historical 'responsibilities'. The fact that more and more universities and conservatoires now offer courses encouraging the interaction of theory and practice, rather than their traditional separation, and that professional performers increasingly present themselves as both 'doers' and 'talkers' (Joseph Kerman's terms) makes the lack of appropriate material all the more regrettable.

The sixteen essays in this volume are intended to unravel the complexities of performance and to bring to light aspects of learning, playing and responding to music relevant to performances at all levels. Broad in aim and accessible in tone, the book is intended for music teachers, students and scholars, as well as music lovers, who are keen to know more about what musical performance entails and who are not content to rely on tradition and intuition alone. It has four parts, corresponding to the stages through which a performance itself evolves: conceptions and preconceptions, learning to perform, making music and interpreting performance. Each part has four chapters, the first of which sets the compass points for the remaining three. Part I begins with a survey of performance through the ages, and this leads to a presentation of fundamental historical, analytical and psychological concepts. The next four chapters address the history of performance teaching, developing the ability to perform, practice and memorisation. Part III considers how music is made from the score, as well as issues related to physical projection, ensemble playing and performance anxiety. The final part investigates the act of listening, the legacy of recordings, music criticism and how performers themselves regard performance.

Each of the authors in this volume is a leading expert in the field, and many are performers of considerable experience and renown. Both of these factors ensure that the writing is vital and cogent, as well as challenging in the best possible ways. The book is intended to appeal widely not only by shunning unnecessary jargon and complexity, but by deliberately avoiding a concentration on one and only one instrument or performance genre. Instead, new light is shed on the principles and procedures underlying performances and the study of performances at least within the Western classical tradition, which is the predominant focus, although other musics and repertoires are addressed along the way (including jazz and rock).

There are a number of common threads running throughout the volume. First and foremost is an emphasis on the *experience* of music through performance, which transforms the score (if there is a score) into a unique musical event, all the while recognising that the score is not 'the music' and that one could never achieve total fidelity to it even if one wished to. (The book also stresses that recordings are not 'how the work goes', despite their potential to reveal a great deal about historical performance practices and of course individual readings.) A distinction thus arises in several chapters between learning 'the notes' and learning 'the music' in developing a view of the work, which, it is argued, is a vital first step – that is, building a sense of the whole. Several authors address the role of analysis in performing or learning to perform, as well as in memorising and in fighting performance anxiety. Various analytical techniques are demonstrated and the role of intuition versus deeper awareness debated. Equally, the modern performer's response to historical precedent is considered early on in the book, in particular the risks associated with 'historically *un*informed' performance.

The nature of practice – a usually solitary act in stark opposition to the highly social experience of performing – is another common theme, attracting discussion of the relation between mental images and physical representations, repetition versus inspiration, problem-solving, and 'forgetting' what one has learned as the music becomes more ingrained, to be recalled 'automatically' in the heat of performance. The way in which music is memorised concerns several authors, who offer practical advice to teachers and performers alike. Moving beyond the preparation stage, comment is offered on the manifold social factors surrounding performances in terms of the relations between performers and audiences and between members of an ensemble, as well as issues of presentation, the role of the body in performing, and the similarities (and differences) between musical performance and acting. Such remarks are addressed to a wide range of performers, including singers (for example, in chapters 9, 11 and 14), pianists (chapters 2, 3, 7 and 9), string players (chapters 8 and 14) and wind players (chapter 14). The tension between trying to find an historically 'right' instrument in order to play certain repertoire, versus the desire of some performers to 'transcribe' music for modern instruments, is confronted head-on in a number of chapters, as is the distinction between listeners' perceptions and the 'facts' about performances as revealed through empirically derived data. This is part of a larger debate about what and how listeners hear, and about the ways in which critics and performers themselves have responded to performance in writing – an act which for some has been as compelling as the need to perform is for many performers.

As these remarks suggest, practical advice is offered in abundance, and the 'Further reading' sections at the end of each chapter present a compact bibliography for those wishing to study particular topics in greater depth. It is keenly hoped that the volume will inspire readers to further investigation about performance, whether by perusing other general literature on performance studies (for instance, my book *The Practice of Performance: Studies in Musical Interpretation*, Jonathan Dunsby's *Performing Music: Shared Concerns*, or Colin Lawson and Robin Stowell's *The Historical Performance of Music: An Introduction*) or by delving into more specialist publications. If indeed appetites to know more about performance are whetted as a result of reading this book, and if answers to at least some of the questions posed above have been provided, then *Musical Performance* will surely have fulfilled its purpose.

I should like to thank Sarah Smith for compiling the index and Lucy Carolan for her careful copy-editing; Ruth Milsom and Mark Wells for preparing the illustrations in chapters 9 and 12; my graduate students at Royal Holloway, University of London for spirited feedback on the manuscript; and Penny Souster for her customary patience and sage advice.

JOHN RINK

PART ONE

Conceptions and preconceptions

1   Performing through history

COLIN LAWSON

Performance in context

At most classical concerts today we expect the audience to remain silent in rapt attention, but this is a quite recent social phenomenon, far removed from music-making of any kind before the beginning of the twentieth century. At the premiere of his 'Paris' Symphony in July 1778, Mozart was delighted by a respectful audience which nevertheless responded actively rather than passively:[1]

Just in the middle of the first Allegro there was a passage which I felt sure must please. The audience were quite carried away – and there was a tremendous burst of applause . . . Having observed that all last as well as first Allegros begin here with all the instruments playing together and generally unisono, I began mine with two violins only, piano for the first eight bars – followed instantly by a forte; the audience, as I expected, said 'hush' at the soft beginning, and when they heard the forte, began at once to clap their hands.[2]

More than a century later, a painting now in the archives of the Royal Opera House, Covent Garden shows the inaugural concert of London's Queen's Hall in 1893; conductor and orchestra are in full flight, yet conversation is also flowing freely in the front rows of the audience.[3] Less controlled was the celebrated riotous premiere of Stravinsky's *Rite of Spring* in Paris in 1913, one of the last documented instances of active audience response within the Western concert tradition.

A freely responding audience is nowadays more characteristic of a pop concert, where performers display their own carefully cultivated set of behaviours. In ritual situations where there is no reason to write down the music, there is less distinction between composing, rehearsing and performing; listeners and bystanders may well contribute. While the notated score acts as a memory and enables dissemination of musical works, it also invites a more distant relationship between composer and performer. Well into the nineteenth century it was taken for granted that performers would have the ability to improvise, and indeed they often did so. Scores were

routinely adapted as occasion demanded, and it was quite usual for specially composed arias to be inserted in operas to suit the singers at hand.
In the early twentieth century there was no reason for Stokowski, Elgar and
others to feel embarrassed about making orchestral transcriptions of Bach's
keyboard music. Even when a composer's original notation was on the music
stand, performers often took a liberated, creative approach. Brahms's violinist friend Joseph Joachim was described as unpredictable by a member of
his quartet: 'To play with him is damned difficult. Always different tempi,
different accents.'[4] Today's overwhelming authority of the score, demanding fidelity and accuracy at all costs, is not at all characteristic of the history
of performance as a whole. Yet musical literature often gives the impression
that true aesthetic meaning resides in the notation and that performance
is at best an imperfect and approximate representation of the work itself.
It is reported that Brahms once refused an invitation to a performance of
Mozart's *Don Giovanni* on the grounds that he would sooner stay at home
and read it, a response which would surely have horrified the supremely
practical Mozart.

A world perspective

The study of world musics calls into question most of the basic
assumptions held by Western performers, thus providing a useful sense of
context. In many cultures the artificial division between performer and audience has never existed; as the player or singer improvises, the audience responds, whether by toe-tapping, finger drumming, hand-clapping, singing
or dancing. Musicians are as likely to be found in streets, markets, fairs or tav-
erns as in more formal surroundings, since music has remained intimately
associated with such ritual events as weddings, funerals or the agricultural
calendar, dealing with perennial subjects like the personal wounds of love.
Surviving oral evidence can sometimes be supplemented by more tangible
primary material; for example, there are distinguished traditions of music
theory from such countries as China, Korea, India and Japan dating back as
far as 5,000 years. Large collections of notated Chinese music survive from
the twelfth century AD onwards, and only a little later appear the beginnings
of the Turkish classical repertoire.

The invention of the phonograph in the late nineteenth century greatly assisted the investigation of oral traditions and living musical systems. Another
milestone was the development of the means to measure intervals smaller
than a semitone, the octave having been divided in a rich variety of ways
unfamiliar in the West. Technical analysis of musical sound and performance practice has been fruitfully allied to anthropological study, so that

fieldwork routinely covers the processes of both creation and performance. In India not only are the instruments, melodies and rhythms unfamiliar to a Western musician, but the ideas behind the music are intimately connected with philosophical and religious concepts which have little to do with Western approaches to time, matter or reality. In these circumstances music cannot be learned from books: a guru must be sought to provide essential secret and esoteric knowledge and to show how a musician's life must be led. From the start a disciple will be taken on stage to observe and interact with his master. In Hindu culture a musician has low-caste ranking not only because of his tradesman status but because his profession involves breaking upper-class taboos such as the handling of animal skins on drums or making lip contact with flutes and reeds which might have been touched by others. The rhythmic complexity of African music and its close integration with dance is likewise far from Western experience. Many African languages do not even have a word for music or musician, useless abstractions alongside their concrete terms for singers, dancers or drummers. In the Far East the religious ceremonies and royal court ritual of Japan have little philosophical connection with the West. The stylised high art of the noh play interweaves literature, theatre and dancing with music that associates drums with the other-worldly sound of the shakuhachi.

The sound world of non-Western music involves many instruments of unfamiliar design and status. An ancient example is the Chinese qin, characterised by its expressive slides and ethereal harmonies. The Indonesian gamelan comprises an ensemble of tuned percussion whose performers partake of a spiritual discipline bound up with the arts of dance, poetry and drama, in which the aim is to reach an ideal state of calm, emotional detachment; naturally, there are no virtuosos or soloists in this non-hierarchical, primarily oral tradition. The Indian sitar, with its characteristic gliding portamento, is an example of an instrument which (like the gamelan) has become known in the West, not least through its interaction with popular culture.

Greece and Rome

Forty thousand years ago, man was making music; Palaeolithic cave paintings discovered in Ariège in France contain the image of an animal-masked man scraping a musical bow to an audience of reindeer. By classical times music was engaging the attention of the great philosophers while also inviting widespread ritual participation. Writers such as Plato and Aristotle regarded musical training as of special educational value. Music's association with poetry demanded profound responses from performer and listener which cannot now be recreated from a mere reading of surviving source material. Choral song was particularly important, often incorporating dance and invariably accompanied by professionals playing wind and stringed instruments. Ritual lay at the heart of performance, as choirs sang in honour of the gods or in celebration of famous men or victorious athletes. Though little actual music survives, there are theoretical treatises by Aristoxenus (fourth century BC), Ptolemy (second century AD) and others. We can surmise that Greek music was primarily homophonic and that voices sang together in unison or at the octave. The Romans also had liturgical and other public music, military music and work songs, assimilating influences of the nations they conquered. Wind players attended sacrificial rites, partly to banish evil spirits and to summon up benevolent deities; they are frequently depicted in reliefs and were highly esteemed. Festivals in honour of the deities were accompanied by processional music, which in the case of Dionysus was sometimes wild and orgiastic. In military music the trumpeters gave fixed signals and played on the march and at ceremonials; in battle their sounds were designed to encourage the ranks and confuse the enemy. Folksongs provided a rhythmical accompaniment for such activities as rowing, reaping and weaving in genres such as lullabies, nursery rhymes, and birthday and wedding songs. Mime and pantomime became important in the theatre, vocal and instrumental music accompanying solo dancers who represented mythological figures.

The church

For centuries the church has been an important focus for music-making. The Romans' association of music with debauchery and immorality of all kinds made early Christian authorities realise that it could either ennoble or debase man's moral fibre. An initial answer to the dilemma was that music should be associated with devout words and instruments banished. Musical education has been an important function of the church ever since the foundation of the Schola Cantorum traditionally ascribed to Gregory the Great (590–604). Boys were trained there, received a complete education in all the principal scholastic subjects, and also took part in secular feasts and carnivals. The sheer length of this tradition is not to be underestimated; when the first modern conservatoire was founded in Paris in 1795 in the wake of the revolution, French musical education was still the responsibility of almost four hundred church-sponsored music schools, each teaching plainchant, counterpoint, some composition, a little French, much Latin and some arithmetic. Though teaching methods were antiquated and instrumental music neglected, about four thousand pupils each year proceeded to theological seminaries or to lives as singers or organists.

No ecclesiastical melody was written down until the sixth century, and only in the twelfth century was a system devised which could indicate pitches if not exact values. One of the main difficulties in recreating medieval music is that improvisation and instrumental accompaniment are not represented in the surviving notation. Small organs and bowed, plucked, wind and percussion instruments found their way into church, but exact personnel was selected according to the occasion and available resources. During several centuries, complexity in church music drew recurrent criticism from the authorities, for example Pope John XXII in 1323. On Good Friday in 1555, Pope Marcellus II instructed the Papal Choir to perform in future with properly modulated voices and so that everything could be heard and understood. From time to time it happened that church composers utterly transcended their professional circumstances, as in the case of J. S. Bach. Lutheran Germany produced many music directors who conscientiously wrote for the greater glory of God, at the same time satisfying their superiors and edifying the congregation. Bach lived at a time when the concepts of genius and masterpiece had not yet been articulated; working from week to week with a small orchestra of eighteen to twenty-four players to accompany his singers, he would doubtless have been astonished at his veneration by later generations.

Secular music

Whereas church music was organised and coordinated, secular music was undertaken without any sense that its method or purpose should be written down. The musical centre of gravity passed from church to the royal and aristocratic courts only in the early renaissance period. Originally music was part of the duty of court entertainers, who were also jugglers, acrobats, dancers, trainers of performing animals and verbal comics. These minstrels would belong either to an aristocratic household or to a touring variety troupe. Accompanied by portable instruments, they would not only entertain but also immortalise glorious royal deeds in song, while dealing with the usual subjects of love, mourning and satire. As towns developed in the Middle Ages, guilds of waits or *Stadtpfeifer* were formed, originally as civic watchmen. They developed into local bands, playing a variety of instruments and training apprentices who worked as servants until they achieved the necessary qualifications. There was often a struggle to defend a monopoly on ceremonial and social music throughout a particular town. Remnants of this system survived into the nineteenth century, when in Leipzig the *Stadtmusiker* became *ex officio* members of the Gewandhaus Orchestra.

Renaissance court establishments followed a consistent pattern of development, with small choirs and a group of instruments for accompaniment and independent music-making. They created well-disciplined, flexible ensembles to perform works usually composed in the most striking and advanced styles of the time. The first printed book on instruments – *Musica getutscht* – was published in Basle in 1511 by Sebastian Virdung. It describes and portrays through woodcuts the clavichord, virginal, lute, viol, dulcimer, harp, shawm, flute, cornett, bagpipe, trombone, trumpet, and various percussion and organs. The printing of music itself originated at the end of the fifteenth century, committing the publisher to the notion that certain works would have a lengthy existence and creating the idea of a musical repertoire. An important aspect of Elizabethan and Jacobean middle-class society was the development of the intimate pleasure of chamber music both for voices and for instruments.

The baroque era

Performance during the baroque period showed a keen appreciation of spontaneity. The rise of instrumental music and opera in the seventeenth century created a new class of musician whose primary emphasis was on technique, demonstrating an ability to extemporise or ornament or to evoke a desired effect. Significantly, female performers won increasing acclaim during the period, not just on the operatic stage but also in Venetian conservatoires such as the Ospedale della Pietà made famous by Vivaldi.

The opera houses were important as the first independent settings for the performance of music to a paying public of all social classes; the earliest opened in Venice in 1637. They were relatively compact; the largest was similar in size to today's small cinema. Their several tiers of boxes were mostly rented by noblemen for a year (in some cases a lifetime), while temporary seating was made available elsewhere for single ticket-holders. The systematic vocabulary of musical signs and gestures developed by Monteverdi and his contemporaries came to represent relationships between the characters on stage, as singers were required to become actors. One cannot assume that similar resources were always used for the same opera; indeed, fluidity of both numbers and personnel could characterise successive performances. Pre-eminent among voice types now obsolete was the castrato, prized for its power and flexibility. There were many aspects of a good singing style which were written in one way but, to be more graceful, effected in quite another. From its beginnings opera engendered that intriguing interaction of commercial and artistic considerations that continues to this day, a prime eighteenth-century example being Handel's colourful career in London.

Like opera, chamber music was usually directed from the harpsichord, often by the composer; detailed performance instructions were therefore unnecessary. Players continued to assume a high degree of responsibility in an age when much material was sketched rather than fully notated, especially in *basso continuo* parts. Penetrating comparisons with jazz technique can be drawn here, not least in the case of *notes inégales* – successions of evenly written notes played unequally in the French style according to the tempo and character of the music. Only around 1700 did instrumental music achieve the status of vocal music, having been largely confined to opera overtures and the service of church worship. But it was significant that Lully's ensemble at the court of Louis XIV had been especially renowned for its discipline and unanimity, establishing stringed instruments as a basis for the orchestra. In Italy there soon arose a new type of virtuoso string writing, exemplified by the Roman violinist-composer Arcangelo Corelli.

The classical period

During the second half of the eighteenth century, music came to be regularly disseminated through published editions. Even a reliable text gives an incomplete idea of what was originally performed, since players and singers continued to have important individual input. But the major treatises by Quantz, Leopold Mozart and C. P. E. Bach cover many aspects of contemporary practice. They draw a close parallel between music and language, placing a premium upon the performer's ability to move an audience. Social conditions favoured the rise of the public concert, which at first flourished in relatively small venues, encouraging an articulate, intimate performing style. Written descriptions of concert standards within reviews are notoriously difficult to interpret. A famous example is Charles Burney's description of the Mannheim orchestra as an army of generals, equally fit to plan a battle as to fight it; he qualified his enthusiasm with a criticism of the wind tuning, whose sourness he reckoned to be a universal orchestral problem.[5] A notorious account of the Lyons orchestra in 1785–6 reported that the leader had neither intelligence nor an accurate style of performance and that there were unauthorised absences among his colleagues for reasons which we should now regard as paltry. Most concerts (unlike opera) could usually count on only one rehearsal and sometimes there were none. Programmes placed a premium on variety and novelty, comprising a mixture of solo, chamber, orchestral and vocal music. For example, on 25 November 1781 the inaugural concert of the Leipzig Gewandhaus Orchestra included a symphony by Joseph Schmitt, a hymn by Reichardt, Berger's Violin Concerto, a quartet of authorship now unknown, a symphony by J. C. Bach, an aria by Sacchini and a symphony by E. W. Wolf.

Burney identifies his century's thirst for new music in his *General History*:

So changeable is taste in Music, and so transient the favour of any particular style, that its history is like that of a ploughed field: such a year it produced wheat, such a year barley, peas, or clover: and such a year it lay fallow. But none of its productions remain, except perhaps a small part of last year's crop, and the corn and weeds that now cover its surface.[6]

An important exception to this general rule is of course Handel's continuing popularity in England long after his death. By the end of the century, impresarios such as Salomon, who attracted Haydn to London after his lengthy service at the Esterházy court, increasingly caused success to be judged in commercial terms as well as by aesthetic approval. Mozart represented a new breed of freelance musician, astutely presenting himself to the Viennese audience of the 1780s in his piano concertos in the role of both composer and performer. He also wrote operatic roles and solo works explicitly tailored to the individual abilities of his performing colleagues. A generation later, Beethoven was to raise fierce challenges to the orchestral player because he made unfamiliar and difficult technical and stylistic demands on individuals at a time when conditions for rehearsal and performance were unfavourable as a result of social and political as well as musical factors.

We are fortunate to have a snapshot of eighteenth-century Austrian training in the form of a 'Musick Plan', a system of education drawn up by Mozart's clarinettist Anton Stadler in 1799 in response to an invitation from the Hungarian Count Georg Festetics. Stadler advocated a six-year course in which all students would learn aspects of theory, performance and composition, including piano, organ or figured bass, violin and wind instruments, to complement their principal study. All music students were to learn the art of singing, whatever the quality of their individual voices. Emphasising the importance of a good general education, he observed that anyone wanting to understand music must know the whole of worldly wisdom and mathematics, poetry, elocution, art and many languages.[7]

The nineteenth century

The industrial age brought sweeping changes, notably transport possibilities which enabled virtuoso careers to flourish and also affected the lives of orchestral musicians. As scores travelled more widely, performance indications tended to become ever more precise. The complexity of German accompaniments gradually rendered singers' freedom to ornament less appropriate; one author warned that 'compositions by Mozart, Haydn, Cherubini and Winter will bear fewer embellishments than those of Salieri, Cimarosa, Martin and Paisiello'.[8] The establishment of conservatoires throughout Europe was bound to encourage technical virtuosity, especially since this is an aspect of performance which can be readily assessed. Not surprisingly, the musical amateur began to disappear from public concert life. The piano maintained a central position both in the domestic environment (almost all orchestral music being arranged for piano duet) and on the concert platform, where Liszt was representative of the new breed of touring virtuosos. Liszt's technical innovations enabled a remarkable transcription of orchestral idioms to the piano, his virtuoso prowess having been inspired by the violinist Niccolò Paganini, one of the most hypnotic of all nineteenth-century figures.

The development of symphony orchestras brought public concert series supported by subscription, while also establishing the role of the conductor. Beethoven was one of the first musicians in Vienna to direct without an instrument, operating from a separate music desk; he is said to have been especially concerned to convey the music's expression, rather than a regular beat. Orchestras varied greatly in size; in the later nineteenth century Brahms's experience ranged from his favourite Meiningen ensemble, with forty-eight players, to the ninety-eight-strong Leipzig Gewandhaus. By his time, detached, contemplative listening had become the very purpose of performance; literary journals and newspapers give a good idea of how concerts were received, as professional criticism became established at the hands of such writers as Eduard Hanslick and George Bernard Shaw. Choral societies in England tended to associate good music with religion rather than musical quality, and were furnished with vast quantities of cheap vocal scores by the publisher Vincent Novello; they continue to supply a now rare opportunity for amateur musicians to appear on the public stage. The brass-band movement was also part of an appetite for self-help and for moral and material improvement.

The revival of earlier music began in earnest, important examples being Mendelssohn's 1829 performance of Bach's *St Matthew Passion* and Brahms's choral repertoire of Morley, Schütz, Palestrina, Bach and Handel. Meanwhile, the publishing of collected editions of the works of Bach, Handel, Mozart and others established the notion of the definitive text. But there was still a widespread belief that old music needed to be updated in performance; in the first edition of Grove's *Dictionary*, Ebenezer Prout's article on 'additional accompaniments' argues that literal performance of music by Bach and Handel fails to realise the intentions of the composer.[9] Conversely, increasing numbers of musicians came to appreciate that contemporary performing styles did not necessarily suit music from earlier times. Individuals such as Arnold Dolmetsch pioneered developments in historical awareness which were to win widespread acceptance during the twentieth century. His activities were timely because Wagner's highly influential conducting had tended to make the music of previous generations sound more like his own, replacing verbal elements of interpretation with pictorial ones.

The twentieth century

The development of communications in the twentieth century enabled musicians to sample and digest interpretations world-wide. The possibilities of recording fundamentally changed the character of music-making, the studio gradually bringing a new reverence for technical accuracy which in turn found its way into the concert hall. The marketing of various kinds of musician has been greatly influenced by the recording industry, both in popular and in classical fields.

In the nineteenth century, popular music still overlapped with concert, theatre and domestic activity. Following the Industrial Revolution the public increasingly sought out music in parks, pleasure gardens, dance halls and music halls, while the latest tunes would also be heard via the street barrel organs. Gradually, serious music was taken out of the reach of the general public, as operetta and music hall filled the accessibility gap created by Verdi and Wagner. From America soon appeared barn dances and Sousa marches, a real breakthrough coming with ragtime and the foxtrot. Jazz initially combined diverse musical elements from Africa, Europe and America, finding an early place on riverboats and advertising wagons and at parades, funerals, dance halls and cabarets. Extempore playing was always a central feature, combining individual and collective skills and drawing on various musical styles, including march, rag, hymn and blues. Jazz performers have increasingly thought of themselves not merely as entertainers but as professional proponents of a subtle and complex art form.

In the interwar period Paul Whiteman provided a highly accessible jazz image, and major American comedies by Kern, Gershwin, Rodgers and Cole Porter achieved enormous popularity. National barriers tended to break down after about 1940, when music could be readily transported and recorded and thus become part of a complex business and financial world. Important individual styles included swing, with its new instrumentation, vibrant sound and powerful rhythmic drive; then in the mid 1950s rock and roll, with a basic difference in sound, instrumentation and expressive intent; then rock in the 1960s and 1970s, with its formal and tonal variety and freedom linked strongly to political sentiments and social radicalism.

Texts ranged from the political to intensely personal experiences, combining with increasingly extensive amplification and electronic gadgetry. The artistic significance of popular music continued to exercise serious critical opinion, Kenneth Tynan claiming in 1967 that the release of the Beatles' album *Sgt. Pepper's Lonely Hearts Club Band* was 'a decisive moment in the history of western civilisation'.[10]

In the concert hall, performers have been required to adapt to new situations and to tackle ever-spiralling technical difficulties. Smaller ensembles of various kinds have challenged the supremacy of the large-scale symphony orchestra. At the beginning of the twentieth century a greater complexity of rhythmic demands was signalled in works such as Stravinsky's *Rite of Spring* and *The Soldier's Tale*. In this period one of the great educational achievements of the Swiss Emile Jaques-Dalcroze was to teach young people to think and feel in different rhythm-patterns simultaneously. Most orchestral musicians in 1910 found it very hard to perform groups of five within a 3/4 or 4/4 metre; this was child's play for those brought up on the Dalcroze method.

Alongside the influences of jazz and ragtime, singers and instrumentalists had to respond to the demands of serial composition and were sometimes required to venture into even more unfamiliar territory such as quarter-tone notation. Extended ranges were demanded of most orchestral instruments, as well as new techniques such as the production of chords on individual woodwind instruments. Where musical sounds end and noises begin became the subject of countless experiments, for example in the works of Varèse and in George Antheil's *Ballet mécanique* of 1924 for ten pianos and electric instruments and machines, including aeroplane propellers. The electronic resources that developed throughout the twentieth century threatened at times to usurp the role of the performer altogether. In 1947 Stravinsky condemned interpretation, demanding from the performer a rigidly objective approach. Yet notation was expanding to include pictures as an inspiration to improvisation, while aleatoric (or chance) principles were also a source of experimentation. Indeterminacy arises when the performer is called upon to choose the order of material or is led by certain devices into an apparently chance or random order. Influenced by Zen Buddhism, John Cage offered his performers such options in his *Variations IV* (1963), 'for any number of players, any sounds or combinations of sounds produced by any means, with or without other activities'.

In succeeding years performers have benefited from the opportunities presented by radio, television, CD and CD-ROM; it seems inevitable that these will be supplemented by the internet, currently poised to offer new possibilities for the dissemination of individual interpretations. Meanwhile, education programmes have increasingly been seen by orchestral management as a way of reaching into the community and of building bridges between everyday life and the concert hall, placing the audience back at the centre of musical activity. As a chief executive from one of the London orchestras recently remarked, 'Perhaps a century of fixed musical etiquette has replaced heart, enjoyment and communication with academia, social order and alienation?'[11]

Approaches to earlier music

Historical awareness was sufficiently developed in 1952 for Hindemith to claim that all music ought to be performed with the means of production that were in use when the composer gave it to his contemporaries. But he also realised the limitations of such an approach: 'Our spirit of life is not identical with that of our ancestors, and therefore their music, even if restored with utter technical perfection, can never have for us precisely the same meaning it had for them.'[12] In response to the widespread acceptance of period performance, some have questioned how historical knowledge in interpreting a score can relate to a performer's individual passion and conviction. Paradoxically, it is this very quality which has always been an important source of inspiration to composers.

Richard Taruskin has argued that strict accountability in fact reduces performance practice to a lottery, for the performer can exercise no control over the state of the evidence. Furthermore, the need to satisfy a composer's intentions (assuming that were possible) bespeaks a failure of nerve, not to say an infantile dependency.[13] He cites Stravinsky as a salutary example of a composer who changed his mind on various interpretative matters throughout his career. Taruskin sees historical music-making as having won its present position as a result of its novelty rather than its antiquity; he also considers it a characteristic phenomenon of our own time. Nevertheless, the stimulus of history can fire the musical imagination, and this can be as important as trying to recover every detail. Margaret Bent recently observed that 'different repertories of early music have their own grammars and their own dialects. As with "dead" languages, these grammars are recoverable, enabling us to understand the written literature, to know quite a lot about how they were performed or pronounced, even without knowing what they really sounded like.'[14]

The fact that detached playing in Mozart's day was the norm is such fundamental historical evidence that we can scarcely afford to ignore it. Knowledge can also usefully complement a performer's own taste in such areas as the interpretation of small-scale slurs or the formulation of an appropriate response to dissonance and its resolution. The use of string vibrato before 1900 as an ornament rather than an all-pervading device positively demands to be taken into account. Indeed, historical awareness can illuminate performance in a myriad of ways. Recently there has been a healthy interaction of modern and period practices, as historical principles have gradually begun to influence mainstream musical life. Meanwhile, claims to authenticity or even historical accuracy ('the most original Beethoven yet recorded')[15] have become ever more muted. Appropriate styles of performance for different periods will surely be one of the great legacies of the twentieth century, and it is creditable that a more intimate relationship with notation has been opened up. However, does an obsession with the past also reflect some terrible rift between contemporary composers and their audiences? It is difficult not to sympathise with the great musicologist Donald Jay Grout, who as long ago as 1957 remarked that if a composer of old music

could by some miracle be brought back to life in the twentieth century to be quizzed about the methods of performance in his own times, his first reaction would certainly be one of astonishment at our own interest in such matters. Have we no living tradition of music, that we must be seeking to revive a dead one? The question might be embarrassing. Musical archaism may be a symptom of a disintegrating civilisation.[16]

During the twentieth century the place of contemporary music was indeed largely substituted by endless repetitions of familiar established repertoire, which now routinely invited detailed comparisons of minor differences in interpretation. The challenges of the new millennium are thus quite distinct from many earlier experiences recounted in this brief survey of performing through history.

Notes

1 See Christopher Small, *Musicking* (Hanover, NH and London: Wesleyan University Press, 1998) for a stimulating examination of relationships between audience and performers.

2 Letter dated 3 July 1778 from Paris to Leopold Mozart in Salzburg; Wolfgang Amadeus Mozart, *The Letters of Mozart and His Family*, 3rd edn, trans. and ed. Emily Anderson, rev. Stanley Sadie and Fiona Smart (London: Macmillan, 1985), 558.

3 Reproduced in Michael Forsyth, *Buildings for Music* (Cambridge, Mass.: MIT Press, 1985), 229.

4 Julius Levin in *Die Musik* (1926), quoted in Joseph Szigeti, *Szigeti on the Violin* (London: Cassell, 1969), 176.

5 Charles Burney, *The Present State of Music in Germany, the Netherlands, and United Provinces* (New York: Broude Brothers, [1773] 1969), 95–7.

6 Charles Burney, *A General History of Music*, 4 vols. (London: Charles Burney, 1776–89), II:380.

7 See Pamela Poulin, 'A view of eighteenth-century musical life and training: Anton Stadler's "Musick Plan"', *Music & Letters*, 71 (1990), 215–24.

8 J. F. Schubert, *Neue Singe-schule* (Leipzig: Breitkopf & Härtel, 1804), 138; my translation.

9 Ebenezer Prout, 'Additional accompaniments', in George Grove (ed.), *A Dictionary of Music and Musicians*, 4 vols. (London: Macmillan, 1879–89), I:30.

10 Quoted from Allan F. Moore, *The Beatles: Sgt. Pepper's Lonely Hearts Club Band* (Cambridge: Cambridge University Press, 1997), 59.

11 Serge Dorny, 'Vital signs', *BBC Music Magazine* (October 1999), 53–4.

12 Paul Hindemith, *A Composer's World* (Cambridge, Mass.: Harvard University Press, 1952), 170–1.

13 Richard Taruskin, *Text and Act: Essays on Music and Performance* (New York and Oxford: Oxford University Press, 1995), 98.

14 Margaret Bent, '"Authentic" listening?', *Early Music*, 25 (1997), 567.

15 Note to The Hanover Band's recording of Beethoven's First Symphony and First Piano Concerto, Nimbus 5003 (1982).

16 Donald Jay Grout, 'On historical authenticity in the performance of old music', in Jacob Maurice Coopersmith (ed.), *Essays on Music in Honor of Archibald Thompson Davison* (Cambridge, Mass.: Harvard University Press, 1957), 346.

Further reading

Brown, Howard Mayer and Stanley Sadie (eds.), *Performance Practice*, 2 vols. (London: Macmillan, 1989)

Haskell, Harry, *The Early Music Revival: A History* (London: Thames and Hudson, 1988)

Kenyon, Nicholas (ed.), *Authenticity and Early Music* (Oxford and New York: Oxford University Press, 1988)

Lawson, Colin and Robin Stowell, *The Historical Performance of Music: An Introduction* (Cambridge: Cambridge University Press, 1999)

Myers, Helen (ed.), *Ethnomusicology: Historical and Regional Studies* (London: Macmillan, 1993)

Raynor, Henry, *A Social History of Music from the Middle Ages to Beethoven* (New York: Taplinger, 1978)

Raynor, Henry, *Music and Society since 1815* (New York: Taplinger, 1978)

2 Historical performance and the modern performer

PETER WALLS

'Interpretation'

This chapter is addressed to 'modern performers' regardless of whether they sing with or play modern or period instruments. We may start by considering the question 'What exactly should we try to do in performing music written before our own time?' In fact, the answer is essentially the same for early music as it would be for a new composition. Most performers would think in terms of being true to the work, of exploring its emotional content, of attempting to honour the composer's intentions. We value imagination and originality in performers, but recognise that (normally) this serves the music they perform, helping to illuminate its character or make palpable its emotional content. By and large, we are not so happy when a performer's imagination distorts or disguises the music on which it is exercised.

This process of realising a musical work in sound is generally called 'interpretation' – though some composers have been very uncomfortable with all that this implies. Famously, Ravel proclaimed, 'I do not ask for my music to be interpreted, but only for it to be played', a remark echoed by Stravinsky when he wrote, 'Music should be transmitted and not interpreted, because interpretation reveals the personality of the interpreter rather than that of the author, and who can guarantee that such an executant will reflect the author's vision without distortion?'[1] Their complaint, clearly, was with wilful renditions in which performers' whims unjustified by anything in the score are conspicuous.

'Interpretation', however, ought to be a good word for what these composers wanted. The *OED* gives as one definition for 'interpret' to 'bring out the meaning of' a musical composition by performance.[2] In this sense, it might be seen to parallel the responsibility borne by foreign-language interpreters not to misrepresent the meaning of what they are given to translate.

Thinking about the ambiguity of the term 'interpret' is quite a useful way of distinguishing between performances which are true to the music being performed and those in which something else (showmanship, for instance) gets in the way. We could, in fact, call the first kind of performance 'interpretation' (anchoring that word to its primary meaning) and the second kind 'appropriation' (since the musical work has, in a sense, become a vehicle for the performer's personal agenda). Interpretation, then, might become synonymous with trying to determine and to realise the composer's intentions.

Score reading

All written music needs 'interpretation'. A musical score awaits realisation in sound. And, just as with a foreign language, expertise in being able to read the music is a prerequisite for doing this. This is something we tend to take for granted until we come across an unfamiliar form of notation such as lute tablature (Example 2.1a), scordatura writing (Example 2.1b) or graphic notation (Example 2.1c). But we need to recognise that, just as the pronunciation and meanings of words change over time, apparently standard musical notation has subtly different meanings depending on where and when it was written. In fact, it always needs contextualising as part of this process of interpretation. In 1717 François Couperin wrote about the particular problem with the music of his own milieu: 'There are in my view some deficiencies in the way we notate music which relate to the manner in which we write our language. It is that we write something different from what we play. This is why foreigners play our music less well than we do theirs.'[3] What specifically he had in mind was that the first in every pair in a series of quavers moving by step would be subtly elongated (*notes inégales*) despite the apparently equal notation.

Many elements in even quite a simple piece of keyboard music presuppose some sense of context. Example 2.2 is the second Gavotte from J. S. Bach's 'Ouverture nach Französischer Art' (Overture in the French Style) BWV 831. The Overture (meaning Suite in this case) was one of the few works by Bach published during his lifetime. It appeared in 1735 in Part II of the *Clavierübung* (Keyboard Exercise), whose title page tells us that it was written for a 'harpsichord with two manuals'. Immediately, the *piano* marking at the beginning assumes a distinctive significance since it is effectively an instruction from the composer to play on the upper manual where the jacks pluck only a single set of strings tuned at written (8′) pitch. In contrast, Gavotte I (which precedes and follows Gavotte II in the kind of relationship we associate with minuet and trio pairs) is marked *forte*, meaning that it is to be played on the lower manual with its coupled sets of strings, possibly even enriched by a third (4′) set tuned an octave higher. Of course, this alternation of manuals creates a dynamic contrast between

(a)

(1)

(b)   written:

violin

basso continuo

6   5

sounding:

violin

basso continuo

6   5

(c)

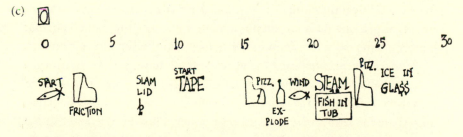

Example 2.1 (a) John Dowland, 'Lachrimae', bars 1–2, with realisation in upper system
(© 1974, 1978, 1981 by Faber Music Ltd. Reproduced by permission of Faber Music Ltd.
from *The Collected Lute Music of John Dowland*, 3rd edn, transcribed and ed. Diana Poulton
and Basil Lam.) (b) Heinrich Biber, 'Rosary Sonata' No. 7 ('The Flagellation of Christ'), bars
1–2 (c) John Cage, *Water Walk*, beginning (Edition Peters No. 6771; © 1961 by Henmar
Press Inc., New York. Reproduced on behalf of the publishers by kind permission of Peters
Edition Limited, London.)

Example 2.2 J. S. Bach, Gavotte II, 'Ouverture nach Französischer Art' BWV 831, bars 1–10

the two gavottes, but more than that, it results in a significant change in timbre.

Such an instrument would have been 'well tempered'. In other words, it would not have been tuned in equal temperament, which is the standard way on modern keyboard instruments of resolving a fundamental problem – namely, that a 'circle' of acoustically pure fifths does not quite return to the point from which it started. In the eighteenth century, the preferred solution lay in a range of circular temperaments in which a few of the fifths (normally four or six) are slightly smaller than pure. This creates a kind of *chiaroscuro* (a term actually used by Tartini[4] in recommending one such temperament) between the sweet consonance of the most commonly used chords and the rather more tense sound of remoter harmonies. Consequently, each key has a distinctive character. There are many quite detailed instructions from the eighteenth century on how to set various circular temperaments. Exactly which one Bach favoured is a matter of conjecture, but all circular temperaments share certain broad principles. One reasonably reliable rule of thumb for conceptualising the effect of these tunings is to regard each note on the keyboard as being tuned to suit its simplest form, meaning the form which is lower in the order of accidentals; hence the note immediately above F on the keyboard will sound better when it functions as an F♯ rather than a G♭, and so on. Thus, D major – the tonic of Gavotte II – is likely to be a sweeter sounding chord than F♯ major (the dominant of Gavotte I, which is in B minor). Within Gavotte II itself, a circular temperament will subtly underline the movement away from and back to D major.[5]

The indication that this work was written to be played on a two-manual harpsichord may be read as implicitly more specific than the actual form of words suggests. There is no definite information about Bach's own harpsichords (though the inventory of his estate shows that he owned five at the time of his death). In 1719 he was responsible for purchasing a two-manual instrument by Michael Mietke for the court at Cöthen (where he was Kapellmeister), and this maker seems to have been well regarded in Leipzig. Bach also worked with the Leipzig-based harpsichord maker Zacharias Hildebrandt. Two years before the publication of the second part of the *Clavierübung*, a Leipzig newspaper had announced the resumption of concerts by Bach's Collegium Musicum which would be graced by 'a new harpsichord [*Clavicymbel*] such as had not been heard here before'.[6]

Regardless of national type, there are features of such instruments that affect technique. The slightly shorter length of key makes orthodox piano fingering impractical (in particular, passing the thumb under the fingers in scale passages). Bach, according to his son Carl Philipp Emanuel, was forward-looking in his fingering methods and used the thumb more than had been normal – but this is still a far cry from standard modern piano fingering. Moreover, the fingering exercises included in the 'Notebook' compiled for his son, Wilhelm Friedemann, show that he expected him to practise the paired fingers then commonly used (see Example 2.3). Such fingerings lend themselves to the subtle lengthening of the first in a pair of conjunct quavers, resulting in *notes inégales*.

Since Gavotte II is quite explicitly a French-style piece (and since Bach was well versed in matters of French performance practice), the stepwise quavers in Example 2.2 should perhaps be treated as *notes inégales*. The ornament signs are also manifestations of a French stylistic trait. Bach, indeed, included an ornament table in Wilhelm Friedemann's 'Notebook' which can be used to decode the signs used in this score. And, last but not least, it is obvious that the fact that this is a gavotte (even though clearly not a danced gavotte) will have a direct bearing on tempo and rhythmic character. Johann Joachim Quantz described the gavotte as being a little slower than a bourrée or rigaudon but sharing the gay and well-articulated character of those dances.

Example 2.4, a short recitative introducing an aria sung by Argante in Handel's 1731 version of *Rinaldo*, presents a case in which it is all but impossible to read the notation accurately without some understanding of matters which fall within the province of performance practice. First, any trained

Example 2.3 J. S. Bach, *Klavierbüchlein für Wilhelm Friedemann Bach*, Applicatio BWV 994, bars 1–4

Example 2.4 Handel, *Rinaldo* (1731 version), recitative 'T'arresta, oh Dio!'

singer in Handel's company would have realised that appoggiaturas should be introduced where the repeated notes on a stressed–unstressed pair of syllables coincide with the changes in harmony and are followed by a rest (in a so-called feminine ending). This is a way of doing justice to the accentuation of the words and has a syntactical (rather than decorative) significance. Depending on the taste of the performer, an appoggiatura might also have been used on 'T'arresta'. The continuo harpsichordist would add a 4–3 suspension on the dominant in the final cadence (bar 4) to avoid an abrasive clash with the singer's appoggiatura. And the cellist playing alongside the harpsichord would have known not to sustain the long notes for their full value.

How would eighteenth-century performers have absorbed these principles? Partly from their music teachers, partly from just hearing colleagues, partly from treatises, partly from written-out exempla. How do we assimilate them today? Directly, only from the last two sources (and indirectly from these sources as they are mediated by our own teachers or by the performers we most admire). Appoggiaturas of this kind are discussed, for example, by Francesco Gasparini in his *L'armonico pratico al cimbalo* (Venice, 1708).[7] An even fuller discussion can be found in Johann Friedrich Agricola's heavily annotated translation of the singing treatise by Pier Francesco Tosi.[8] Alessandro Scarlatti habitually wrote exactly what notes he expected from the singer in cadences like the one ending the recitative in Example 2.4. The aria that follows assumes an equal familiarity with unnotated conventions – particularly in regard to ornamentation. Again, this is discussed by Tosi (and Agricola), but there are a few fascinating written-out examples of operatic arias which can be traced to Handel himself.[9]

Who should sing this music? For his 1731 production Handel had the famous castrato Francesco Bernardi, known as Senesino, singing the title role of Rinaldo. But Argante (another male role) was sung by the contralto

Francesca Bertolli. These days, high male roles in baroque opera tend to be assigned to falsettists (countertenors). The operatic countertenor is an invention of the twentieth century – an unnecessary answer to the problem of not having castrati available. When Handel found himself in a similar situation (that is, when he lacked castrati who were good enough), he simply cast the best female singer in his company. To be historically accurate, we ought to follow his example.

It is tempting to regard notation as prescriptive only, or at least primarily, in relation to pitch and duration. But the Bach and Handel examples considered here help us to identify a number of other parameters which are implicit in the way the music is written. We could thus create a checklist of basic questions with the aim of arriving at a thickly contextualised understanding of a musical score:

- What voice-types or instrument(s) are intended?
- How will they be set up (tuned etc.)?
- What kind of technique is assumed and what are the implications of this for articulation, phrasing, tonal colour etc.?
- Would the composer have assumed familiarity with rhythmic or syntactical conventions not made explicit in the score?
- What kind of ornamentation, if any, is appropriate?
- Are there expressive devices which would have seemed natural when the music was composed but which no longer form part of the well-trained musician's vocabulary?
- Are there aspects of modern expressiveness which are not suitable for this repertoire?

All these questions are so closely related to a properly nuanced understanding of the notation that I hestitate even to describe them as aspects of context. But to this list of questions (the 'A list') others could be added (the 'B list') which might also affect the way we approach the performance of a particular work. For what circumstances was it written? Was the piece composed with a particular kind of acoustic in mind? And so on.

Being able to come up with 'right' answers to all of these questions is never easy and often impossible; moreover, such answers are no substitute for the performer's imagination. At best, the arena within which imagination functions is one in which a set of received assumptions is displaced by an alternative range of stylistic possibilities. That process of displacement can itself act as a stimulus to musical imagination. Carl Dahlhaus argued that what made a history of music – and, by extension, any history of the arts – distinct from other kinds of histories is its concern not just with things from the past (events, documents) but with an aesthetic present.[10]

A similar statement could be made about the role of performers. The performer, whose task it is to realise that score for contemporary audiences, is especially concerned with this act of mediation between an historic past and an aesthetic present.

The 'right' instrument

At this point, I want to look at the most obvious of the parameters outlined above – the choice of instrument – to consider how integral it is to a proper understanding of music written before our own time. This in turn leads us to a related question: to what extent should performers be free to ignore (or remain ignorant of) historically verifiable information about how the music they play originally sounded?

Interest in period instruments has been driven by a conviction that music of earlier eras is best served by recreating the instrumental timbres envisaged by the composer (in so far as they can be established). There is, of course, an alternative point of view, most eloquently put in the 1870s by Philipp Spitta, who proclaimed that the modern pianoforte 'floated in the mind of Bach'.[11] Spitta, incapable of appreciating the beauty of a fine eighteenth-century German harpsichord (and perhaps even unable to hear such an instrument in playing order), was convinced that Bach's intellectual conception was ahead of instrument technology – in other words, that his keyboard works came into their own only once an instrument worthy of them had been developed.

It is, in fact, interesting to speculate about what, say, Mozart's attitude might have been to a mid nineteenth-century piano or even a modern nine-foot Steinway. He might (in the manner of Spitta) have thought, 'This is the instrument of my dreams; this is what I really wanted for my concertos', or, alternatively, 'If only I'd known about this wonderful instrument I'd have written some music for it.' On the other hand, he might have dismissed it as a crude and rather vulgar product of an industrialised society. We cannot know for certain which (if any) of those responses the piano would have evoked – but we do know that he was excited by the fortepianos that he encountered in the late 1770s. That in itself should be more than enough to make any performer who wants to play Mozart take them seriously.

The first thing one notices about Mozart performed on instruments of the kind he knew and loved is that the common view of his music as an expression of classical restraint and elegance tends to evaporate fairly quickly. Even a work like the Piano Concerto in B♭ major K. 450, which seems to evoke a *Figaro*-like world of *dramma giocoso*, uses the resources of the piano to the full. Example 2.5 begins at the point where the piano takes over an idea first outlined in the opening bars in a beautiful dialogue between winds and

Example 2.5 Mozart, Piano Concerto in B♭ major K. 450, i, bars 71–87 (piano with orchestral reduction)

strings. As the solo part approaches the cadence at bar 86 (where the strings effect a one-bar transition to the relative minor), it expands out to cover the full five-octave (F_1 to f^3) range of Mozart's instrument. Furthermore, the transparent tone of the instrument suits both the double thirds so prevalent in this example and the agile semiquavers.

The autograph manuscript of Haydn's Sonata in E♭ major Hob. XVI:49 allocates it to the 'Forte-piano' – the first sonata to be thus described by the composer. Moreover, three letters written to Maria Anna von Genzinger at the time of its completion in June 1790 make it quite clear that he had composed it with a specific instrument in mind:

This Sonata was destined for Your Grace a year ago, and only the Adagio is quite new, and I especially recommend this movement to your attention, for it contains many things which I shall analyse for Your Grace when the time comes; it is rather difficult but full of feeling. It's a pity, however, that Your Grace has not one of Schantz's [sic] fortepianos, for Your Grace could then produce twice the effect.[12]

The preference not just for a fortepiano but for a Schanz instrument is explained and reinforced in two subsequent letters. First, Haydn insists that this sonata really will not work very well on the harpsichord:

It's only a pity that Your Grace doesn't own a Schantz [sic] fortepiano, on which everything is better expressed. I thought that Your Grace might turn over your still tolerable harpsichord [Flügl] to Fräulein Peperl, and buy a new one for yourself. Your beautiful hands and their facility of execution deserve this and much more. I know I ought to have composed this Sonata in accordance with the capabilities of your keyboard [Clavier], but I found this impossible because I was no longer accustomed to it . . . [13]

In the next letter (4 July 1790) Haydn explains in detail why he preferred Schanz instruments to those by other Viennese makers, emphasising their lightness of touch. Noticeable here is his stress on the role that the feel of the instrument had for him as a *composer*: the fact that he was no longer accustomed to even a good harpsichord made it 'impossible' for him to write in a way that would have suited Maria Anna von Genzinger. And from that it followed that the best way to *perform* this was to replicate not just the sound but the feel of the instrument he had in mind.

There are a few places in this sonata where Haydn uses markings that seem to presuppose the use of a fortepiano. The outer movements have a single crescendo marking while the central Adagio e cantabile has a number of sforzandos and dynamic changes within a phrase (which could not convincingly be realised by changing manuals). Mostly, though, the specifically pianistic features are more subtle – a matter of the kind of cantabile phrasing at which the fortepiano excelled (see Example 2.6). For anyone determined enough, however, this sonata could be played on a harpsichord.

As we saw, Haydn urged the good friend for whom he had written the Eb major Sonata to acquire a more appropriate (in this case, more up-to-date) instrument. We might imagine him adapting his letter for our benefit. After all, he would be equally justified in telling pianists in the twenty-first century that an instrument with a Schanz-like lightness of touch would suit the sonata better than the Steinway with its much heavier action. And, as in the Mozart example cited earlier, the more transparent sound of a late eighteenth-century Viennese fortepiano will serve the prevalent thirds in this sonata so much better. A. Peter Brown comments:

the differences between the harpsichord and *fortepiano* of the eighteenth century are not nearly as pronounced as the disparity beteen the modern Steinway or Bösendorfer piano and the old Stein or Walter *fortepiano*. The instrument made in Germany and Austria during the eighteenth century had a brightness and

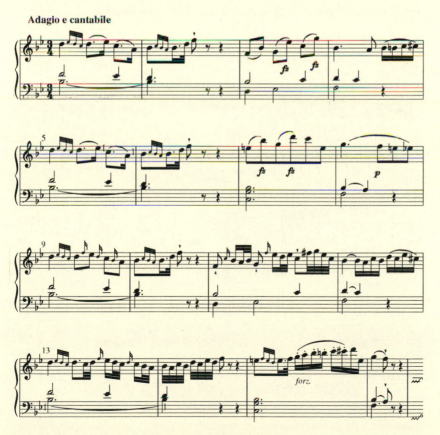

Example 2.6 Haydn, Sonata in Eb major Hob. XVI:49, ii, bars 1–16

crispness of articulation that seems to have had little aesthetic connection to the more massive and darker-sounding large English pianos that are the true ancestors of the modern instrument.[14]

Similar points – about the 'rightness' of the instrument for the music – could be made about later music. The marked pedalling in the opening bars of the slow movement in Beethoven's Third Piano Concerto Op. 37 (Example 2.7) is puzzling to the point of impossibility on a modern concert Steinway, but an evocative colouristic device on the instrument for which it was written.[15] Carl Czerny, who studied with Beethoven, said that the opening 'must sound like a holy, distant, and celestial harmony'.[16]

The increase in the piano's range and power over the first thirty years of the nineteenth century redefined the relationship between soloist and orchestra in piano concertos. Schumann was very aware of this. He did not advocate that pianists should find old instruments on which to perform their Mozart or Beethoven concertos, but he did think that composers had to discover a new way of approaching the genre. In an article from 1839 entitled 'Das Clavier-Concert' (The Piano Concerto) in the *Neue Zeitschrift für Musik* (the journal he had founded in 1832), he wrote:

This severing of the bond with the orchestra, as we have seen, was long in preparation. Modern pianistic art wants to challenge the symphony [orchestra],

Example 2.7 Beethoven, Third Piano Concerto Op. 37, ii, bars 1–12 (piano part only)

and rule supreme through its own resources; this may account for the recent dearth of piano concertos . . . Surely it would be a loss, should the piano concerto with orchestra become entirely obsolete; but on the other hand, we can hardly contradict the pianists when they say, 'We have no need of any assistance; our instrument can achieve a complete effect entirely by itself.' And so we must confidently await the genius who will show us a brilliant new way of combining orchestra and piano, so that the autocrat at the keyboard may reveal the richness of his instrument and of his art, while the orchestra, more than a mere onlooker, with its many expressive capabilities adds to the artistic whole.[17]

It is all too easy for first-time listeners to hear an early piano in terms of its incapacity to do what a nine-foot concert grand is so good at. Getting beyond this brings rich rewards – hearing its dynamic flexibility, tonal gradations and brilliant mobility in ways which explain Mozart's, Haydn's and Beethoven's enthusiasm for the instrument.

The same kind of adjustment might initially be demanded by other instruments. In the case of the violin, we live out the absurd paradox that, although Antonio Stradivari is popularly acknowledged to have been the greatest violin maker of all time, we do not in practice trust that he knew what he was doing. Not one of the Stradivari instruments being used by virtuosos today is set up as it was when it left the workshop in Cremona. Bass bars have been strengthened, thicker sound posts inserted, bridges altered, the necks re-set at a different angle, string types changed and chin rests added. The sound is thus significantly altered in ways which may well suit the performance of nineteenth-century concertos but which do a disservice to the music of Stradivari's own age.

The art of the possible

Once we have accepted that Haydn's (or whoever's) intentions are likely to be better realised on the instruments for which these works were conceived, there is another practical and contingent question that we as musicians living in the twenty-first century must confront: how narrowly should we set our focus in our efforts to match instruments to repertoires? After all, Haydn is recommending not just a Viennese fortepiano but a particular maker's instruments. But by the time he composed his next, and wonderfully flamboyant, Sonata in E♭ major Hob. XVI:52 in 1794, he had been won over to the instruments of John Broadwood and his contemporaries that he had encountered in England, which were more robust, heavier in action and fuller in tone. When Haydn returned to Vienna in 1795 after his second English visit, he took with him a new 'Grand Piano Forte' by Longman and Broderip (whose compass extended to c^4). So, were the late

'English' sonatas off-limits for Maria Anna von Genzinger (so soon after she had persuaded her husband to invest in a Schanz), and should they be avoided now by fortepianists without access to a piano of the late eighteenth-century English style? Actually, the last three Haydn sonatas never go beyond the compass of the Viennese instruments (though they exploit that to the full), so perhaps Haydn wanted to ensure that these works, for all that they might have been inspired by the sonority of the English piano, remained accessible to his compatriots.

Beethoven provides an interesting parallel case since his piano compositions span the period of greatest change in the instrument's history. The late sonatas simply cannot be played on the instrument for which his early works were conceived. Should pianists wishing to perform all of Beethoven's solo piano works be expected to acquire half a dozen instruments on which to do this?

In a case like this, a distinction needs to be made between an ideal solution (one which can quite often be approached in commercial recording projects) and a more generally practical one. Here it is interesting to reflect on the historical evidence for the kind of pragmatism that is, for most musicians, the only alternative to being confined to an ever-decreasing segment of the repertoire for their instrument. All the composers examined in this essay combine very precise instrumental preferences with a willingness to acknowledge the exigencies of real performing situations.

The history of the genesis and revisions of numerous works by Bach testifies to his willingness to adapt to circumstance, to change his mind or to explore alternatives. In the *St John Passion*, for instance, the lutes and violas d'amore in 'Erwäge, wie sein blutgefärbter Rücken' are replaced by organ and muted violins in the third and fourth versions. All seven of Bach's solo harpsichord concertos (BWV 1052–8) are thought to be transcriptions of works originally composed for other instruments. Certainly, two of them – the Concertos in D major BWV 1054 and in G minor BWV 1058 – are arrangements of the Violin Concertos in E major BWV 1042 and in A minor BWV 1041 respectively.

Mozart, we know, loved clarinets. After visiting Mannheim in 1778, he went into rhapsodies in a letter to his father about their effectiveness in an orchestral ensemble: 'Ah, if only we had clarinets too! You cannot imagine the glorious effect of a symphony with flutes, oboes, and clarinets.'[18] He did, of course, go on to write most memorably for the instrument. But he was prepared to contemplate substitutions in circumstances where, as he had just experienced in Salzburg, clarinets were not available. In 1786, when sending parts of the Piano Concerto in A major K. 488 to be used in the household of Prince von Fürstenberg, he wrote:

There are two clarinets in the A major concerto. Should his Highness not have any clarinets at his court, a competent copyist might transpose the parts into the suitable keys, in which case the first part should be played by a violin and the second by a viola.[19]

Similarly, Beethoven offered violin as an alternative to clarinet in his Trio in B♭ major Op. 11 (1798), and, as with Haydn, the title pages of many of his piano sonatas give piano or harpsichord as alternatives (though this is more related to the publishers' commercial priorities rather than to a direct wish on the composer's part to be flexible).

Modern performers should be encouraged by the apparent readiness of these composers to adjust to circumstance. At least on certain occasions, they were prepared to contemplate substitutions if exactly the instrument they had in mind for a particular work was not available. But that realism is not the same as indifference, and it cannot be used to justify a total flouting of composers' intentions in the matter of instrumental choices. Besides, it would be folly to do so, since getting as near as we can – literally – to the intended sound world of works from the past is part and parcel of engaging with their essence. (There is, alas, not room here to deal with the fallacy that achieving something like the original impact involves scaling-up decibel levels and timbres for ears used to modern-day spectaculars.)

Conclusion

At this point, we might return to the idea of 'interpretation' discussed at the beginning of this chapter. If it is the responsibility of the performer to realise the composer's intentions, then the first step is, clearly, to try to understand the music as fully as possible. Some aspects of this understanding will not directly (or at least not conspicuously) involve a sense of history. Analysis, obviously, is a central part of this process. But so many other aspects of understanding the music (ultimately the same thing as reading it properly) demand an historical perspective.

As indicated above, this perspective may be seen simply as a matter of reading a score properly with as full an awareness of its nuances as possible. I have described this as a thickly contextualised reading. But the crucial concept of historical context needs refining since, in approaching virtually any piece of music, a musical judgement has to be made about what aspects of the historical circumstance belong in our understanding of the score and what might be discarded as irrelevant or unnecessary. In other words, one needs to decide which questions belong to my 'A' and 'B' lists above and which can be relegated to a 'C list' – features of historical performances which, however interesting as history, we would never choose to emulate.[20] The decision about what not to incorporate from the historical record in safeguarding the aesthetic presence of the music we perform is the beginning of musical judgement. The boundary here between 'mere' context and details which are seen as integral to our understanding of a musical work is not fixed, however. We need to remain open to the possibility of discovering the relevance of seemingly unimportant details.

The point of view espoused in this essay has often been characterised as a quest for historical authenticity. That concept, however, is surrounded by pitfalls. As Peter Kivy and others have pointed out, it is impossible in practice to satisfy the various facets involved in a comprehensive authenticity – or, at least, it would be unrealistic to expect general agreement that in any specific instance it had been achieved.[21] So let us forget authenticity – a term which has caused more trouble than it is worth. Of the various alternatives that have been suggested, 'historically informed performance' has found most favour. But this too has been challenged. According to Richard Taruskin, it is unacceptable because it fails the 'invidious-antonym test', being unhelpful as a way of characterising valid alternatives.[22] Taruskin's objection nevertheless presupposes that it is the free choice of every performer to adopt or reject an approach that takes account of what can be demonstrated of composers' intentions. This is true only if we accept that it is also up to performers whether or not to play the right notes. In the final analysis, it could be argued that to play Bach on the instruments appropriate for Brahms and without taking account of his expectations in relation to such matters as articulation and ornamentation is not acceptable. We should perhaps face up to the fact that performers who think they can do justice to the aesthetic presence of music while ignoring the score's historical implications deserve to be regarded not as 'differently abled', but as 'historically uninformed'.

Notes

1 Respectively, Maurice Ravel, quoted in Marguerite Long, *At the Piano with Maurice Ravel* (London: Dent, 1973), 16; Igor Stravinsky, *Autobiography* (New York: Simon and Schuster, 1936; repr. New York: Norton, 1962), 75. Long also reports an exchange between Ravel and Toscanini which ran as follows: Ravel – 'That's not my tempo'; Toscanini – 'When I play your tempo the piece is ineffective'; Ravel – 'Then don't play it' (*At the Piano*, 18).

2 The full definition (1.c.) reads: 'To bring out the meaning of (a dramatic or musical composition, a landscape, etc.) by artistic representation or performance; to give one's own interpretation of; to render.'

3 François Couperin, *L'Art de toucher le clavecin* (Paris: François Couperin, 1717), 39; my translation.

4 Giuseppe Tartini, *Trattato di musica secondo la vera scienza dell'armonia* (Padua: Seminario, 1754), 100, quoted from Mark Lindley, 'La "Pratica ben regolata" di Francescantonio Vallotti', *Rivista Italiana di Musicologia*, 16 (1981), 72.

5 For a contrary view see Rudolf Rasch, 'Does "well-tempered" mean "equal-tempered"?', in Peter Williams (ed.), *Bach, Handel, Scarlatti: Tercentenary Essays* (Cambridge: Cambridge University Press, 1985), 293–310.

6 Quoted from Hans T. David and Alfred Mendel (eds.), *The New Bach Reader*, revised and enlarged by Christoph Wolff (New York and London: Norton, 1998), 156. See also the entry on 'harpsichord' in Malcolm Boyd (ed.), *Oxford Composer Companions: J. S. Bach* (Oxford: Oxford University Press, 1999), 207–8; John Koster, 'The quest for Bach's *Clavier*: an historiographical interpretation', *Early Keyboard Journal*, 14 (1996), 65–84; and Sheridan Germann, 'The Mietkes, the Margraves and Bach', in Williams (ed.), *Bach, Handel, Scarlatti*, 119–48.

7 Translated by Frank S. Stillings and Donald L. Burrows as *The Practical Harmonist at the Harpsichord* (New Haven and London: Yale University Press, 1963).

8 Johann Friedrich Agricola, *Anleitung zur Singekunst* (Berlin: Winter, 1757); on the use of appoggiaturas in recitative see Julianne C. Baird's English translation, *An Introduction to the Art of Singing by Johann Friedrich Agricola* (Cambridge: Cambridge University Press, 1995), 174ff.

9 See George Frideric Handel, *Three Ornamented Arias*, ed. Winton Dean (London: Oxford University Press, [c. 1976]); and Winton Dean, 'Vocal embellishment in a Handel aria', in H. C. Robbins Landon (ed.), *Studies in Eighteenth-Century Music* (London: Allen & Unwin, 1970), 151–9.

10 Carl Dahlhaus, *Foundations of Music History*, trans. J. B. Robinson (Cambridge: Cambridge University Press, 1983), 4ff.

11 Philipp Spitta, *Johann Sebastian Bach*, trans. Clara Bell and J. A. Fuller-Maitland, 2 vols. (London: Novello, 1884–5; repr. New York: Dover, 1951), II:44.

12 Letter dated 20 June 1790 from Esterháza to Maria Anna von Genzinger in Vienna; H. C. Robbins Landon, *Haydn, Chronicle and Works*, vol. II: *Haydn at Esterháza 1766–1790* (London: Thames and Hudson, 1978), 743–4.

13 Letter dated 27 June 1790 from Esterháza to Maria Anna von Genzinger in Vienna; ibid., 745. I have altered Landon's translation of *Clavier* from 'piano' to 'keyboard'; according to A. Peter Brown (*Joseph Haydn's Keyboard Music: Sources and Style* (Bloomington: Indiana University Press, 1986), 146), 'Haydn uses the term *Clavier* in a generic sense.' See the original text in Dénes Bartha and H. C. Robbins Landon (eds.), *Joseph Haydn: Gesammelte Briefe und Aufzeichnungen* (Kassel: Bärenreiter, 1965), 242.

14 Brown, *Joseph Haydn's Keyboard Music*, 171.

15 It is not easy to determine exactly what instrument Beethoven had in mind here. Given that the last movement goes up to c^4 (in bars 346–9), the most likely candidate is an Erard of the kind he acquired in 1804 (after the first performance of Op. 37 in April 1803). There were, however, other instruments of that kind in Vienna already.

16 Quoted from Leon Plantinga, *Beethoven's Concertos* (New York and London: Norton, 1999), 143–4.

17 Quoted from Leon Plantinga, *Schumann as Critic* (New Haven: Yale University Press, 1967), 204.

18 Letter dated 3 December 1778 from Mannheim to Leopold Mozart in Salzburg; Wolfgang Amadeus Mozart, *The Letters of Mozart and His Family*, 3rd edn, trans. and ed. Emily Anderson, rev. Stanley Sadie and Fiona Smart (London: Macmillan, 1985), 638.

19 Letter dated 30 September 1786 from Vienna to Sebastian Winter in Donaueschingen; ibid., 900.

20 It would be silly, for example, to take the fact that in 1778 Mozart performed his Variations on a Minuet of J. C. Fischer K. 179 in the freezing cold to an inattentive audience in Paris as encouragement to replicate those conditions when performing this work today. See Mozart's letter dated 1 May 1778 from Paris to his father Leopold in Salzburg, in ibid., 531.

21 See Peter Kivy, *Authenticities: Philosophical Reflections on Musical Performance* (Ithaca and London: Cornell University Press, 1995).

22 Richard Taruskin, 'The pastness of the present and the presence of the past', in Nicholas Kenyon (ed.), *Authenticity and Early Music* (Oxford and New York: Oxford University Press, 1988), 140.

Further reading

Brown, Clive, *Classical and Romantic Performing Practice 1750–1900* (Oxford: Oxford University Press, 1999)

Brown, Howard Mayer and Stanley Sadie (eds.), *Performance Practice*, 2 vols. (London: Macmillan, 1989)

Cyr, Mary, *Performing Baroque Music* (Portland, Ore.: Amadeus, 1992)

Donington, Robert, *The Interpretation of Early Music* (London: Faber, [1963] 1989)

Dreyfus, Laurence, 'Early music defended against its devotees: a theory of historical performance in the twentieth century', *Musical Quarterly*, 49 (1983), 297–322

Haskell, Harry, *The Early Music Revival: A History* (London: Thames and Hudson, 1988)

Kenyon, Nicholas (ed.), *Authenticity and Early Music* (Oxford and New York: Oxford University Press, 1988)

Kivy, Peter, *Authenticities: Philosophical Reflections on Musical Performance* (Ithaca and London: Cornell University Press, 1995)

Lawson, Colin and Robin Stowell, *The Historical Performance of Music: An Introduction* (Cambridge: Cambridge University Press, 1999)

MacClintock, Carol (ed.), *Readings in the History of Music in Performance* (Bloomington and London: Indiana University Press, 1979)

3   Analysis and (or?) performance

JOHN RINK

Confusion and controversy tend to reign whenever the term
'analysis' is used in relation to musical performance. Some authors regard analysis as 'implicit in what the performer does', however 'intuitive
and unsystematic' it might be,[1] while for others, performers *must* engage
in rigorous and theoretically informed analysis of a work's 'parametric
elements' if its 'aesthetic depth' is to be plumbed.[2] It cannot be denied that
the interpretation of music requires decisions – conscious or otherwise –
about the contextual functions of particular musical features and the means
of projecting them. Even the simplest passage – a scale or perfect cadence,
for instance – will be shaped according to the performer's understanding
of how it fits into a given piece and the expressive prerogatives that he or
she brings to bear upon it. Such decisions might well be intuitive and unsystematic, but not necessarily: most performers carefully consider how the
music 'works' and how to overcome its various conceptual challenges. That
process is in many respects an analytical one – but what that means requires
explanation.

The aim of this chapter is to explore the dynamic between intuitive and
conscious thought that potentially characterises the act of analysis in relation
to performance. After surveying some of the literature in this domain,
I shall describe a mode of analysis which might benefit rather than constrain
performers.[3] This will be illustrated in a case study of Chopin's Nocturne in
C♯ minor Op. 27 No. 1.

Perspectives on analysis and performance

In a fascinating essay from 1985, Janet Schmalfeldt gives voice to
two different personae – those of analyst and performer – to consider how
their respective interpretations of two Beethoven Bagatelles might influence one another. Though clever, their dialogue is problematic: the analyst
speaks far more authoritatively than the performer, who seems subservient
to her counterpart's theoretical edicts; moreover, the division into split

personalities hardly reflects how most musicians operate. Schmalfeldt's ultimate conclusion nevertheless rings true: 'there is no single, one-and-only performance decision that can be dictated by an analytic observation'.[4] This point echoes Edward Cone's comment in his classic *Musical Form and Musical Performance*, that 'every valid interpretation . . . represents, not an approximation of some ideal, but a choice: which of the relationships implicit in this piece are to be emphasized, to be made explicit?'[5]

Similar remarks occur elsewhere in the literature, but, as noted, so does a more doctrinaire school of thought virtually requiring performers to base their interpretations on the findings of rigorous analysis. One such author is Eugene Narmour, who in 1988 insisted that 'performers, as co-creators . . . must acquire theoretical and analytical competence . . . to know how to interpret', and that 'many negative consequences' will follow 'if formal relations are not properly analyzed by the performer'.[6] Wallace Berry likewise stated that 'musical interpretation must be informed by penetrating analysis'; for him, unlike Schmalfeldt and Cone, 'every analytical finding has an implication for performance'.[7]

In 1989 Jonathan Dunsby questioned the legitimacy of such injunctions, claiming that 'understanding and trying to explain musical structure is not the same kind of activity as understanding and communicating music. There is a genuine overlap between these poles of activity, but it cannot be a complete overlap.' According to Dunsby, a more deliberate analytical approach might help performers cope with difficult passages, but their generally pragmatic approach precludes the methodological rigour normally associated with analysis.[8] In a later response, I countered that 'performers are continually engaged in a process of "analysis", only of a kind different from that employed in published analyses. This sort of "analysis" is not some independent procedure applied to the act of interpretation' but rather 'an integral part of the performing process'. Referring to this as 'performer's analysis' (that is, 'considered study of the score with particular attention to contextual functions and [the] means of projecting them'), I noted the importance of musical 'shape', rather than structure, in the performer's conceptualisation of music – an elusive but elucidatory notion more temporally conceived than that of structure. Music's temporality is indeed critical in this regard, a factor either ignored or downplayed in at least some 'rigorous analysis',[9] to invidious effect when the results thereof are directly harnessed to performance. I also proposed the term 'informed intuition', which recognises the importance of intuition in the interpretative process but also that considerable knowledge and experience generally lie behind it – in other words, that intuition need not come out of the blue, and need not be merely capricious.[10]

Purpose and approach

Despite the many discrepancies within the literature, performance-related analysis can be divided into two principal categories:

(1) analysis prior to, and possibly serving as the basis of, a given performance
(2) analysis of the performance itself.

The first of these, whether rigorous or more pragmatic in nature, is potentially *prescriptive* with regard to performance, whereas the second type of analysis is *descriptive*. Post facto analysis is not my primary concern here, although its importance should be noted. The tempo and dynamic graphs in Figure 3.1 (based on recorded and live performances respectively) offer an example;[11] moreover, musicians themselves regularly analyse (that is, break down and evaluate) their performances after the fact, attempting to find different and better ways of understanding the music for the sake of the next rendition, in an ongoing evolution.

I have already identified the problems associated with some 'prescription', the moral being that performers are perhaps wise to resist any *systematic* attempt to correlate the findings of rigorous analytical methodologies and actual performance. For example, analytical demonstrations of motivic unity can be fascinating on paper but are usually better seen than heard; doggedly bringing out each instance of a seminal motif in performance

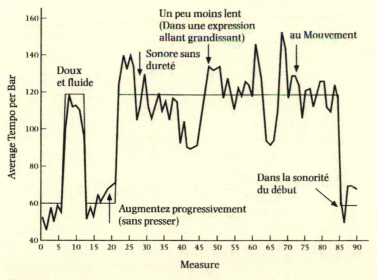

Figure 3.1 (a) 'Tempo map' of Claude Debussy's piano-roll performance (1913) of 'La Cathédrale engloutie', reproduced by permission of Oxford University Press from José A. Bowen, 'Finding the music in musicology: performance history and musical works', in Nicholas Cook and Mark Everist (eds.), *Rethinking Music* (Oxford: Oxford University Press, 1999), 440.

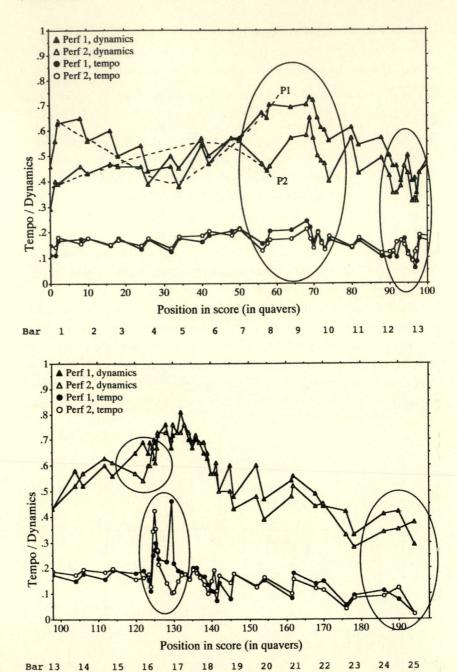

Figure 3.1 (b) Data depicting dynamic and tempo fluctuation in two performances of Chopin's Prelude in E minor Op. 28 No. 4 (right hand only; the vertical axis is in arbitrary units but starts from a true zero), reproduced from Eric Clarke, 'Expression in performance: generativity, perception and semiosis', in John Rink (ed.), *The Practice of Performance: Studies in Musical Interpretation* (Cambridge: Cambridge University Press, 1995), 32.

could lead to ludicrous results, even if an awareness of the motivic workings within a given piece might prove useful to the performer (for instance, in shaping the music timbrally or dynamically). Similarly, although a Schenkerian analysis can elegantly depict a tonal structure in its hierarchical complexity, to make the performance deliberately conform to and try to recreate the analysis in sound would be dubious, however valuable a knowledge of the processes and relationships implicit in that analysis might be in building the interpretation.

Nevertheless, more rigorous analytical study can assist performers in solving conceptual or technical problems (as noted before), as well as in memorising and in combating performance anxiety. Chapters 8 and 12 deal respectively with the latter, while the problem-solving role of analysis will be demonstrated here, along with instances not so much of mediation between the rigorous and the pragmatic as of parallel conception, by which I mean that performers often understand music along the same lines as those carrying out 'rigorous analysis', but in different terms – a parallelism that we ignore at our peril.

To understand that parallelism (which is a central theme of my case study) requires further consideration of what 'performer's analysis' might entail. Five principles can be outlined on the basis of the discussion above:

(1) Temporality lies at the heart of performance and is therefore fundamental to 'performer's analysis'.
(2) Its primary goal is to discover the music's 'shape', as opposed to structure, as well as the means of projecting it.
(3) The score is not 'the music'; 'the music' is not confined to the score.
(4) Any analytical element that impinges on performance will ideally be incorporated within a larger synthesis influenced by considerations of style (broadly defined), genre, performance tradition, technique, instrument and so on, as well as the performer's individual artistic prerogatives. In other words, analytically determined decisions should not be systematically prioritised.
(5) 'Informed intuition' guides, or at least influences, the process of 'performer's analysis', although a more deliberate analytical approach can also be useful.

It must be stressed that 'performer's analysis' primarily takes place as an interpretation is being formulated and subsequently re-evaluated – that is, while one is practising rather than performing. This does not deny its potential influence on actual performance or that new discoveries are sometimes made during performances. In general, however, the analytical process occurs at the (evolving) design stage, and its findings are assimilated into the

(a)

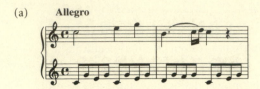

(b)

Example 3.1 Mozart, Piano Sonata in C major K. 545, i (a) bars 1–2 (b) bars 69–73

generalised body of knowledge that lies behind but does not dominate any given performance act.

This mode of analysis can be illustrated by looking at the first two bars of Mozart's Piano Sonata in C major K. 545 (Example 3.1a). The passage consists of an Alberti-bass accompaniment supporting an initially arpeggiated right-hand melody which then reaches an embellished, more registrally confined cadential close. The cadence is weak: the left hand's dominant-seventh harmony in bar 2 is not in root position, and the quaver pattern carries on unabated. Moreover, the cadence occurs just into the piece and lacks finality. Now whether or not a performer conceives the passage in precisely those terms, he or she will undoubtedly be aware of these features and the interpretation will be influenced accordingly. Most pianists, for example, would make much less of the C major cadence in bar 2 than the one at the end of the movement in bars 69–71, which is far more definitive and structurally significant (Example 3.1b).[12] To play bar 2's cadence with the same weight and conviction would be hard to justify (although a Glenn Gould might just manage it!). In short, the pianist's awareness of the contextual function of each cadence will determine how it is shaped – the amount of temporal stretching (if any in bar 2), the dynamic levels of the constituent elements relative to each other and to the surrounding music, the kind of articulation (pedalling, touch, timbre) and so on.

Similar decisions will be taken about the opening melody in bar 1, which most pianists would imbue with a small-scale crescendo while gently emphasising and perhaps sustaining the first note in each left-hand group of four quavers. Stylistic tradition and innumerable other factors naturally influence one's decisions, but first the pianist must explicitly recognise the triadic, ascending arpeggiation in the right hand and the broken-chord accompaniment in the left – and by 'explicitly' I do not necessarily mean in those terms. The point is that without a parsing of this music and an identification of each element's function both locally and in the context of the whole, one could hardly conceive a viable interpretation.

Parsing and identifying function – the essence of each and every analytical act – can, and for the experienced musician probably will, initially take place at sight, on the basis of the 'informed intuition' referred to above (that is, drawing upon an assimilated understanding of syntax, melodic structure, rhythmic patterning and so on). But immediate apprehension by no means precludes later and more deliberate reconsideration of how the various elements operate in a piece, and at that stage something beyond intuition may be required.

One way for musicians to satisfy their 'thirst for musical knowledge'[13] is to learn more rigorous techniques not so much for eventual direct application to performance, but in order to assimilate terminology and concepts which might heighten their ability to articulate to themselves and others (students, teachers and so on) what is happening in the music. It is not knowledge that some performers fear as much as the possible *requirements* associated with it: performers understandably do not like being told what to do by scholars employing a dictatorial language that threatens their musical freedom. Nevertheless, to be able to employ a more sophisticated vocabulary supplementary to the 'arcane sign-gesture-and-grunt system'[14] often used in rehearsal, and also to understand more fully the ways in which music might be organised, can prove liberating to musicians striving for more informed intuition, more profound conscious thought and greater powers of verbal articulation.

These techniques include the following:

(1) identifying formal divisions and basic tonal plan
(2) graphing tempo
(3) graphing dynamics
(4) analysing melodic shape and constituent motifs/ideas
(5) preparing a rhythmic reduction
(6) renotating the music.

I shall describe these and demonstrate their role in preparing Chopin's Nocturne Op. 27 No. 1 for performance, having first observed that their potential application is by no means limited to solo piano music. In principle, any musician could find these techniques beneficial, as long as they are regarded not as an end in themselves but as a means of heightening one's sense of musical process. Once again, temporality and 'shape' are fundamental to this analytical enterprise, as indeed is recognition of the need for a larger synthesis.

A performer's analysis of Chopin's C♯ minor Nocturne

Chopin composed the Nocturnes Op. 27 in 1835. The first of the two opens bleakly (Example 3.2a), but eventually the music starts building until a powerful climax is reached, after which it falls back only to build again (Example 3.2b–d). A triumphant melody then enters (Example 3.2e), followed by an almost immediate retraction (Example 3.2f) and a sudden breakdown, culminating in a cathartic cadenza that leads to the return of the futile opening melody (Example 3.2g). But the mood turns more hopeful in the C♯ major coda (Example 3.2h), which anticipates the lyrical D♭ major of the second nocturne.[15]

The pianist's most immediate technical challenge is to control the widely spaced, *pianissimo* accompaniment in the opening section and reprise, as

Example 3.2 Chopin, Nocturne in C♯ minor Op. 27 No. 1 (a) bars 1–7 (b) bars 29–32 (c) bars 45–52 (d) bars 53–6 (e) bars 65–8 (f) bars 73–7 (g) bars 78–84 (h) bars 94–101

(c)

(d)

(e)

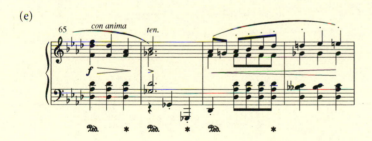

(f)

Example 3.2 (*cont.*)

(g)

(h)

Example 3.2 (*cont.*)

well as the more vehement left-hand figuration that increases in intensity and registral convolution as climax approaches. More subtle challenges include sustaining the energy of the 'bleak' sections and judiciously pacing the unfolding drama in the middle in order to achieve graded expansions and appropriately abrupt moments of retraction. Some of the analytical tools presented below might help to those ends.

Identifying formal divisions and basic tonal plan

One of the first 'deliberate' analytical tasks a performer could undertake is to determine the music's form and tonal foundation. Such models as binary and ternary form, sonata form, rondo form and so on are familiar to most musicians, and analysing a work in these terms early on can be productive, followed perhaps by a more detailed, individually tailored outline showing the music's principal sections and subsections, tonal plan and other features as relevant. Nevertheless, diagrams of this sort have no more musical value than an electrical circuitboard unless one understands their architectural attributes in diachronic terms, that is, in terms of time and process. This is especially vital for the performer, for the reasons stated earlier.

The structure of Chopin's Nocturne is relatively simple, as Figure 3.2 demonstrates. It has a ternary form – A–B–A' plus coda – with a two-part division of section B defined by the 'con anima' melody in Db major, the tonic major's enharmonic equivalent (see Example 3.2e). Db major is prepared by a move from C♯ minor (section A) through E major to the dominant (notated as Ab major in Example 3.2c), which acts as an important pivot in section B and the piece as a whole. After the new melody in bar 65 and the rupture in bars 78–80, the dominant briefly returns, remaining in force until the abbreviated[16] reprise of section A.

As before, the way in which performers understand the Nocturne need not conform to this 'rigorous' description. A pianist would instead tend to *feel* the various tonal areas as points of gravitation towards or away

Bars	1–28				29–64	65–83		84–94	
Section	A				B			A'	
Subsection	intro	A₁	A₂	'coda'	B₁	B₂	cadenza	intro	A₂'
Bar	1	3	19	27	29	65	83	84	86
Tonality	C♯ minor				- - - - - - E – Ab	Db - - - - - - - G♯		C♯ minor	
	i				- - - - - - - III – V	=I V		i	

Figure 3.2 Chopin, Nocturne in C♯ minor Op. 27 No. 1: formal and tonal plan

from which the music flows – areas weighted according to their perceived importance, the transient E major meriting less emphasis (in dynamics and temporal stretching) than, say, the ensuing dominant, which enters at the point of climax. Equally, pianists would typically regard the A–B–A′ form not as a sequence of sectional blocks but as a diachronic unfolding – possibly as an interplay between stable and unstable or static and active phases, or as a statement followed by departure and then return.[17] Although none of these formulations fully captures what happens in the piece, at least they indicate one's basic feel of the music in performance as it expands and contracts, remains fixed or moves forward, and so on. A *sense* of form-as-process is what really matters to the performer, although to achieve that might require some hands-on dissection rather than just intuitive assimilation. Charts like the one in Figure 3.2 can assist in that respect despite their ossified appearance.

Graphing tempo

Although the graphs in Figure 3.1 provide a valuable snapshot of tempo fluctuation in performance, neither performers nor listeners are likely to perceive such fluctuations in a literal sense: the 'facts' of the performance expressed by the data reveal only a partial and somewhat misleading truth.[18] Whatever implications this might have for post facto performance analysis, charting tempo fluctuation can prove beneficial to performers as an act of analysis *prior to* performance, that is, while developing an interpretation. One way of doing so is to determine the broad tempo divisions in a work and then to sketch by hand the contour of the prevailing tempos while taking into account the smaller-scale accelerations or retardations that occur in performance. Although this freehand method lacks the rigour behind Figure 3.1's diagrams, it may better approximate how the music is 'heard' by the performer while also producing an enlightening visual image of temporal process.

Diagrams like these are much easier to devise when the composer specifies metronome markings, and the Nocturnes Op. 27 happen to be the last of Chopin's works with such indications. In Op. 27 No. 1, section A is marked 'Larghetto ♩ = 42', and section B 'Più mosso ♩. = 54' (the minim and dotted minim respectively acting as the basic pulse in each section). The opening tempo returns at the reprise, and the last three bars are played Adagio (after gradual slowing in bars 93–6). The piece could therefore be viewed as three temporal plateaux in turn, followed by the Adagio. As before, performers would typically understand these states not as entities but as an ongoing succession of governing pulses subject to moment-by-moment adjustment. I have depicted that succession in Figure 3.3 in a graph simulating the post

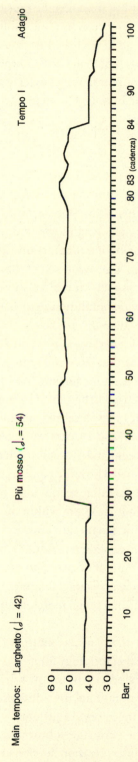

Figure 3.3 Tempo fluctuation in Chopin, Nocturne in C♯ minor Op. 27 No. 1

facto analyses seen previously but mapping the music's temporal landscape as traversed in the performer's inner ear. While it similarly offers a synchronic snapshot, the graph should also be viewed from start to finish, in other words as the Nocturne unfolds. The dialectical interplay between diachronic process and the synchronic whole is in fact characteristic of the way in which performers conceive of music in general – an important point to which we shall return.[19]

Graphing dynamics

One's sense of musical process can be enhanced by charting a work's changing dynamic levels, again in the manner of Figure 3.1 but with a potentially prescriptive purpose. This involves preparing a diagram like the one in Figure 3.4, in which the principal dynamic markings appear on the vertical axis, with a line tracing the bar-by-bar progression according to the many indications provided by Chopin. One weakness of this approach is its limited attention to context, which usually influences a given dynamic marking's meaning. (For example, a *piano* marking might have a different meaning within a prevailing *fortissimo* than in a passage marked *pianissimo*.) Nevertheless, even though dynamic markings are interpreted here at face value, and though once more lacking the rigour of Figure 3.1b, the graph provides an excellent overview of the dynamic terrain as well as the opportunity to sense it as it passes by. That sense can be gained by imagining the first part of the piece proceeding on more or less level ground, followed by a rapid climb and then a steep drop, a more gradual ascent leading to another abrupt drop, and finally a third phase of ascent and descent which more tortuously makes its way back to the level plane on which the piece began. In my view, Chopin pours the Nocturne's entire potential energy into the dynamics, or at least represents that energy flux in microcosm within the dynamic markings. In any case, the chart of dynamic fluctuation amounts to an 'intensity curve' for the whole piece – that is, 'a graphic representation of the music's ebb and flow, its "contour" in time',[20] and if one tried to capture how the Nocturne feels to the player, a diagram like this might emerge, a diagram which again is both diachronic and synchronic in its representational import.

Analysing melodic shape and constituent motifs/ideas

Although a general methodology for analysing melody is elusive, it can be instructive to trace melodic contours on a sheet of paper without the stems, noteheads and other notational impediments that distract one's eye from the underlying pitch trajectory. In general, and as suggested earlier, music's representation in the performer's inner ear little resembles its appearance in the score: as the interpretation develops, notation is transformed

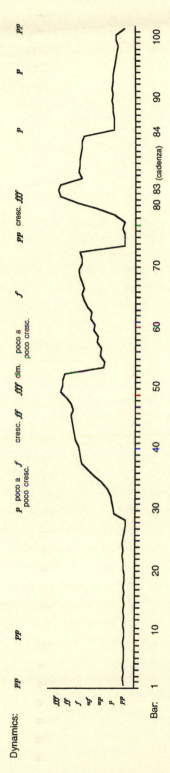

Figure 3.4 Dynamics in Chopin, Nocturne in C♯ minor Op. 27 No. 1

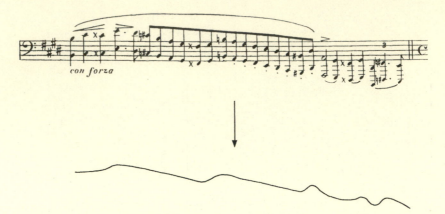

Figure 3.5 Chopin, Nocturne in C♯ minor Op. 27 No. 1: registral contour of the cadenza (score reproduced from German first edition; Leipzig: Breitkopf & Härtel, 1836)

into a series of physical actions corresponding to mental images of various kinds, including aural ones (as discussed in chapter 4). Performers typically conceive of melody as a line (whether continuous or not) that they sing to themselves while making music, and a literal graph of melodic contour or shape, over brief or extended passages (in the latter case perhaps depicting successive registral high or low points), may come closer than the original notation to that aural image. Figure 3.5 traces the melodic contour of the Nocturne's cadenza, the undulation and gestural properties of which become all the more palpable when thus highlighted.[21]

An awareness of significant pitch configurations within a melody as well as more generally will also affect how performers project the music, even if demonstrations of motivic unity are not their primary goal. Such patterns could invite a characteristic timbre or articulation, likewise recurrent textures, rhythms and other elements that affect the music's shape. In Chopin's Nocturne, sections A and A′ – which feature a tight registral compass and predominantly conjunct, monodic melodic motion – present an evocative countermelody in bars 20–6 and (in abbreviated form) bars 89–93 which might be played 'nostalgically', that is, with a weighted but paradoxically detached touch and a less reticent dynamic than the bleak melody it counterpoints, especially in the two cadential passages (bars 25–6 and 92–3), the first of which is left hanging, while the second ends the main body of the piece with the telling 'con duolo' indication.

These cadences have such expressive potency partly because of the suggestive D♮ within the melodic descent, which recurs throughout A and A′ in one of two harmonic settings. The first (Example 3.3a) uses a Neapolitan D major over an insistent tonic pedal, followed by a cadence. The second setting (Example 3.3b) sets the dominant harmony against the D♮, now a dissonant counterpart to the expected diatonic D♯. Again, the terminology

Example 3.3 Chopin, Nocturne in C♯ minor Op. 27 No. 1: melodic D♮ in sections A and A′ (a) bars 5 and 21 (see also bars 9–10, 25, 26–8, 88, 92 and 93) (b) bars 13 and 17

is not what matters: the issue is one of analytical technique relevant to the performer – which in this case involves extracting all the different manifestations from the score, juxtaposing them on paper for the sake of comparison and then weighing up their respective roles within the per-formance conception. In my view, the D♮s offer a key to understanding sections A and A′, their proximity to the tonic somehow suggesting futility (particularly when harmonised by the Neapolitan), while the modal disso-nance of bars 13 and 17 seems archaic and elegiac, starkly contrasting with the middle section's bellicosity and triumph.

Preparing a rhythmic reduction

Each section in the Nocturne has a distinctive rhythmic character, and parsing and identifying the function of the main rhythmic elements reveals their role in generating, sustaining or suspending momentum. For example, the unchanging quaver backdrop in sections A and A′ and the coda engenders the static quality mentioned earlier; the dotted figure (♩. ♪ ♩) used

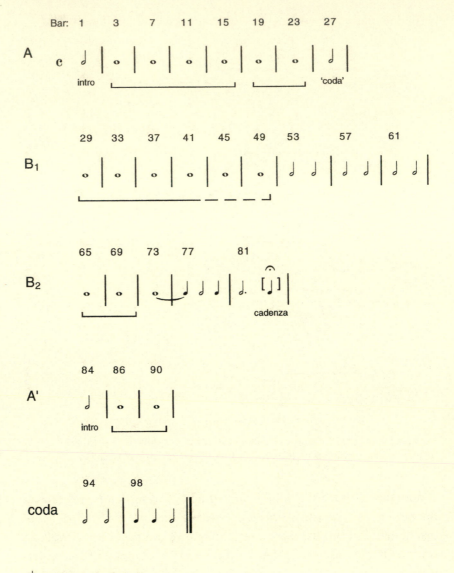

Figure 3.6 Chopin, Nocturne in C♯ minor Op. 27 No. 1: rhythmic reduction of phrase structure

virtually throughout B_1 drives the music towards climax in two phases; and the repeated crotchet and crotchet–quaver figures in B_2 (♩ ♩ ♩ and ♩ ♫♫ respectively) help create the transient sense of triumph.

But the rhythmic reduction referred to above relates not to rhythmic details such as these but to higher-level rhythmic properties, namely phrase structure. Various techniques of rhythmic reduction are described in the analytical literature,[22] although the most valuable and accessible one from the performer's standpoint could be to represent each bar (or other unit) as a proportionally smaller rhythmic value like a crotchet, and then to combine these rhythms according to phrase groupings perceived within the music. The next step is to discern the shape inherent within the emergent diagram, by which I mean instances of truncation, extension, contraction, elision and so on at the level of the phrase or above. This reductive technique works particularly well with Chopin, whose predilection for four-bar phrases is well known, although there is no lack of momentum in the phrase structure of our Nocturne. Each semibreve in Figure 3.6 stands for a four-bar phrase (or 'hypermeasure'),[23] while minims represent two-bar units and crotchets a single bar. The diagram reveals section A's entirely regular four-bar phrase pattern save for the introduction and the 'coda' framing it (two bars each), and as in section A′ this regularity contributes to the intentionally static character identified earlier. In section B_1, which starts with a 4 + 2 arrangement emphasising the climactic bars 45–52, the phrase rhythm quickens in bars 53–64 with six two-bar units in rapid succession. This is an extended anacrusis to section B_2, where an initially balanced four-bar phrase pattern breaks down at bar 77, the ensuing irregularities in phrase structure fuelling the collapse at this critical juncture. Although all of these features could conceivably be intuited by performers, they involve a higher level of structure that might be hard merely to sense. A diagram like Figure 3.6 helps to show that phrase structure and musical shape are two sides of the same coin in Chopin's Nocturne.

Renotating the music

Conventional notation by no means captures music's full complexity, as every performer knows. Rhythmic subtleties are notoriously difficult to pin down, as indeed are dynamic nuances, minor deviations in pitch and the huge range of articulation used by musicians. Rescoring the music can sometimes mitigate the original notation's inadequacies by shedding light on properties obscured by or absent from the score itself. For instance, an alternative metrical scheme latent in the original might be revealed by rewriting the music with the new metre(s) in the relevant parts, rebarring as necessary to shift otherwise hidden downbeats and associated patterns of emphasis.[24] This does not mean the new notation fully captures 'the music': indeed, it is the tension between the original and the new versions that is potentially of greatest interest to the performer, who must recognise that 'the music' conforms to neither but exists as it were in the interstices between

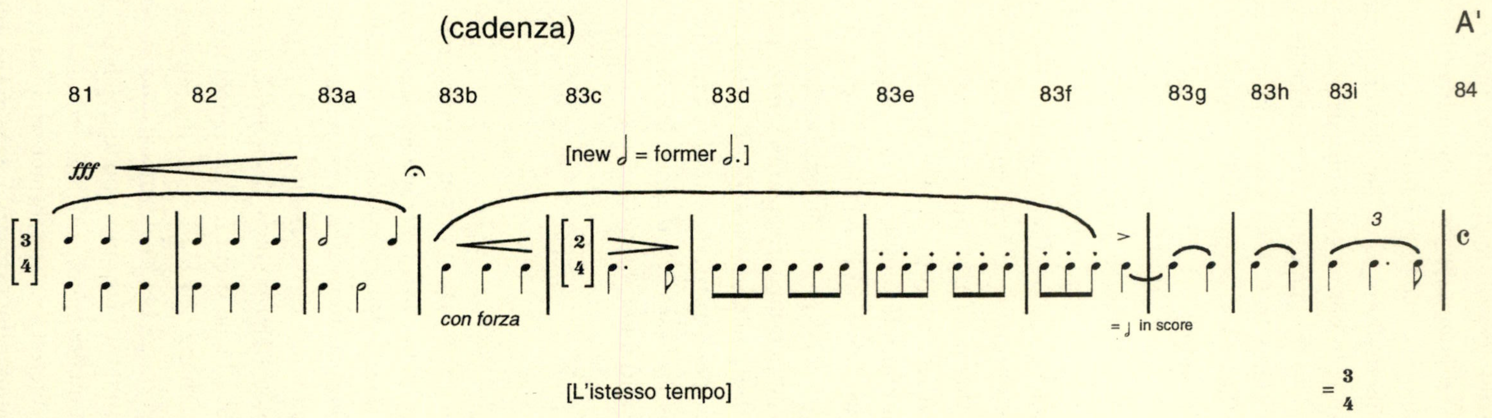

Figure 3.7 Chopin, Nocturne in C♯ minor Op. 27 No. 1: rescoring of bars 81–4 (with Chopin's dynamics and slurs)

them. Renotation might also succeed in depicting such features as lower-level rhythmic play, the contrapuntal layering that can be masked especially in keyboard music, the distribution of parts between the pianist's hands or the members of an ensemble, and so on.

Figure 3.7 presents a renotated version of bars 81–4 of Chopin's Nocturne, elaborating the cadenza's metrical properties in particular. This diagram resulted from ongoing uncertainty on my part about how to shape the cadenza in actual performance: it is the product of a deliberate analytical act undertaken when mere intuition failed to crack an intractable problem. The fact that the passage is unbarred in the original made it difficult to determine where metric accents should fall as well as the internal rhythmic organisation of the fifteen-quaver group (see Example 3.2g), factors which would affect dynamics, rubato and articulation and thus stretch or compress the registral contour shown in Figure 3.5. In my analysis, which fulfilled the problem-solving role I referred to earlier, bar 83b perpetuates the 3/4 metre of bars 81–3a, but at bar 83c a new 2/4 metre is implied, with the duration of the bar kept constant by equating the new minim with the former dotted minim (so in retrospect bar 83b seems like a crotchet triplet). Chopin's fifteen-quaver group is broken down into the four sets of triplets in bars 83d–e, followed by another in bar 83f which catapults the music towards the syncopated octave on A (notated as a minim in the score). A slower, more regular rhythm then leads to the crotchet triplet in bar 83i (the '3' is Chopin's), which implicitly reinstates the 3/4 metre of bars 81–3b while preparing for the return of **C** in section A'.

It is interesting to contemplate whether Chopin had this sort of organisational scheme in mind when composing the Nocturne. Certainly his slurs, dynamics and articulation markings indicate that possibility, as perhaps does the presence of an eight-bar phrase structure consistent with his usual practice. Now whether or not the pianist 'should' have this sort of scheme in mind when performing the Nocturne is a different matter. Having produced a diagram like Figure 3.7, one need not stay wedded to it in performance; in fact, I play the music much more freely than this new notation suggests, however enlightening it once proved to be.[25] The fruits of such an exercise need to be assimilated like any other knowledge acquired in the process of building an interpretation – perhaps to be forgotten yet unconsciously remembered on each occasion the music is brought to life thereafter.

Towards synthesis

I have stressed throughout this chapter that the insights gained from analysis – whether intuitive or deliberate – are but one factor influencing the performer's conception of the music. The success of a performance will be measured by oneself and one's audience not so much by its analytical rigour, historical fidelity or even technical accuracy (at least in some circles) as by the degree to which 'resonance' is achieved in drawing together the constituent elements into something greater than the sum of those parts, into a musically cogent and coherent synthesis. Analysis may well be 'implicit in what the performer does', and it may also be explicitly undertaken by performers employing the techniques described here or indeed others. But it is important not to elevate it above the performance it gives rise to, or to use it as a means of subjugating and shackling musicians. Instead, its potential utility must be recognised as well as its limitations, by which I mean simply that 'the music' transcends it and any other approach to understanding it. Projecting 'the music' is what matters most, and all the rest is but a means to that end.

Notes

1 'The performance of a piece of music is ... the actualization of an analytic act – even though such analysis may have been intuitive and unsystematic ... analysis is implicit in what the performer does.' Leonard Meyer, *Explaining Music* (Chicago: University of Chicago Press, 1973), 29.

2 '[P]erformers can never plumb the aesthetic depth of a great work without an intense scrutiny of its parametric elements.' Eugene Narmour, 'On the relationship of analytical theory to performance and interpretation', in Eugene Narmour and Ruth A. Solie (eds.), *Explorations in Music, the Arts, and Ideas* (Stuyvesant: Pendragon, 1988), 340.

3 By 'performers' I principally mean soloists as opposed to ensemble or orchestral musicians, although the analytical techniques proposed here could be used in preparing performances with two or more musicians. They could also be applied to other repertoires despite this chapter's focus on tonal music in the Western classical tradition.

4 Janet Schmalfeldt, 'On the relation of analysis to performance: Beethoven's Bagatelles Op. 126, Nos. 2 and 5', *Journal of Music Theory*, 29 (1985), 28; italicised in the original.

5 Edward T. Cone, *Musical Form and Musical Performance* (New York: Norton, 1968), 34.

6 Narmour, 'On the relationship', 319, 340; see also Narmour's comment in note 2 above.

7 Respectively, *Form in Music*, 2nd edn (Englewood Cliffs: Prentice-Hall, 1986), 415, and *Musical Structure and Performance* (New Haven: Yale University Press, 1989), 44.

8 Jonathan Dunsby, 'Guest editorial: performance and analysis of music', *Music Analysis*, 8 (1989), 7, 9ff. Cf. page 232 in this book, where Dunsby comments:

'structural analysis in some form simply must be part of the performer's work'; 'the performer has to identify the structure, assimilate it and control it well enough in real time to represent and, ideally, accurately convey it'.

9 The crudity of the terms 'rigorous analysis' and 'performer's analysis' must be acknowledged, although the distinction will prove useful. Techniques of 'rigorous analysis' include Schenkerian, set-theoretic and paradigmatic approaches.

10 John Rink, review of Berry, *Musical Structure*, in *Music Analysis*, 9 (1990), 323, 324, 328. For a more detailed summary of the analysis-and-performance literature see Nicholas Cook, 'Analysing performance, and performing analysis', in Nicholas Cook and Mark Everist (eds.), *Rethinking Music* (Oxford: Oxford University Press, 1999), 239–61.

11 See also chapters 11 and 14 in this volume (especially Figures 11.1–11.3 and 14.1–14.3). Quite different techniques were used to prepare the various diagrams in Figure 3.1. Tempo fluctuation in CD recordings can be graphed by tapping a key on a computer with CD-ROM player to mark where each beat or bar begins; the computer then transforms successive taps into lines, as in Figure 3.1a. Alternatively, software like 'Sforzando' can track tempo and dynamic fluctuation in recorded performances. As for live piano performance, the digital data obtained from a Yamaha Disklavier define the expressive properties (i.e. timing, dynamics and articulation) of each note, which can be represented graphically as in Figure 3.1b (see also Figures 11.2 and 11.3). Such data are less readily available for voice and other instruments, which partly explains why investigations of piano music are predominant in the literature.

12 The short coda in bars 71–3 reinforces the cadence.

13 Jonathan Dunsby, *Performing Music: Shared Concerns* (Oxford: Clarendon Press, 1995), 46.

14 Joseph Kerman, *Musicology* (London: Fontana, 1985), 196.

15 Readers are advised to consult an Urtext score and to listen to as many recordings as possible.

16 Both A_2 and A_2' lack a counterpart to bars 11–18.

17 The new melody in B_2 can be seen as a further statement and the coda as a return at least of the tonic major from B_2 if not its triumphant mood.

18 See Bruno H. Repp, 'Probing the cognitive representation of musical time: structural constraints on the perception of timing perturbations', *Cognition*, 44 (1992), 241–81; see also chapter 13 in this volume.

19 See Cone, *Musical Form*, 88–98.

20 An intensity curve is 'determined by all active elements (harmony, melody, rhythm, dynamics, etc.) working either independently, in sync, or out of phase with one another to create the changing degrees of energy and thus the overall shape'; John Rink, 'Translating musical meaning: the nineteenth-century performer as narrator', in Cook and Everist (eds.), *Rethinking Music*, 234.

21 Cf. the graphs in Rink, 'Translating', 231–2.

22 For example, see Carl Schachter, *Unfoldings: Essays in Schenkerian Theory and Analysis*, ed. Joseph N. Straus (New York and Oxford: Oxford University Press,

1999), and William Rothstein, *Phrase Rhythm in Tonal Music* (New York: Schirmer Books, 1989).

23 For discussion see Rothstein, *Phrase Rhythm*. Note the hypermetre in Figure 3.6, **C**, which indicates that four-bar hypermeasures are the norm.

24 For examples see John Rink, 'Playing in time: rhythm, metre and tempo in Brahms's *Fantasien* Op. 116', in Rink (ed.), *The Practice of Performance: Studies in Musical Interpretation* (Cambridge: Cambridge University Press, 1995), 274–5, and Rink, 'Opposition and integration in the piano music', in Michael Musgrave (ed.), *The Cambridge Companion to Brahms* (Cambridge: Cambridge University Press, 1999), 93.

25 It is instructive to compare other performers' interpretations (live or recorded). For instance, Alfred Cortot (EMI CDZ 7673652) shapes the cadenza more or less as in Figure 3.7 – presumably without having first devised such a diagram!

Further reading

Cone, Edward T., *Musical Form and Musical Performance* (New York: Norton, 1968)

Cook, Nicholas, 'Analysing performance, and performing analysis', in Nicholas Cook and Mark Everist (eds.), *Rethinking Music* (Oxford: Oxford University Press, 1999), 239–61

Dunsby, Jonathan, 'Guest editorial: performance and analysis of music', *Music Analysis*, 8 (1989), 5–20

Lester, Joel, 'Performance and analysis: interaction and interpretation', in John Rink (ed.), *The Practice of Performance: Studies in Musical Interpretation* (Cambridge: Cambridge University Press, 1995), 197–216

Rink, John, review of Wallace Berry, *Musical Structure and Performance*, in *Music Analysis*, 9 (1990), 319–39

Rink, John, 'Playing in time: rhythm, metre and tempo in Brahms's *Fantasien* Op. 116', in Rink (ed.), *Practice of Performance*, 254–82

Rothstein, William, 'Analysis and the act of performance', in Rink (ed.), *Practice of Performance*, 217–40

4 Understanding the psychology of performance

ERIC CLARKE

Introduction: what performers do

Musical performance at its highest level demands a remarkable combination of physical and mental skills. It is not uncommon for concert pianists to play at speeds of ten or more notes per second in both hands simultaneously, in complex and constantly changing spatial patterns on the keyboard, and with distinct patterns of rhythm, dynamics and articulation. Equally, a performer has to have an awareness and understanding of the immediate and larger-scale structure of the music itself, an expressive 'strategy' with which to bring the music to life, and the resilience to withstand the physical demands and psychological stresses of public performance. Abilities such as these do not develop overnight, and by the time the best performers have reached the age of twenty-one, they are likely to have spent over 10,000 hours practising their instrument,[1] quite apart from the time devoted to other aspects of formal music education and the more informal components of what can be termed 'musical enculturation'. The message of even these simple observations is that musical performance represents a striking human achievement and is the result of a massive investment of time and effort.

What, then, do performers do? At one level the answer to this question is obvious: they produce physical realisations of musical ideas whether these 'ideas' have been recorded in a written notation, passed on aurally (as in a non-literate culture) or invented on the spur of the moment (as in free improvisation). The most basic requirement is that a performer should produce (more or less) the correct notes, rhythms, dynamics etc. of a musical idea – if an appropriate reference point exists (notational or conceptual) against which 'correctness' can be measured. However, over and above that, performers are expected to animate the music, to go *beyond* what is explicitly provided by the notation or aurally transmitted standard – to be 'expressive'. Not surprisingly, a substantial amount of research on the psychology of performance has in one way or another been focused on questions of interpretation and expression.

This chapter will be concerned with three aspects of the psychology of performance: the physical and mental skills of performing, expression in performance and the body in performance. These three topics will be considered primarily from the perspective of the Western concert tradition, since very little work thus far has investigated the psychology of any other kinds of performance – although arguably many of the same psychological skills and attributes that can be identified and studied within the Western tradition also apply to other traditions of performance, allowing at least some generalisation to other cultural contexts. There is also a rich ethnomusicological literature on many different performance traditions, some of which makes direct reference to psychological theory.[2]

Performance skills

As a physical skill, musical performance has attracted the interest of psychologists studying complex movement and timing skills. The origins of this interest are in the work of Carl Seashore,[3] who was the first to develop methods for recording the detailed timing and dynamic characteristics of performances. Seashore was primarily concerned with the accuracy and reproducibility of performance, and with analysing pitch production and control in non-keyboard performance. Henry Shaffer[4] and Caroline Palmer[5] developed these interests in various ways. For instance, Shaffer focused on three main issues: the control of movement, timing mechanisms in performance, and coordination and independence between the hands in solo piano performance and between players in duet performance. His work traced the way in which the mental image of a piece of music is translated into the movements of performance, arguing that the control of movement remains quite abstract and conceptual until comparatively late in this process. He showed, for example, how a performer sight-reading a Bach fugue missed a change of clef from one page to the next, and produced a sequence of errors which nevertheless preserved the underlying harmony of the passage and were not simply the notes that would result from misreading the clef.[6] It seemed that as soon as the player realised something was wrong, he essentially improvised with appropriate rhythm and harmony while correcting the mistake. It is the presence of information about musical structure within the mental program for controlling movement that makes this emergency improvisation possible.

One of the ways in which the abstract control of movement must be made definite is in terms of timing. Timing is particularly important for music performance, since it is a crucial aspect of musical structure as well as a medium for expression. Shaffer and others[7] have shown that expert performers have remarkable control of performance timing at levels ranging from the individual note to sections or complete pieces. Performers possess the capacity to judge and set the absolute tempo of a performance with varying degrees of reliability and reproducibility, with some reputedly having the tempo equivalent of absolute pitch (that is, the ability to set their tempo to a particular metronome mark without reference to an external timekeeper). There is no generally accepted explanation for the human sense of tempo, though various kinds of 'internal clock' or internal oscillator have been suggested.[8] It has been widely proposed that temporal shaping above the note or beat level is controlled by the performer's mental representation (or 'image') of the music. The stability (or otherwise) of the higher-level tempo shape can therefore be directly attributed to the stability of the performer's representation of the music: a performer with a clear and definite conception of a piece of music, and the requisite technical skills, is more likely to be able to play it in a controlled and reproducible manner.

An obvious feature of keyboard performance is the question of coordination between the two hands – and the related issue of coordination between players in an ensemble. Shaffer demonstrated the considerable independence between the hands that pianists can achieve, either where the polyrhythms of the music demand it or for expressive purposes.[9] Once again this independence, and the complementary skill of hand coordination, is attributed to the structure of the mental image. It is impossible to achieve the kind of independence needed to play even a simple polyrhythm flexibly unless there are separate representations or images for the left- and right-hand parts. Equally, the coordination between two players in a piano duet does not (or perhaps should not!) depend on one player rigidly following the other: Shaffer's analysis of two skilled pianists playing music for four hands by Beethoven indicated that a significant element of prediction on the part of both pianists about the future course of each other's expressive performance is involved.[10] This can be explained by assuming that the two players had a shared representation of the music and used this as the stable reference point from which to anticipate each other's expressive shaping. Despite the obvious importance of listening and an awareness of each other's breathing, bodily movement, facial gesture etc. as channels of communication, the role of auditory and visual feedback in this whole process remains almost completely uninvestigated.[11]

Two skills of central concern in the Western concert tradition are those of reading notation and memorising. In the mid 1970s, Sloboda carried out a significant programme of research into the psychology of music-reading,[12] for which he used the 'eye–hand span' as his primary indicator – a measure of how far ahead a music reader processes the notation. In his experiments, Sloboda gauged this by asking pianists to continue playing after the notation had been made to disappear suddenly and without warning, using whatever image of the notation remained in the 'mind's eye'. Sloboda found that skilled readers had an eye–hand span of about seven notes, and that for the more skilled readers this value expanded and contracted to coincide with phrase boundaries in the music, suggesting that an important factor in skilled music-reading is a sensitivity to musical structure. Evidence for this structural awareness also comes from the equivalent of proof-readers' errors in music. Sloboda showed that skilled readers tended not to notice isolated misprints in music, unconsciously playing the 'correct' (that is, intended) note rather than the misprint. Indeed, in repeated readings of a piece containing deliberate misprints, while the overall number of errors decreased (as one would expect) the number of unconscious 'corrections' *increased*, presumably as the readers became familiar with the material and made more assumptions about its structure. It is worth noting that skilled music-reading is not simply a visual skill: one study[13] has shown that success at sight-reading was associated with success in matching visual notation to sound – in other words, the ability to hear music from notation 'in the mind's ear'.

Systematic studies of the process of memorising music from notation for performance are surprisingly scarce,[14] and comparatively little is known about the processes that occur during memorisation and the range of different strategies that performers may use. The ability to memorise music for performance has a particular cultural value, although some might argue that there is as much to be said against it as for it. In a study evaluating the effect of memorisation on audience perceptions, Aaron Williamon found some evidence for better musical communication,[15] though only for musically trained observers/listeners. Another study[16] showed that a visual approach was more effective (in terms of the time taken to memorise) than an aural approach, which in turn was more effective than a kinaesthetic ('muscle-memory') approach; and that those with better memorising abilities were also better sight-readers. A further study investigated an autistic man (N.P.) with an exceptional aural musical memory,[17] demonstrating that despite having never seen the score, this individual could remember and reproduce a sixty-bar piano piece by Grieg virtually note-perfect after just four hearings, while an equally experienced 'control' pianist could manage only a fraction of the piece after equivalent exposure. This apparently remarkable feat depended on stylistic familiarity: a much shorter piece by Bartók, which was stylistically unfamiliar to N.P., was remembered dramatically less well, the 'control' pianist in this case achieving a

far better result. The authors concluded that 'the ability [of N.P.] is structurally based', that he 'needs to code material in terms of tonal structures and
relations and that his exceptional ability cannot at present survive outside
that framework'.[18]

Expression in performance

Expression, or 'feel', is so fundamental to performances of every
kind that, paradoxically, it is easy to ignore: we become deaf to its presence.
A close look at the phenomenon, however, opens up a rich topic that has
generated abundant research. Seashore, one of the pioneers of empirical
research on performance in the 1930s, defined expression as follows: 'the
artistic expression of feeling in music consists in esthetic deviation from
the regular – from pure tone, true pitch, even dynamics, metronomic time,
rigid rhythms etc.'[19] Because his work and the overwhelming majority of the
research that has followed have been concerned with the notated Western
tradition, the phrase 'esthetic deviation from the regular' has often been
interpreted as 'deliberate departures from the indications of the score'. But
how are deliberate departures to be distinguished from accidents? How is
music that has no score to be treated? What should be done about expressive
markings already in the score (accelerandos and ritardandos, crescendos and
decrescendos etc.) – must the corresponding tempo and dynamic changes
in the performance be regarded as inexpressive simply because there is a
marking in the score? Other proposed definitions of expression have tried to
overcome such problems while retaining the basic principle that expression
is a departure from some norm.[20]

There are, of course, limits to how far performers are conventionally
expected or allowed to 'deviate' from either norms or the score. Within
the Western concert tradition, performers are not expected to change the
notes and rhythms of a piece of music (although this is a comparatively
recent attitude: in the nineteenth century, and still more so prior to that,
performers commonly embellished or otherwise altered the compositions
they performed), or to change the order of movements or sections (except
when this option is explicitly allowed in the score, as in a work such as
Stockhausen's *Klavierstück XI*), or to play the music very much faster or
slower than the composition indicates (though a great deal of music exists
from before the era of the metronome for which the composer has provided
no firm tempo indication). But within these limits there is still enormous
scope for performers to adopt different approaches, raising an interesting
problem for the psychology of music: to determine what makes a performance sound 'human' and musically effective, and to distinguish such a

performance from one which sounds lifeless, implausibly mannered or wayward, or simply incompetent.

One general perspective on expression is that a performer aims for transparency between conception and action, so that every aspect of his or her understanding of the music finds an outlet in the performance itself. There are at least two problems with this perspective. First, it is an idealised view of performance, and the reality is bound to fall short for practical reasons if nothing else: a performer may have more than one understanding of an event or passage in a piece, but in any given performance is obliged to settle for one interpretation; or he or she may have an understanding of some large-scale feature of the organisation of the work which may be impossible to project in a concrete fashion within the performance. Second, and more fundamentally, this approach tends to present the score as 'the music', and expressive performance as some kind of modification thereof. The score is of course not the music but simply one of a number of possible representations (CD recordings, videos and written descriptions are others), and can be seen as something like a blueprint for a performance – and a rather sketchy one at that, which 'makes sense' only when understood within some cultural context.

In recent years a considerable body of research has aimed at specifying the psychological principles that govern expressive performance in music.[21] This research has used a mixture of detailed analysis and computer modelling to explore the ways in which human performers expressively employ a variety of musical dimensions (tempo, loudness, attack, timbre, tuning, vibrato etc.) in performance. Experimental studies have demonstrated that expression can be extremely stable over repeated performances that may sometimes span a number of years,[22] is found even in sight-read performances[23] and can be changed by a performer at a moment's notice.[24] These observations have been used to argue that expression cannot be a learned pattern of timing, dynamics and articulation, remembered and applied to a piece each time it is played, but must arise out of a performer's understanding of the music in the course of performance.

In principle every aspect of musical structure contributes to the specification of an expressive profile for a piece, but some authors have shown that phrase structure is particularly salient. Neil Todd developed a model which produces an expressive timing pattern on the basis of the hierarchical phrase structure of the music, using one simple rule.[25] The resulting timing profiles compare well with the data of real performances by professional players. Similarly, in a study of twenty-eight performances of a short piano piece by Schumann, taken from commercial recordings by many of the twentieth century's greatest pianists, Repp found a high level of agreement in the timing profiles of the performances, all of which were organised around the phrase structure.[26] He also showed increasing diversity between the performers at more superficial levels of expression, suggesting that performers agree substantially about the larger shape of a piece of music, and express their individuality by manipulating the finer details of structure and its expressive implementation. Subsequent studies by Repp with even larger samples (over one hundred performances of the same music) have confirmed these conclusions.[27]

Expression can be understood as the inevitable and insuppressible consequence of understanding musical structure, yet it is also a conscious and deliberate attempt by performers to make their interpretations audible. As evidence for its unconscious and inevitable presence in performance, some authors have shown that when performers are explicitly asked to play without expression, the degree of tempo and dynamic variation is reduced but never eliminated, and that it keeps the same general pattern that is observed under normal conditions.[28] This aspect of performance expression can be seen as a consequence of the performer's spontaneous and unconscious grasp of the basic elements of musical structure: crudely put, it seems impossible *not* to play a note at the end of a phrase with different expressive features compared to notes in the middle of a phrase. However, it is obvious that performers also consciously and deliberately shape expression in their performances in order to achieve particular structural and stylistic results. This is one function of practice (along with overcoming purely technical problems), and it involves changes in the performer's understanding of the music and in the use of, and balance between, different expressive devices. These are all processes which either emphasise expressive properties already implicit in the music or superimpose a pattern upon it, and as Shaffer among others has pointed out, small differences in the precise implementation and relative balance of even a small number of expressive principles will result in potentially distinct characterisations of a piece.[29] As with memorising, there have been comparatively few systematic studies of the psychological processes involved in practice and rehearsal.[30]

Although expression may have a 'rule-like' quality, performers also have a (variable) ability to mimic an expressive pattern they hear – even when it has no reasonable structural basis.[31] In these circumstances they may create some kind of direct auditory 'image' of the performance which they then try to imitate (rather like an impersonator); or they may try to remember a verbal description of the performance (for instance, 'speed up towards the end of the first phrase, slow down during the middle of the second phrase, and then rush towards the end'); or they may try to conceive of the performance as a bodily image – a kind of mental choreography capturing and representing the shape of the performance. These strategies are loosely analogous to those that students might use in trying to imitate their teachers or in mimicking (perhaps unconsciously) aspects of other live or recorded performances which might have influenced them. They remind us that interpretation and expression are far from being the unique contributions of isolated individuals, but go on within a sometimes deafeningly 'noisy' culture of other performances. Whatever the attitude and strategy of different performers to this wealth of influence, it is clear that a theory of performance which is presented as a set of rules relating structure to expression is too abstract and cerebral, and that the reality is far more practical, tangible and indeed messy. In particular, the body is not just an 'input/output device', but is intimately bound up with our whole response to music, and needs to be recognised as having a more central role than a rule-based model suggests.

Movement and the body in performance

A concern with the human body and the role of bodily movement recognises that structure is not the sole determinant of expression. A wide range of other factors will shape the result, including the possibilities of the instrument, the acoustics of the performing environment, the nature of the audience, the mood and intentions of the performer, stylistic and cultural norms, and even the performance ideology espoused (for example, 'historically informed' performance practice). Movement and the human body are particularly significant in this complex set of relationships for many reasons – the most obvious being that music is produced by movements of the body and instrument, and is thus indelibly stamped with those origins. The ebb and flow of apparent movement and tension/relaxation that listeners experience in music come in part from an identification with the physical means of musical production – whether or not we have direct experience of the actual instruments involved. In a broader context, ethnomusicological research has demonstrated how the development of the characteristic structures of a musical style can be traced in some cases to physical factors associated with the instrument on which that music developed. For instance, John Baily has shown how the music of the dutar, a stringed instrument from Afghanistan, evolved from music associated with a different instrument in a neighbouring region, and in the process acquired characteristics specifically related to physical properties of the dutar itself.[32]

The close relationship between music and human movement has been recognised for a long time. In the 1930s Alexander Truslit carried out experimental research showing that different kinds of movement instruction (or movement image) given to performers resulted in measurably different performances.[33] Independently of this, other researchers have demonstrated that performers' spontaneous timing patterns follow the temporal curve of objects moving in a gravitational field, suggesting that a natural-sounding performance mimics the behaviour of physical objects moving in the real world.[34] Todd showed that a model of performance timing and dynamics based on the speed and force of movement of objects moving under the influence of gravity can account for a considerable proportion of the expression found in spontaneous musical performances, providing evidence for the idea that expression in musical performance is in certain respects a concrete and physical phenomenon upon which more rarefied elements are overlaid.

Movement is itself a part of performance as an audio-visual event and has been the subject of investigation and debate. While some movement is inevitably needed simply to produce music on an instrument, the majority of the movements observed and studied in published research by Jane Davidson[35] are over and above this purely ergonomic baseline – and can therefore be regarded as expressive, rather than practical. The movements concerned include swaying movements of the whole body, as well as discrete bodily gestures which are, strictly speaking, 'unnecessary' for the basic task of producing sound from the instrument. In one study (also discussed in chapter 10), Davidson concluded that a professional pianist made use of something like a lexicon of expressive gestures in his performances. Different gestures appeared to be associated with specific musical functions, and were so bound up with his conception of the music that they were observed even when he produced an imaginary performance of the same music on a table top rather than the keyboard. The performer had only limited conscious awareness of the expressive movements that he made, and there was no evidence to suggest that the movements had been deliberately developed or rehearsed at any time. The overriding impression (as intuition might suggest) was that the movements were integral to his conception and production of the music, and were generated in performance in just the same way as the expressive features of the sound (timing, dynamics, articulation etc.) are generated from an idea of the music.

This chapter's consideration of how the mind and the body interact in performance reflects a persistent and more general mind/body dualism. When composing, playing, teaching, researching and listening to music, it is all too easy to think of the constraints of the body simply as impediments to the all-powerful and self-sufficient mind. The difficulty of escaping from this way of thinking, and the damage that it does to our view of musical performance, remains profound. The reality is both more diverse and more integrated, as the mind is neither divorced from the body nor confined within the skull. Even a pianist's apparently pragmatic activity of choosing a fingering is just as concerned with thinking about what the music means as it is about getting to the right notes at the right time.[36] Playing music is a concrete form of musical thinking, and the body is as much a part of finding out about music as it is a means for its actualisation.

Conclusions: mind, body and meaning in performance

A rather stark separation between structure and expression has at times threatened to dominate a psychological view of performance. Musical structure is undoubtedly an important component in what motivates and shapes expression, but it is only one element in a wide-ranging network of relationships. As discussed above, Shaffer has proposed that expression in performance is concerned with the characterisation of a piece in performance, and that two performers with the same structural interpretation of a piece could conceivably give distinct performances based on how they characterised the music.[37] This raises a question about the limits of the notion of structure in music, and whether 'characterisation' is viable as a concept. More than that, it suggests that the crucial term – largely absent from the discussion so far – is *meaning*, and that when a performer 'characterises' a piece in performance, he or she is constructing meaning through expression. One option would be to regard performers as using their view of the meaning of the music as the 'generative source' of expression, but since expression itself is part of the meaning of the music, and not just a vehicle for it, this casts into doubt the 'generative' view as a whole – the idea that expression is generated *from* either structure or meaning.[38] Pursuing this a step further, performance research has mostly adopted a thoroughly individualistic view of the performer and his or her mind. The social context of performance (including co-performers, the audience and the influence of teachers and mentors, as well as recordings and performances by others, social attitudes to performance and performance 'fashions') is of paramount importance but as yet is poorly understood in any explicit manner. It only requires a consideration of the specific example of stage fright to see how dramatically the social and individual components of performance may interact.

Raising these concerns at the end of a chapter which has tried to separate out different components of performance and the mind might seem a perverse undoing of all that has gone before. Not so: although it is in many ways productive to break down a complex phenomenon into identifiable components in order to study it carefully and systematically, it is also important to remember that the individual components are not independent, and that an attempt must also be made to reintegrate and synthesise. Musical performance is the construction and articulation of musical meaning, in which the cerebral, bodily, social and historical attributes of a performer all converge, and if we choose to regard this convergence as an expression of the performer's mind, then we must remember that the mind is neither driving the body nor confined within the head.

Notes

1 See Ralf Th. Krampe and K. Anders Ericsson, 'Deliberate practice and elite musical performance', in John Rink (ed.), *The Practice of Performance: Studies in Musical Interpretation* (Cambridge: Cambridge University Press, 1995), 84–102; see also chapter 7 in this volume.

2 For example, see John Baily, 'Music structure and human movement', in Peter Howell, Ian Cross and Robert West (eds.), *Musical Structure and Cognition* (London: Academic Press), 237–58, and Benjamin Brinner, *Knowing Music, Making Music* (Chicago: University of Chicago Press, 1995).

3 Carl E. Seashore, *Psychology of Music* (New York: Dover, [1938] 1967).

4 L. Henry Shaffer, 'Performances of Chopin, Bach and Bartók: studies in motor programming', *Cognitive Psychology*, 13 (1981), 326–76, and 'Timing in solo and duet piano performances', *Quarterly Journal of Experimental Psychology*, 36A (1984), 577–95.

5 Caroline Palmer, 'Music performance', *Annual Review of Psychology*, 48 (1997), 115–38.

6 Shaffer, 'Performances', 365.

7 For example, see Manfred Clynes and Janice Walker, 'Neurobiologic functions of rhythm, time and pulse in music', in Manfred Clynes (ed.), *Music, Mind, and Brain: The Neuropsychology of Music* (New York: Plenum, 1982), 171–216.

8 For example, see Shaffer, 'Performances', and David Epstein, *Shaping Time: Music, the Brain, and Performance* (New York: Schirmer Books, 1995).

9 Shaffer, 'Performances' and 'Timing'.

10 Shaffer, 'Timing'.

11 For preliminary attempts see Lucy J. Appleton, W. Luke Windsor and Eric F. Clarke, 'Cooperation in piano duet performance', in Alf Gabrielsson (ed.), *Proceedings of the Third Triennial European Society for the Cognitive Sciences of Music (ESCOM) Conference* (Uppsala: Uppsala University Press, 1997), 471–4.

12 John A. Sloboda, 'Experimental studies of music reading: a review', *Music Perception*, 2 (1982), 222–36.

13 Andrew J. Waters, Ellen Townsend and Geoffrey Underwood, 'Expertise in musical sight reading: a study of pianists', *British Journal of Psychology*, 89 (1998), 123–49.

14 See for example George R. Marek, 'Toscanini's memory', in Ulric Neisser (ed.), *Memory Observed: Remembering in Natural Contexts* (San Francisco: W. H. Freeman, 1982), 414–17; Grace Rubin-Rabson, 'Studies in the psychology of

memorizing piano music. VI: A comparison of two forms of mental rehearsal and keyboard overlearning', *Journal of Educational Psychology*, 32 (1941), 593–602 (see also papers I–V in this series); Michiko Nuki, 'Memorization of piano music', *Psychologia*, 27 (1984), 157–63; and Roger Chaffin, Gabriela Imreh and Mary Crawford, *Practicing Perfection: Memory and Piano Performance* (Mahwah, NJ: Erlbaum, 2002). For an account of memory research in general, see Alan D. Baddeley, *Human Memory: Theory and Practice* (Hove: Erlbaum, 1990).

15 Aaron Williamon, 'The value of performing from memory', *Psychology of Music*, 27 (1999), 84–95; see also chapter 8 in this volume.

16 Nuki, 'Memorization', 160.

17 John A. Sloboda, Beate Hermelin and Neil O'Connor, 'An exceptional musical memory', *Music Perception*, 3 (1985), 155–70.

18 Ibid., 165.

19 Seashore, *Psychology of Music*, 9.

20 For example, see Peter Desain and Henkjan Honing, *Music, Mind and Machine* (Amsterdam: Thesis Publishers, 1992), 175; see also Bruno H. Repp, 'The aesthetic quality of a quantitatively average music performance: two preliminary experiments', *Music Perception*, 14 (1997), 419–44, which evaluates the aesthetic qualities of an artificially generated 'average' performance.

21 For example, see Eric F. Clarke, 'Generative principles in music performance', in John A. Sloboda (ed.), *Generative Processes in Music: The Psychology of Performance, Improvisation, and Composition* (Oxford: Clarendon Press, 1988), 1–26; Johan Sundberg, 'Computer synthesis of music performance', in Sloboda (ed.), *Generative Processes*, 52–69; and Neil P. McA. Todd, 'A computational model of rubato', *Contemporary Music Review*, 3 (1989), 69–89.

22 See Clynes and Walker, 'Neurobiologic functions'.

23 See Shaffer, 'Performances'.

24 See Eric F. Clarke, 'Structure and expression in rhythmic performance', in Howell, Cross and West (eds.), *Musical Structure*, 209–36.

25 Neil P. McA. Todd, 'A model of expressive timing in tonal music', *Music Perception*, 3 (1985), 33–58; see also Todd, 'Computational model'.

26 Bruno H. Repp, 'Diversity and commonality in music performance: an analysis of timing microstructure in Schumann's *Träumerei*', *Journal of the Acoustical Society of America*, 92 (1992), 2546–68.

27 Bruno H. Repp, 'A microcosm of musical expression: I. Quantitative analysis of pianists' timing in the initial measures of Chopin's Etude in E major', *Journal of the Acoustical Society of America*, 104 (1998), 1085–100, and 'A microcosm of musical expression: II. Quantitative analysis of pianists' dynamics in the initial measures of Chopin's Etude in E major', *Journal of the Acoustical Society of America*, 105 (1999), 1972–88.

28 See for example Seashore, *Psychology*, and Caroline Palmer, 'Mapping musical thought to musical performance', *Journal of Experimental Psychology: Human Perception and Performance*, 15 (1989), 331–46.

29 L. Henry Shaffer, 'Musical performance as interpretation', *Psychology of Music*, 23 (1995), 17–38.

30 See for example Linda M. Gruson, 'Rehearsal skill and musical competence: does practice make perfect?', in Sloboda (ed.), *Generative Processes*, 91–112; Susan Hallam, 'Professional musicians' approaches to the learning and interpretation of music', *Psychology of Music*, 23 (1995), 111–28; Kacper Miklaszewski, 'A case study of a pianist preparing a musical performance', *Psychology of Music*, 17 (1989), 95–109; Chaffin et al., *Practicing Perfection*; and chapter 7 in this volume.

31 See Eric F. Clarke, 'Imitating and evaluating real and transformed musical performances', *Music Perception*, 10 (1993), 317–43.

32 Baily, 'Music structure', 242–56.

33 Alexander Truslit, *Gestaltung und Bewegung in der Musik* (Berlin-Lichterfelde: Chr. Friedrich Vieweg, 1938); for discussion see Patrick Shove and Bruno H. Repp, 'Musical motion and performance: theoretical and empirical perspectives', in Rink (ed.), *Practice of Performance*, 55–83.

34 Neil P. McA. Todd, 'The kinematics of musical expression', *Journal of the Acoustical Society of America*, 97 (1995), 1940–9.

35 Jane W. Davidson, 'Visual perception of performance manner in the movements of solo musicians', *Psychology of Music*, 21 (1993), 103–13, and 'What does the visual information contained in music performances offer the observer? Some preliminary thoughts', in Reinhart Steinberg (ed.), *Music and the Mind Machine: The Psychophysiology and Psychopathology of the Sense of Music* (Berlin: Springer Verlag, 1995), 105–13; see also chapter 10 in this volume.

36 See Eric F. Clarke, Richard Parncutt, Matti Raekallio and John A. Sloboda, 'Talking fingers: an interview study of pianists' views on fingering', *Musicae Scientiae*, 1 (1997), 87–109.

37 See also Repp, 'Microcosm of musical expression: I'.

38 For related views see John Rink, 'Translating musical meaning: the nineteenth-century performer as narrator', and Nicholas Cook, 'Analysing performance and performing analysis', in Nicholas Cook and Mark Everist (eds.), *Rethinking Music* (Oxford: Oxford University Press, 1999), 217–38 and 239–61 respectively.

Further reading

Chaffin, Roger, Gabriela Imreh and Mary Crawford, *Practicing Perfection: Memory and Piano Performance* (Mahwah, NJ: Erlbaum, 2002)

Clarke, Eric and Jane Davidson, 'The body in performance', in Wyndham Thomas (ed.), *Composition, Performance, Reception: Studies in the Creative Process in Music* (Aldershot: Ashgate, 1998), 74–92

Davidson, Jane W., 'The social in musical performance', in David J. Hargreaves and Adrian C. North (eds.), *The Social Psychology of Music* (Oxford: Oxford University Press, 1997), 209–28

Dunsby, Jonathan, *Performing Music: Shared Concerns* (Oxford: Clarendon Press, 1995)

Gabrielsson, Alf, 'The performance of music', in Diana Deutsch (ed.), *The Psychology of Music*, 2nd edn (San Diego and London: Academic Press, 1999), 501–602

Palmer, Caroline, 'Music performance', *Annual Review of Psychology*, 48 (1997), 115–38

Rink, John (ed.), *The Practice of Performance: Studies in Musical Interpretation* (Cambridge: Cambridge University Press, 1995)

Wilson, Glenn D., 'Performance anxiety', in David J. Hargreaves and Adrian C. North (eds.), *The Social Psychology of Music* (Oxford: Oxford University Press, 1997), 229–48

PART TWO

Learning to perform

5   On teaching performance

JANET RITTERMAN

Play from the soul, not like a trained bird!   C. P. E. BACH[1]

Introduction

This chapter concentrates on performances in which a musician or group of musicians 'self-consciously enacts music for an audience', in which a pre-existing work is 'realised'.[2] Its particular focus is on the teaching of solo instrumental performance of Western art music. The timespan is from the late eighteenth century onwards, the geographical boundaries those of Western Europe, the emphasis on the teaching of those aspiring to professional standards, rather than of amateurs or beginners. Although instrumentalists are frequently advised to learn from singers, the teaching of singing itself is not addressed in this chapter, given the scope of the subject and the numerous strands particular to the history of voice teaching. Instead, the examples cited relate mainly to the piano and violin literature. Because of the popularity of these instruments and the emphasis placed on the mastery of solo repertoire and its presentation in concert, it is through them that the trends in instrumental performance teaching since the late eighteenth century can be seen most clearly. Since the phrase 'teaching performance' is used here with the implication that performance involves a consideration of the relationship between performer and audience, these are trends in the interpretation and communication of music in performance, rather than in instrumental technique. While performance teaching in most Western art music traditions has focused as least as much on the latter as the former, it is the teaching of style and interpretation that provides the context for this chapter.

Musical treatises as guides to performance

The attention given to issues of interpretation is a noticeable feature in the most influential of the treatises that began to proliferate in the second half of the eighteenth century. In earlier treatises, which generally were briefer, the emphasis tended to be on the initial stages of learning and the focus mainly on rudiments of theory and basic technique. While passing reference was often made to the importance of expressive playing and critical judgement, most remained virtually silent on the means by which these qualities were demonstrated or developed, presumably on the assumption that such matters were best communicated by the teacher and were likely to be particular to the repertoire – frequently the teacher's own compositions – that the student was learning.

As the numbers of those wishing to learn music increased, treatises tended to include more extended discussion of the qualities key to effective performance. In his flute treatise of 1752, Quantz, while reiterating the advice of earlier authors that a performer needed to cultivate good taste, related this to the ability to identify with the various 'passions' in the music and adjust the playing style accordingly – a sentiment echoed by many later writers:

The performer of a piece must seek to enter into the principal and related passions that he is to express. And since in the majority of pieces one passion constantly alternates with another, the performer must know how to judge the nature of the passion that each idea contains, and constantly make his execution conform to it. Only in this manner will he do justice to the intentions of the composer, and to the ideas that he had in mind when he wrote the piece.[3]

The need for experienced teaching to help aspiring performers develop this judgement was assumed. Although he elaborated the implications of his advice in the text, Quantz nevertheless regarded a good teacher as essential, as he explains at some length in his introduction.[4]

The emphasis in this treatise on what the art of performance demanded of performers in general – not only of flautists – singled it out from most preceding publications. Though wide-ranging, however, it was essentially retrospective in outlook, whereas the *Versuch über die wahre Art das Clavier zu spielen* – a treatise by C. P. E. Bach, Quantz's younger colleague at the court of Frederick the Great in Potsdam – had more direct impact on the teaching of performance in the following decades. Published in two parts, the first of which appeared in 1753, Bach's *Versuch* was reissued three times by 1787 and soon became the most widely circulated, frequently cited and generally admired publication of its kind.[5] It was this treatise that the young Carl Czerny was required to take to his first piano lesson with Beethoven in Vienna.[6]

Its focus is principally on the teaching of solo keyboard performance. As the author made clear in subsequent correspondence, it was addressed to 'those for whom music is a goal', rather than to amateurs.[7] Good performance is therefore given prominence in the opening paragraph as one of the qualities on which the true art of playing keyboard instruments depends.[8] For Bach, as for Quantz, this involved 'the ability . . . to make the ear conscious of the true content and affect of a composition'. But Bach's definition, while acknowledging through its emphasis on 'true content' the need to identify with the composer's intentions, emphasised the judgement of the ear. For Bach, good performance demanded that the listener 'hears all notes and their embellishments played in correct time with fitting volume produced by a touch which is related to the true content of a piece'.[9]

For those wishing to become accomplished performers, 'study by listening', which Bach wryly characterised as 'a kind of tolerated larceny', was essential: it was only in this way, he maintained, that matters 'which cannot be easily demonstrated, much less written down', became apparent.[10] Like Quantz, Bach was concerned by the lack of good performance teaching. He deplored the fact that most students, required to play the compositions of their teacher, were not exposed to works by composers of earlier periods or other national traditions, 'under the pretext that they are obsolete or too difficult'.[11] As with Quantz's treatise, however, the *Versuch* included no guidance on repertoire by other composers which would be appropriate for study.

Sources of performance teaching

Most of what C. P. E. Bach learned as a performer came from his father and from constant 'study by listening', particularly at court. In most parts of Western Europe before 1800, the musical tuition of those expected to become professional musicians was usually of this kind – provided within the family, the court or the church, or through apprenticeship schemes. Biographies of Haydn, Mozart and Beethoven show that they developed their performing skills in these ways, receiving tuition which often emphasised the skills of composition as much as it did those of performance itself.

Performance training of a more intensive kind was provided by conservatoires in Naples and Venice – institutions established from the end of the sixteenth century by certain charitable foundations for the care of orphans and others in need of protection. At a number of these, performance training became a prominent activity, and they gained enviable reputations for their music-making. By the closing decades of the eighteenth century, however, political upheaval had caused most of these institutions to decline. But from these roots a different type of conservatoire began to emerge. These new institutions were usually established with city or state support, rather than linked with the church or with charitable organisations, and they reflected the importance that was increasingly attached to public music-making. Through performances given by students or under the institution's auspices, many became integral to the development of public concert life in their respective cities.

By the turn of the century, the social, economic and cultural changes sweeping Europe helped to ensure that the teaching of performance became more widespread, increasingly sought by members of the middle classes and less influenced by earlier apprenticeship traditions. In the major cities, the demand for music teaching escalated at a remarkable rate, as is evident from directories, music periodicals and other informed comment of the time.[12] Private teaching of performance flourished, but in general it was the new conservatoires that exerted most influence on the gradual systematisation of performance teaching at an advanced level. Many attracted to their instrumental teaching staff leading performers of the day, whose reputations were known through Western Europe from their careers as touring concert artists. Their influence did much to determine what became accepted as standard instrumental repertoire.

The first of these new-style conservatoires emerged in Paris in the wake of the revolution. Founded in 1795 with a national remit, and building on earlier, more specialised schools, the Paris Conservatoire was established with joint responsibilities for teaching and performance: thus, students were trained to perform for national festivals and other types of public music-making. Initially 600 in number,[13] they were selected from all parts of the country and received tuition without charge.

The influence and reputation of the new institution quickly spread, and by the 1820s Prague, Vienna, Milan, Brussels, London and The Hague had followed suit. The trend continued, with conservatoires eventually being established in many German-speaking centres, Russia (St Petersburg and Moscow), Britain and America, some of which drew extensively on the approaches to performance teaching developed in Paris. Many began with a relatively narrow range of specialisms, reflecting local priorities and possibilities. In Paris, despite the expressed intention to train students in 'all branches of the art of music',[14] instrumental tuition in 1806 was focused on flute, oboe, clarinet, bassoon, horn, violin, cello and piano. Other specialisms emerged only gradually: for instance, harp was introduced in 1825, trumpet and trombone during the 1830s.

The need to establish systems and standards of performance teaching led in Paris to the publication of a series of method books.[15] These were specially commissioned from the Conservatoire's professors and subject to a process of formal institutional approval. Even where comparable in organisation and general content to what had preceded them, these new method books ranged well beyond the scope of earlier instrumental treatises. Most provided extensive and detailed instruction on matters of technique, style and interpretation, complemented by copious musical illustrations and teaching material, including compositions of earlier periods and different national schools as well as contemporary works. Among the most widely influential method books to emanate from the Paris Conservatoire in the first decade of its existence were those for strings and for piano. The method book for piano, first produced by Adam and Lachnith in 1798,[16] provides an extensive collection of excerpts, thus giving insight into the breadth of repertoire studied. Similar principles informed the *Méthode de violon* published in 1803 by Baillot, Rode and Kreutzer,[17] and the *Méthode de violoncelle* of 1804, in which Baillot collaborated with Baudiot, Levasseur and Catel.

Where Paris led, others followed. The nineteenth century saw a veritable flood of method books, particularly for the most popular instruments.[18] Many bore a considerable debt to earlier treatises, although without always acknowledging it. Some were from teachers connected with other conservatoires; others from established performer-teachers who had no institutional affiliation, such as Czerny, who, with Vienna as his base, taught piano for about fifty years, attracting talented students from many parts of Europe. As with Czerny's three-volume *Complete Theoretical and Practical Piano Forte School* Op. 500,[19] method books produced by distinguished performers of the time – such as the pianists Hummel[20] and Moscheles[21] and the violinist Spohr,[22] who had well-established reputations in many of the major musical centres of Europe from their years as touring virtuosos – readily crossed national boundaries. Attentively reviewed in the major music periodicals of the time, the most highly regarded of these publications were reissued in translation – usually appearing in Vienna, Paris and London – and were among the forces that helped to develop increasingly cosmopolitan approaches to the teaching of performance as the century progressed.

National schools of performance teaching

Despite these unifying trends, the existence of national schools of performance associated with particular instruments was generally acknowledged throughout the nineteenth century and well into the twentieth. By some commentators the term 'national' was used historically. Czerny applied it in this sense, distinguishing six schools of piano playing which he associated with particular composers: Clementi; Cramer and Dussek; Mozart; Beethoven; Hummel, Kalkbrenner and Moscheles; and a newly emerging school, represented by three young artists of the time, Thalberg, Chopin and Liszt. Even within these groupings, the music of each composer needed to be 'executed in the style in which he wrote'; Czerny rejected out of hand any thought that these could all be performed in the same style.[23]

Particularly from mid-century onwards, others used the concept of national schools of performance to differentiate contemporary trends in performing and teaching. Frequently a subject of comment in accounts by teachers or students, the distinctions tended initially to strengthen with the formalisation of teaching approaches by the leading national conservatoires, in some cases gaining impetus from nationalist trends. This can be seen in the emergence of Russian schools of instrumental performance. It was only from the second half of the century – after the St Petersburg and Moscow Conservatoires were established in the 1860s – that references to Russian schools of playing became commonplace. Until then, instrumental teaching at an advanced level in Russia had been provided principally by performer-teachers identified with other mainstream European performing traditions.[24]

Descriptions of national schools of performance often reflect the contributions of both composers and performers: the phrase has been variously used to identify particular approaches to musical expression, playing technique, choice of repertoire and even the organisation of curricula. In terms of technical approach, for much of the nineteenth century there undoubtedly were differences which distinguished certain schools of playing from others. However, in the case of piano and strings, these differences were gradually eroded by the patterns of travel of leading performer-teachers and the increasing mobility of students. By the close of the century, a great deal of permeation had occurred: although certain teachers continued to be identified with individual technical methods and specialist repertoires, the similarities in approach in matters of style and interpretation had become stronger and the differences less easy to categorise.

Such a trend is reflected in the French school of violin playing. At the beginning of the nineteenth century, this school of playing, identified with the teaching at the Paris Conservatoire, had become the main focus of attention, in part through its assimilation of aspects of the eighteenth-century Italian school, brought to Paris in the 1780s by Viotti.[25] Continuity of teaching played an important part in maintaining this position: Baillot, a professor at the Paris Conservatoire from 1795 to 1842,[26] was succeeded by violinists who had studied with him and who remained in post until the early 1890s. The thoroughness of the documentation of the French school of playing and its continued reappraisal was also a contributory factor. The production in 1834 by Baillot of a new and comprehensive method book, *L'Art du violon*, which provided an updated overview of the teaching of the French violin school and the repertoire studied by students in Paris, helped to ensure that its characteristic features continued to influence string playing in the decades that followed.[27]

By the time of Baillot's death in 1842, new influences were impinging on these traditions: a distinctive Franco-Belgian school was developing, based on the conservatoire in Brussels and influenced by the playing of Paganini. A further fusion of styles followed. During the second half of the century, as foreign students were more readily admitted to the Paris Conservatoire,[28] features of the French school of playing spread in ever-widening circles, modifying and being modified by other violin playing traditions. Among those who studied in Paris and contributed to this trend were Marsick, Wieniawski and Kreisler. The artistry of Kreisler, Viennese by birth, became known world-wide through his performances and recordings. Wieniawski, Polish-born, taught at the newly founded St Petersburg Conservatoire in the 1860s and later in Brussels. Marsick, a Belgian, who after his time as a student in Paris studied in Berlin with Joachim, returned to Paris to teach at the Conservatoire in the 1890s; his pupils included the Hungarian-born Carl Flesch and the Romanian Georges Enescu, both of whom had studied in Vienna. By the beginning of the twentieth century, relatively few of the leading performer-teachers could be neatly categorised as representatives of a particular national school. Styles of playing, once associated with composer or nationality, were increasingly identifed more with the performer or teacher than with one geographic location.

Style and interpretation

Even while national differences were perceived to exist, most discussions of style and interpretation in nineteenth-century treatises presented broadly similar views on the features essential to expressive performance and the centrality of the performer's contribution to this. A constant theme was the performer's ability to impress his or her individuality on the performance – a theme articulated by Adam[29] and developed by others. Spohr, elaborating the distinction between what he regarded as merely '*correct style* or *delivery*' and '*fine style*', affirmed Quantz's emphasis on the composer's intentions. A '*fine style*', he asserted, meant not simply that performers added ideas of their own but that they were 'capable of intellectually animating the subject so that the hearer may discover and participate in the intentions of the composer'.[30]

Of the various ways in which performers were expected to introduce their own ideas, considerable attention was given by nineteenth-century commentators to the importance of well-judged fluctuations or alterations of tempo. In the final section of his method book, Hummel illustrated this with lengthy extracts from his Piano Concerto in A minor Op. 85, showing by verbal instructions written into the score (e.g. 'somewhat accelerated', 'somewhat slower', 'somewhat relaxing in the time') the extent to which tempo modifications were expected.[31] Devoted exclusively to 'playing with expression', the third volume of Czerny's *School* included a chapter on the tasteful use of ritardandos and accelerandos. While this begins with the assurance that every composition 'must be played in the tempo prescribed by the composer', Czerny's musical examples support his statement that 'in almost every line of music there are certain notes and passages where a little ritardando or accelerando is necessary, to beautify the reading and to augment the interest'.[32]

Tasteful variations of the pitch and rhythm of the notated score, for rhetorical effect or to give spontaneity to the playing, were similarly seen as a desirable part of an experienced performer's contribution. These could involve changes to the detail of passagework or to notated rhythms, the interpolation of cadenza-like passages or, in the case of pianists, the arpeggiation of chords. Most method books, while counselling that sound musical judgement was required and that context determined appropriateness, presented the view that too little was at least as great a fault as too much. Both Hummel and Kalkbrenner produced editions of Mozart's concertos in which figuration was modernised in accordance with contemporary taste. Czerny's teaching, amplified in separate publications on ornamentation and expression 'in the modern style',[33] took a similar stance. There is ample evidence that this practice was perpetuated by influential teachers such as Liszt and Leschetizky, both of whom made textual changes in works they performed and taught. Liszt is known to have 'enriched' the passagework in one of Weber's concertos where he regarded it as thin,[34] while Leschetizky exercised 'great freedom and leeway' in interpretations of the printed score.[35]

But at the same time, there were signs that attitudes to the relationship between performer and work were changing and that these changes were impacting on performance teaching. Clara Schumann was influential in this regard: her teaching, which ran parallel to her performing career for over fifty years, influenced generations of performers and teachers in mainland Europe as well as in England.[36] When she performed in Vienna in 1856, the critic Eduard Hanslick observed that 'the artistic subordination of her own personality to the intentions of the composer' was 'a principle' for her, and he described her playing as 'a most truthful representation of magnificent compositions, but not an outpouring of a magnificent personality'. Other features of her playing singled out as unusual by Hanslick were its clarity ('Everything is distinct, clear, sharp as a pencil sketch') and, with certain reservations about its appropriateness, her 'strict confirmity to measure'.[37]

In these respects Clara Schumann's approach differed markedly from that of Anton Rubinstein. Widely admired for 'the fire and passion of his playing, and for his imagination and spontaneity',[38] Rubinstein, the first director of the St Petersburg Conservatoire and a dominant figure in European musical life throughout the second half of the century, took a more liberal approach to the works he performed. According to Josef Hofmann, arguably the most famous of his students, Rubinstein maintained that one should: 'Just play first exactly what is written. If you have done full justice to it and then still feel like adding or changing anything, why, do so.'[39] But by Rubinstein's death in 1894, such views, already challenged from various directions, were no longer unquestioningly accepted. Hofmann, who in 1926 was to become the first Director of the Curtis Institute in Philadelphia, believed that the player 'should always feel convinced that he plays only what is written', asserting that the correct understanding of a work – the prerequisite of a 'true interpretation' – depended 'solely upon scrupulously exact reading'.[40] The development during the mid nineteenth century of the concept of the performer as interpreter rather than as co-creator, which led some critics to adopt quasi-religious metaphors to describe the act of performance, encouraged this sense of performance as observance. During the twentieth century 'respect for the text' came increasingly to dominate the teaching of performance.

Challenges for performance teaching

The violinist Duncan Druce is among those who lament the tendency for modern musicians to produce performances that are commendably clear and accurate but 'comparatively bland and lacking in personality'. In his account of historical approaches to violin playing, he characterises this as 'part of a general and gradual decline in the creative role of the performer'.[41] While the teaching of instruments with extensive nineteenth-century solo repertoires has increasingly embraced the move towards a more historically informed approach to performance, it is true that this has only rarely been accompanied by a seizing of the creative freedom that such an influence implies. All too often it has tended to encourage the belief that the score should be interpreted literally. The obligation to be individually responsive to the spirit of the work – unequivocally advocated in earlier times – has all too readily, in a less confident age, been overtaken by a misplaced belief that conformity to the letter of the score offers security against critical challenge. Urtext editions, along with performance examination systems and their attendant assessment criteria, have contributed to this normalising trend, as has the authoritative status increasingly accorded to recordings.

Observing this trend, Alfred Brendel, in an essay from 1966, roundly refuted the notion that a work 'will speak for itself as long as the interpreter does not interpose his personality', reminding performers that 'musical notes can only suggest, that expression marks can only supplement and confirm what we must, first and foremost, read from the face of the composition itself'. Echoing the sentiments of much earlier writers, he described the process as demanding 'one's own engaged emotions, one's own sense, one's own intellect, one's own refined ears'.[42] Yet in much performance teaching, while lip service is paid to the role of the student's musical judgement and intuition in the shaping of an interpretation, it can be all too easy in practice to neutralise their impact.

Valuable though it has been in many ways, the surge of interest in 'authentic' performance that took place during the 1980s and 1990s has done nothing to resolve this inherent tension. While avowedly 'authentic' approaches often say as much about contemporary taste as they do about the tastes and musical values of earlier times (as Richard Taruskin and others have argued),[43] they nevertheless accentuate the need for performers and teachers to steer a course in which they remain true to themselves as well as to the music they choose to perform. In an age of increasing diversity of approach and attitude, performance teaching needs to help musicians to clarify their personal convictions as performers; as Jonathan Dunsby maintains, 'Like it or not, there cannot now be an innocent performer, if ever there could.'[44] One of the enduring effects of the period performance movement should be to encourage performers to adopt a less trammelled and more creative approach to the music they perform, whatever the repertoire. As Nicholas Kenyon has argued, 'tradition isn't what it used to be'.[45] In view of the range of repertoire now regarded as the norm for performers, a well-grounded understanding of the insights that disciplines such as aesthetics, analysis, musicology (including ethnomusicology) and psychology can bring, can no longer be the exception. Their importance to the developing performer is now greater than ever.

But young performers need to be helped to acquire this knowledge gradually and to wear it lightly: it cannot be a substitute for musical instinct, or become so weighty that it silences the personal voice. Schnabel valued Leschetizky's teaching because it acted as 'a current which activated or released all the latent vitality in the student's nature. It was addressed to the imagination, to taste, and to personal responsibility.'[46] It is these qualities that good performance teaching has always encouraged. Stylistic integrity demands this wholeness of approach, in which composers' ideas are complemented by performers' understanding – understanding of themselves as well as of the music they play. Only then can performers confidently clothe themselves in their own individuality, as Baillot described it, and perform with conviction and integrity – not like C. P. E. Bach's 'trained bird', but in ways that draw with confidence on 'the inspirations of the heart and the bursts of the imagination'.[47]

Notes

1 Carl Philipp Emanuel Bach, *Essay on the True Art of Playing Keyboard Instruments* [*Versuch über die wahre Art das Clavier zu spielen*], trans. and ed. William J. Mitchell (London: Eulenburg, [1753, 1762] 1949), 150.

2 See John A. Sloboda, *The Musical Mind: The Cognitive Psychology of Music* (Oxford: Oxford University Press, 1985), 67.

3 Johann Joachim Quantz, *On Playing the Flute*, 2nd edn, trans. Edward R. Reilly (London: Faber and Faber, [1752] 1985), 124–5.

4 Ibid., 15–17.

5 For discussion see Bach, *Essay*, 1–23 passim.

6 See Carl Czerny, 'Recollections from my life', *Musical Quarterly*, 62 (1956), 307.

7 Letter published in *Hamburger unpartheiischer Correspondent*, 7 (1773); quoted from Bach, *Essay*, 8.

8 The other qualities – also advocated by earlier writers – are described as correct fingering and appropriate embellishments; Bach, *Essay*, 30.

9 Ibid., 148.

10 Ibid., 28.

11 Ibid., 30–1.

12 See for example César Gardeton, *Annales de la musique ou Almanach musical . . .* (Geneva: Minkoff, [1819, 1820] 1978), 39–43, which lists thirteen music schools recently established in Paris. Mendelssohn, in a letter from Paris to Carl Friedrich Zelter in Berlin (15 February 1832) refers to there being 1,800 piano teachers, but 'still not enough' to meet demand (Felix Mendelssohn, *Letters*, trans. and ed. G. Selden-Goth (London: Paul Elek, 1946), 190). In *Musique et musiciens* (Paris: Pagnerre, 1862), Oscar Comettant, a prominent Parisian critic of the time, refers to the number of piano teachers in Paris alone as having risen to 20,000. For comment on the situation in England, see Cyril Ehrlich, *The Musical Profession in England since the Eighteenth Century* (Oxford: Clarendon Press, 1985), 76–120.

13 The number of students varied from year to year (see Constant Pierre, *Le Conservatoire National de Musique et de Déclamation . . .* (Paris: Imprimerie nationale, 1900), 873). By 1828, 11,000 students had enrolled; of the 3,800 who had completed their studies, 1,127 were pianists or accompanists (see François-Joseph Fétis, 'Statistique musicale de la France. Premier Article', *Revue musicale*, 6 (1828–9), 126–7).

14 Pierre, *Conservatoire*, 125; my translation.

15 These method books, ten in all, were for flute, clarinet, bassoon, horn (two), serpent, violin, cello and voice, with another on harmony, solfège and the rudiments of music.

16 The method by Louis Adam and Louis-Wenceslas Lachnith, *Méthode ou principe général du doigté pour le forté-piano* (Paris: Sieber, [1798]), was edited and

reissued by Adam in 1802 and again in 1804, under the title *Méthode de piano du Conservatoire adoptée pour servir à l'enseignement dans cet établissement* (Paris: Conservatoire Royal, 1802, 1804). In the version reissued in 1805, *Méthode complète pour le piano* (Paris: Conservatoire impérial de musique, [1805]), it achieved further popularity, appearing in two German and two Italian editions.

17 This replaced the method book by Jean-Baptiste Cartier, *L'Art du violon . . .* (Paris: Decombe, [1798]), which the author dedicated to the newly established Conservatoire. The 1803 edition remained in use for teaching until replaced by Pierre Baillot's *L'Art du violon* (Paris: Dépôt Central de la Musique, [1834]).

18 For details of method books for violin, see Robin Stowell, *Violin Technique and Performance Practice in the Late Eighteenth and Early Nineteenth Centuries* (Cambridge: Cambridge University Press, 1985), 5–10, 368–74. For a list of the main cello method books, see Valerie Walden, *One Hundred Years of Violoncello: A History of Technique and Performance Practice, 1740–1840* (Cambridge: Cambridge University Press, 1998), 300–1. For keyboard treatises, see Glyn Jenkins, 'The legato touch and the "ordinary" manner of keyboard-playing from 1750 to 1850: some aspects of the early development of piano technique' (Ph.D. thesis, University of Cambridge, 1976).

19 Czerny's Op. 500 (trans. J. A. Hamilton, 3 vols. (London: R. Cocks & Co., [1839])) was also published in Paris and Vienna.

20 Johann Nepomuk Hummel, *Ausführlich theoretisch-practische Ausweisung zum Piano-forte Spiel*, 3 vols. (Vienna: Haslinger, 1828).

21 François-Joseph Fétis and Ignaz Moscheles, *Méthode des méthodes de piano* (Paris: Schlesinger, 1837).

22 Louis Spohr, *Violinschule* (Vienna: Haslinger, [1832]).

23 Czerny, *School*, III:99–100. This echoes comments by Adam (*Méthode* (1802), 234).

24 Piano teaching in St Petersburg before the establishment of the Conservatoire, for example, was strongly influenced by John Field (a student of Clementi) and subsequently by Adolphe Henselt (a student of Hummel).

25 In 1792, as a result of revolutionary pressures, Viotti moved to London where he was a key figure in the city's musical life for the next five years.

26 Baillot's teaching was described by his pupil Eugène Sauzay, who later taught at the Conservatoire (from 1860 to 1892); see Brigitte François-Sappey, 'La Vie musicale à Paris à travers les *Mémoires* d'Eugène Sauzay', *Revue de musicologie*, 60 (1974), 159–210.

27 Two German editions appeared in 1835; further editions followed in French and Spanish. It is published in English as *The Art of the Violin*, ed. and trans. Louise Goldberg (Evanston, Ill.: Northwestern University Press, 1991).

28 At first, foreign students were admitted to the Paris Conservatoire only with ministerial approval.

29 'Performers, like composers, must each have an individual style.' Adam, *Méthode* (1802), 233; my translation.

30 Louis Spohr, *Grand Violin School*, trans. C. Rodolphus (London: Wessel, n.d.), 179; italics in original.

31 Johann Nepomuk Hummel, *A Complete Theoretical and Practical Course of Instructions on the Art of Playing the Piano Forte*, 3 vols. (London: T. Boosey & Co., [1828] 1830), III:43–50.

32 Czerny, *School*, III:34–5. For a later account, dealing with a wider repertoire, see chapter 16, 'The accelerando and rallentando', in Adolph Kullak, *The Aesthetics of Pianoforte-Playing*, trans. Theodore Kullak, ed. Hans Bischoff, 3rd edn (New York: G. Schirmer, 1903), 280–94.

33 The title page of Czerny's *L'Ecole des expressions* (London: R. Cocks & Co., n.d.) describes the melodies it contains as including 'Elegant Embellishments, in the Modern Style Composed expressly to serve as Models, for Extemporaneous Ornament'. Similar examples are contained in Czerny's *L'Ecole des ornemens* (London: R. Cocks & Co., n.d.).

34 See Mme Auguste Boissier, *Liszt Pédagogue* (Paris: Honoré Champion, 1927), 32.

35 Harold C. Schonberg, *The Great Pianists* (London: Victor Gollancz, 1964), 280. For further examples see William S. Newman, *The Sonata since Beethoven* (Chapel Hill: University of North Carolina Press, 1969), 104–8.

36 For an account of Clara Schumann as teacher, see Nancy B. Reich, *Clara Schumann: The Artist and the Woman* (Ithaca and London: Cornell University Press, 1985), 288–96.

37 Eduard Hanslick, *Vienna's Golden Years of Music, 1850–1900*, trans. and ed. Henry Pleasants (London: Victor Gollancz, 1951), 39–44 passim.

38 Amy Fay, *Music-Study in Germany* (New York: Dover, 1965), 275.

39 Quoted from Schonberg, *Pianists*, 355–6.

40 Josef Hofmann, *Piano Playing* (New York: Dover, 1976), 54–5.

41 Duncan Druce, 'Historical approaches to violin playing', in John Paynter, Tim Howell, Richard Orton and Peter Seymour (eds.), *Companion to Contemporary Musical Thought*, 2 vols. (London and New York: Routledge, 1992), II:1013.

42 Alfred Brendel, 'Notes on a complete recording of Beethoven's piano works', *Musical Thoughts and Afterthoughts* (London: Robson, 1976), 23, 25.

43 See for example Richard Taruskin, 'The pastness of the present and the presence of the past', in Taruskin, *Text and Act: Essays on Music and Performance* (New York and Oxford: Oxford University Press, 1995), 90–154, and Robert Philip, *Early Recordings and Musical Style: Changing Tastes in Instrumental Performance, 1900–1950* (Cambridge: Cambridge University Press, 1992), 239–40.

44 Jonathan Dunsby, *Performing Music: Shared Concerns* (Oxford: Clarendon Press, 1995), 41.

45 Nicholas Kenyon, 'Tradition isn't what it used to be', 2001 Royal Philharmonic Society Lecture, London, 24 February 2001.

46 Artur Schnabel, *My Life and Music* (Gerrards Cross, Bucks.: Colin Smythe, 1970), 125.

47 Baillot, *Art of the Violin*, 13, 477.

Further reading

Dunsby, Jonathan, *Performing Music: Shared Concerns* (Oxford: Clarendon Press, 1995)

Godlovitch, Stan, *Musical Performance: A Philosophical Study* (London and New York: Routledge, 1998)

Howat, Roy, 'What do we perform?', in John Rink (ed.), *The Practice of Performance: Studies in Musical Interpretation* (Cambridge: Cambridge University Press, 1995), 3–20

Kivy, Peter, 'Live performances and dead composers: on the ethics of musical interpretation', in Kivy, *The Fine Art of Repetition: Essays in the Philosophy of Music* (Cambridge: Cambridge University Press, 1993), 95–116

Sessions, Roger, 'The performer', in Sessions, *The Musical Experience of Composer, Performer, Listener* (Princeton: Princeton University Press, [1950] 1971), 68–86

Taruskin, Richard, 'On letting the music speak for itself', in Taruskin, *Text and Act: Essays on Music and Performance* (New York and Oxford: Oxford University Press, 1995), 51–66

6   Developing the ability to perform

JANE DAVIDSON

This chapter examines the key factors involved in developing musical skills. Initially, the concept of musical potentiality is explored, followed by an investigation of the specific skills required for learning an instrument. Finally, a discussion is undertaken of how best to nurture the ability to perform for an audience. A balance between theory and practice is achieved by referring both to research literature on the psychology of music and music education and to anecdotal evidence and material from teaching manuals. Though some reference is made to musical learning in other cultures, the focus here is on a child developing the ability to perform within a Western cultural framework.

The relative roles of biology and environment in shaping musical potentiality

There has been considerable interest in the seeming differences in musical achievement among the population in general. Most of the debate has centred on the relative roles of biological and environmental influences on human abilities – the 'nature versus nurture' debate.[1] Assessing the scientific findings, it seems that genetic factors influence general development in a number of ways:

- *maturational staged development*
  An example of this is the need to crawl before walking, or in musical terms, the gradual development of the hand and eye dexterity and coordination necessary to enable bow and string synchronisation in violin playing.
- *some physical advantages*
  For instance, tall, lean-limbed people tend to be better at high-jumping than short, more heavily built ones. In music, people with wide hand spans have a better potential to develop as pianists than those with small hand spans.

- *some mental advantages*

  Generally, for example, some people can 'tune into' problem-solving tasks more quickly than others. They may therefore be able to identify musical patterns and thus carry out aural discrimination tasks more rapidly.

A biological component is clearly important, and researchers like Robert Plomin[2] suggest that it is only a matter of time before a gene will be identified for the determination of musical accomplishments. Nevertheless, if the concept of a 'normal distribution'[3] is accepted, it seems that the vast majority of people – around 95 per cent of the population – fall within 'norms' for both physical and mental capacity and structure, suggesting that more or less everyone has similar potential.[4] This applies to the development of musical skills as well, in which the importance of innate abilities is often exaggerated. It would therefore be useful to explore the issues associated with environmental influence on musical abilities.

To highlight the critical role of environment, consider the politically sensitive area of race stereotyping and the various 'nature versus nurture' explanations that have been offered to account for musical abilities. Black Africans, for instance, have often been referred to by white people as having 'rhythm in their veins', while the Japanese have been perceived as possessing naturally high intellectual capacities and displaying technical virtuosity in their music-making. Although at some level genetic factors may have come into play, an examination of the respective cultures and social practices indicates that these stereotypes developed from socio-cultural rules of engagement and behaviour. For instance, the Anang Ibibo tribe in Nigeria makes music a part of everyday life. All children are expected to participate in music from birth. By five years of age, the vast majority of these children have a huge repertoire of songs, dances and drum patterns which they can perform. The notion of being unmusical does not exist. Also, although some individuals are slightly better than others, all are expected to participate at a high level. Within the culture, the normal distribution principle operates: music is for all, and performing accomplishments are fairly evenly distributed. In Japan, the discipline imposed by society on the individual is far more intense than that experienced in the West. Therefore, children invest many hours on homework of all kinds, including music. As there tend to be a more systematic approach to learning and thus more disciplined and structured patterns of associated behaviour, Japanese children acquire a higher level of musical skill than their Western counterparts.

Perhaps one of the best ways to consider the key influence of the environment on the acquisition of musical skills is by examining an individual who at first glance appears to have had no environmental support whatsoever but who became one of the most 'talented' musicians of the Western world: the jazz trumpeter Louis Armstrong. Born into dire poverty, he spent large amounts of time fending for himself in the street (his mother was a prostitute), and he received almost no formal education. It seems remarkable that as a boy he did not even own a trumpet. However, if Armstrong's biography[5] is examined closely, five critically important environmental factors can be identified:

(1) *casual but frequent exposure to musical stimuli*
    Armstrong grew up in New Orleans and was constantly surrounded by jazz.

(2) *ample opportunities over an extended period of time for freely exploring the jazz medium and for developing performance presentation skills*
    Armstrong formed and sang in a street-corner choir as a boy, and had opportunities to participate in communal jazz activities where mistakes were tolerated and where he could choose the level of risk and difficulty of his performance. Thus, he was able informally to learn the 'rules' of jazz harmony, improvisation and performance etiquette.

(3) *an early opportunity to experience intense positive emotional or aesthetic states in response to music*
    It is fair to assume that Armstrong developed a 'love' of jazz based on some emotional experience allied to the music.

(4) *an opportunity to amass large numbers of hours of practice*
    Armstrong spent his entire day with jazz musicians and could borrow a trumpet to play.

(5) *a number of externally motivating factors such as a key adult*
    Armstrong received informal instruction from the older jazz musicians with whom he spent time, and this contact developed his musical knowledge, performance skills and desire to engage with music.

The five factors that seem critical in the determination of Armstrong's musical interest and engagement have been fairly systematically studied by music psychologists and have now been identified as key factors in the development of musical skills.[6] These will be traced in depth below, and some suggestions will be made as to how performance skills might best be promoted.

Early opportunities for musical engagement

There is increasing evidence that the environment starts to influence individuals before birth. For instance, the foetus is able to hear music and speech several weeks prior to birth and to recognise that music after birth,[7] meaning that some learning must have occurred. It is also possible to deduce that the foetal experience is largely 'musical' in that the foetus feels the rhythms of the mother's body and hears the inflections – the melodic contours – of external noises including speech and music. It could be that pre-natal stimulation is one of the most important of all environmental experiences and that infants stimulated in such a manner receive benefits in terms of their overall education as well as their particular musical development. If nothing else, the commercial music market assumes the viability of the pre-natal learning environment, thus offering pregnant women a variety of special music programmes which supposedly have a positive effect on the unborn child.

It has been demonstrated that in infancy, 'motherese'[8] is the basis for the development of turn-taking skills.[9] Gestural communication is also crucial, with the rhythm, tempo and dynamics of interactions[10] being determined by playful movements and actions such as clapping. 'Motherese' and gestural play are developed to communicate basic emotional states and needs. Thus, the link between emotion, physical gesture and musical meaning is formed. An expressive musical feature like rubato may demonstrate a link to early infant experience. For instance, slowing occurs in physical and vocal interactions when they are about to end, and so when playing music, this idea is abstracted further as a means of anticipating and prolonging the musical ending. Quasi-musical interaction between guardians and infants in the course of childcare thus leads to the almost incidental development of musical meaning and some performing competencies.[11]

Early and frequent exposure to music has long-term investment potential in terms of engaging the child's interest in and commitment to learning. For instance, researchers[12] have discovered that children who later developed high-level musical skills were sung to and engaged in musical play during a critical period from birth to two years of age. This very early engagement was not structured or formalised, however. The children were allowed to explore the musical instruments in their home or to listen to the music playing on the hi-fi. The children who gave up music, by contrast, tended not to have much musical stimulation before two years, and when it did occur, it either appears to have been too infrequent to amount to an influence or was thought to be intimidating by being formally structured. For instance, one boy had a violin teacher who came to his house from the age of two, and he was so fearful of the experience that he would run and hide under his bed.

Thus, available data suggest that informal, free engagement with musical stimuli at a very early age is of great importance for future development. It seems to enable the child to build up a knowledge and an understanding of musical communication.

The power of music: emotional experience as a prerequisite for committed engagement with learning

Jeanne d'Albret, the mother of Henri IV of France, had court musicians play to her during pregnancy in the hope that her child would develop a mild manner from hearing the 'sweet' sounds. Interestingly, chroniclers of the day reported on the King's calm nature. This anecdote reveals a possible link between physiological arousal, emotional response, music-liking and temperament. Anthony Kemp[13] has written about this issue at some length, discussing whether it is the music which attracts certain personalities to engage with it or the personalities which are shaped by the music. There can be no firm answer, but it is now fairly well established that musical engagement has some positive emotional effect. Indeed, those working in the domains of music therapy[14] and music education[15] explore music as a means of calming, soothing and invigorating individuals. Some of the results are impressive: in one case, a class of unruly children with 'special educational needs' worked better and achieved more by listening to Mozart in the background of their science lessons.

It has been argued that an emotional response to musical content is a key trigger to intrinsic musical motivation.[16] One study[17] revealed that individuals with a lifelong commitment to music were far more likely to report key emotional experiences in response to musical content during early childhood than those who never learned a musical instrument beyond an initial stage. For example, one woman described hearing classical clarinet music for the first time at seven years of age; the instrument sounded 'liquid' and 'beautiful' to her, causing her to feel 'tingles' through her body.

It is important to note that in addition to musical content, musical context is a key motivational stimulus. For instance, being with a close friend when hearing a particular piece might encourage future engagement with such music, whereas, conversely, music heard in a distressing situation is likely to be avoided thereafter.

Practice to make perfect

A number of studies have shown that the most directly effective activity for acquiring skill is deliberate practice.[18] In music, a clear relationship has been found between the accumulated hours spent engaging in 'formal' practice (scales, technical exercises and repertoire) and achievement. For instance, in a study of student violinists,[19] K. Anders Ericsson et al. discovered that the best students had amassed almost 10,000 hours of formal practice by the age of twenty-one, whereas students of far lesser achievement had accumulated under half that total. Additionally, a study by John Sloboda et al.[20]

revealed that not only did students with higher achievements engage in much more practice than their less successful peers, but there was a direct correlation between the amount of practice done and the quality of performance in musical examinations. The researchers studied five groups of young people ranging from those who had given up music after less than two years of learning to those who were receiving a specialist musical education with a view to professional careers in music. They found that the students in specialist education advanced much more quickly through the practical musical examination system than the other students. Yet when the hours of practice were calculated, they discovered that it took all students, irrespective of group, exactly the same total practice time to achieve a particular grade. The students in the specialist education advanced far more quickly because they were practising in a more concentrated way than the other students.

In addition to formal practice, Sloboda et al. also found that students who advanced quickly were those who engaged in informal practice, which involved improvising and playing familiar tunes by ear. Thus, in addition to acquiring the technical skills to control both instrument and repertoire, the successful students were also investing time and effort in exploring how musical structures function. As in the case of Armstrong, there was considerable opportunity for trial and error, allowing an understanding of musical structure and expression to emerge.

The style and structure of practice also have a significant bearing on how a student advances in learning music. For instance, separate projects by Linda Gruson[21] and Kacper Miklaszewski[22] revealed that fragments of a piece would initially be worked on for extended periods of time, and as these fragments became more fluent, larger sections would gradually be studied, at first in a serial manner until a holistic strategy evolved. Susan Hallam[23] demonstrated that serial and holistic strategies are two broadly different approaches to practice, with some individuals preferring one over the other. Her detailed studies showed that practising strategies are highly idiosyncratic, with no simple correspondence between a single strategy and success.

While practising is significant to skill acquisition, as the case of Louis Armstrong attests, finding sources of motivation for musical engagement is also very important.

Motivation for learning

Without doubt, people's drives, arousal, anxiety levels, and thoughts and beliefs – in other words, their individual characteristics – have critical roles in shaping how they approach a task such as learning music.

In particular, self-esteem and self-awareness have profound impacts on the development of personal goals and aims.[24] A number of theories of motivation have emerged, and one which effectively explains why some young people find it more rewarding than others to engage in musical activities is 'expectancy-value theory'.[25] This argues that people learn tasks if they value the activity or product or anticipate being successful. Value depends on a number of types of motivation:

- *extrinsic* (when tasks are carried out because of some external reward potential such as passing an examination)
- *social* (a wish to please or fit in with others)
- *achievement* (for enhancement of the ego, to do better than others)
- *intrinsic* (interest in the activity itself, engagement for simple personal enjoyment).

Existing research into how children engage with music suggests that the three external sources of motivation – extrinsic, social and achievement – often precede and develop into intrinsic motivation. Earlier in this chapter, when the power of emotional responses was considered, intrinsic motivation was shown to be the type of motivation that facilitates long-term commitment to music. Hallam[26] has written at length about how to help develop intrinsic motivation, and she suggests the following teaching strategies:

(1) students should be exposed to many different types of music in a free manner, in order to open the possibilities of emotional response to music
(2) students should be involved in making decisions about the style and difficulty of music to be learned and whether or not to perform in public or enter for examinations
(3) to stimulate the learners, teachers should generate surprise, perplexity, contradiction and debate.

In other words, the musical tasks need to be meaningful to the learners and at an optimum level of complexity which is both challenging and manageable. Hallam's strategies have evolved by observing many students but also by examining the biographical characteristics shared by successful musicians.[27]

As for external motivators, it seems that social reinforcers are the most common – for example, friends, family and teachers. These individuals can and do use material reinforcers such as sweets, money, tokens, treats, hugs and smiles to encourage, but their presence and involvement with the learner are most critical for progress in learning.

Social reinforcement and learning

In addition to the early stimulation of musical interest that goes on in 'motherese' and gestural play, later, once an instrument has been taken up, parents or guardians can have a critical role in developing skills of engagement. A large-scale psychological investigation[28] demonstrated that it was not uncommon for children to give up learning a musical instrument because they did not receive sufficient parental support. Two hundred and fifty-seven children between the ages of eight and eighteen who had instrumental lessons and performed with varying levels of achievement were interviewed with regard to the role that parents and teachers played. The highest-achieving group was supported the most frequently and consistently by their parents, with the adults often attending lessons and making notes as to what their children had to practise at home, and then, once home, supporting them either by regularly sitting in during or listening to the practice activity itself.

Parents therefore need to establish certain attitudes towards music. Siblings can also enhance the learning environment, as can role models. In Louis Armstrong's case, other jazz musicians provided a safe and supportive environment where praise and success had reinforcing roles. In that regard, they were like teachers within the more conventional Western music-learning framework.

The role of the teacher

Research[29] has shown that students with high achievements in music found their teachers to be entertaining and friendly as well as proficient musicians, whereas the low-achieving students remembered their teachers as unfriendly and incompetent. With increasing age, this combination of teacher characteristics did not change for the lowest group, but the higher achievers started to distinguish between professional and personal attributes on the part of their teachers, the professional qualities becoming more relevant. Children who abandoned their lessons did not make this distinction. When the teacher's personality was deemed pleasant, he or she was also perceived as professionally satisfactory. We see here how crucial the personal aspects are in addition to the professional ones; especially at young ages, they may motivate students to play. This highlights the emotional climate in which musical experiences are gathered. Children who developed outstanding instrumental achievements learned in a positive atmosphere which was enjoyable and free of anxiety. In contrast, the learning context of the drop-out children was negative and characterised by anxieties.

The researchers also discovered that after the age of eleven, many children did not need external sources for motivation, instead developing their
intrinsic link with the instrument.[30] Indeed, a study[31] of adolescent musicians and their activities revealed that sense of self was highly bound up
with playing musical instruments. In other domains such as pop music, this
has also been found to be the case, with musical rewards becoming tied to
self-identity.[32]

Exploration of the broader research literature thus reveals that
Armstrong's biography demonstrates the key environmental factors linked
to musical skill acquisition. But what about the particularities of the skills
themselves?

Performance skills

According to Hallam,[33] a critical first stage in motivating instrumental learning is to select the correct instrument. That involves choosing
an instrument which appeals to the child, perhaps even conforming to sex
stereotyping (for instance, girls prefer flutes, boys prefer drums). With the
instrument selected, with practice duly supported by parents and with a
warm and friendly teacher directing the child, the following elements appear
to form the basis of the skills to be developed:

(1) *structure, notation and reading skills*
    These are acquired by developing a knowledge base for the rules of
    musical structure, such as how phrases are arranged and how harmony
    functions; examining how music looks on the page, and thus learning
    how to decipher the code of music notation; discovering how to sight-
    read so that more music can be learned and processed more quickly
    through greater reading fluency; learning how to memorise so that music
    can be played without focusing completely on the notation; and from
    this, developing strong mental maps linking knowledge about structure
    to execution of the music.
(2) *aural skills*
    Aural abilities are particularly necessary to enable the learner to de-
    velop good intonation and tone quality on the instrument. Acquiring
    the ability to manipulate knowledge about musical structure practically
    through improvisation is critical, as is learning how music will sound
    without playing it.
(3) *technical and motor skills*
    Allied to building mental structures for understanding music is the need
    to train the body to automatise the note-playing process so that fluency
    and agility can be achieved.

(4) *expressive skills*

These involve knowing how to manipulate the structural rules to create music that is perceived to have emotional content and is original to the performer.

(5) *presentation skills*

Such skills include learning how to present both the music and the performer's body in a confident manner on stage so that the performer, co-performers and audience feel a sense of ease about the act of performance and what it is communicating. They also include mastery of the rules of stage etiquette – for example, bowing after the performance.

Many manuals are available to help develop the sub-skills listed above, and it is now acknowledged that with a persistent and determined attitude, the first three sets of sub-skills can be developed to high levels.[34] Nevertheless, it has long been thought that expressive skills are highly decisive in separating average from excellent performers, with some mysterious, untrainable 'gift' determining the extent to which an individual can be expressive in music. However, research[35] indicates that 'expressive devices' conform to a series of characteristics. First, they are *systematic*. For example, the use of slowing will always occur at certain structural moments in a piece, like phrase boundaries. Second, these devices improve the *communicability* of the structural feature to the perceiver, so that, for instance, the metre will be clearer if the first beat is accented. Third, these devices are used in a *stable manner*, so a performer can repeatedly achieve similar expressive effects in multiple performances, often over large time spans. Fourth, *flexibility* is possible, with skilled performers being able to change or exaggerate the shape of an expressive line. Finally, these expressive devices are *used automatically*, with performers often not conscious of what they are doing. From these findings, it is evident that the five characteristics can potentially be taught, given their stability.

Are presentation skills a decisive factor in separating the good from the great? From the literature, they appear to be no more dependent on 'talent' than the other sub-skills. Recent research[36] has shown that individuals learn to attune to one another and conform to social convention in the performance context, and there are training programmes such as Dalcroze's Eurythmics which centralise the importance of non-verbal cues and interpersonal interaction in the development of performing abilities. However, as Andrew Evans insightfully comments,[37] much more cultural and teaching investment needs to take place in the development of presentation skills. For example, he discusses at length the dreadful anxieties reported by musicians at all levels associated with a lack of self-confidence about performance context and evaluation. The research literature suggests that familiarity with a variety of performing contexts, playing repertoire that is well known and and having plenty of performance opportunities are ways of overcoming potential problems with presentation skills.

One of the major difficulties with the way in which performance is taught and conceived of as a performance act in Western culture is that it takes place in isolation: practice is a solitary activity, and lessons are typically on a one-to-one basis. To develop performing skills requires a pull against the dominant cultural trend. Although the nature of the musical material is very different, classical musicians and music educators in the West could learn a great deal from the Anang Ibibo of Nigeria. For the Anang, music is part of daily life: it is not threatening, stressful or attainable by only a few. Music is for all, with everyone participating as creators, listeners and performers.

Notes

1 See John A. Sloboda, Jane W. Davidson and Michael J. A. Howe, 'Is everyone musical?', *The Psychologist*, 7 (1994), 349–54.

2 Robert Plomin, John C. DeFries and John C. Loehlin, 'Genotype-environment interaction and correlation in the analysis of human behaviour', *Psychological Bulletin*, 84 (1977), 309–22.

3 See Rita L. Atkinson, Richard C. Atkinson, Edward E. Smith, Daryl J. Bem and Ernest R. Hilgard, *Introduction to Psychology*, 10th edn (Orlando, Fla: Harcourt Brace Jovanovich, 1990), 779–80.

4 There are equal numbers at both the bottom and the top of that distribution who will be either impaired or advantaged in some way, but since these total only 5 per cent, they are rare instances.

5 James L. Collier, *Louis Armstrong: An American Genius* (New York: Oxford University Press, 1983).

6 See John A. Sloboda, Jane W. Davidson, Michael J. A. Howe and Derek G. Moore, 'The role of practice in the development of expert musical performance', *British Journal of Psychology*, 87 (1996), 287–309.

7 See Peter G. Hepper, 'An examination of foetal learning before and after birth', *Irish Journal of Psychology*, 12 (1991), 95–107, and Jean-Pierre Lecanuet, 'Prenatal auditory experience', in Irène Deliège and John A. Sloboda (eds.), *Musical Beginnings: Origins and Development of Musical Competence* (Oxford: Oxford University Press, 1996), 3–34.

8 That is, the 'goo-goo gah-gah' vocalisations of the guardian and infant.

9 See Colwyn Trevarthen, 'Musicality and the intrinsic motive pulse: evidence from human psychobiology and infant communication', *Musicae Scientiae*, Special Issue (1999–2000), 155–215.

10 See Mechthild Papousek, 'Intuitive parenting: a hidden source of musical stimulation in infancy', in Deliège and Sloboda (eds.), *Musical Beginnings*, 88–114.

11 See Hanus and Mechthild Papousek, 'Beginning of human musicality', in Reinhart Steinberg (ed.), *Music and the Mind Machine: The Psychophysiology and Psychopathology of the Sense of Music* (Berlin: Springer Verlag, 1995), 27–34.

12 Michael J. A. Howe, Jane W. Davidson, Derek G. Moore and John A. Sloboda, 'Are there early childhood signs of musical ability?', *Psychology of Music*, 23 (1995), 162–76.

13 Anthony Kemp, *The Musical Temperament* (Oxford: Oxford University Press, 1996), viii, 234–55.

14 E.g. Gary Ansdell, *Music for Life: Aspects of Creative Music Therapy with Adult Clients* (London: Jessica Kingsley, 1995).

15 E.g. Anne Savan, 'The effect of background music on learning', *Psychology of Music*, 27 (1999), 138–46.

16 John A. Sloboda, 'Musical structure and emotional response: some empirical findings', *Psychology of Music*, 19 (1991), 110–20.

17 John A. Sloboda, 'Empirical studies of emotional response to music', in Mari R. Jones and Stephen Holleran (eds.), *Cognitive Bases of Musical Communication* (Washington, D.C.: American Psychological Association, 1992), 33–46.

18 See chapter 7 in this volume. A case discussed in the psychology literature is that of S.F., a man able to increase his normal memory span from five to seven items for immediate recall, to eighty items after over 200 hours of systematic practice of the task. For discussion see William G. Chase and K. Anders Ericsson, 'Skilled memory', in John R. Anderson (ed.), *Cognitive Skills and their Acquisition* (Hillsdale, NJ: Erlbaum, 1981), 141–89.

19 K. Anders Ericsson, Ralf Th. Krampe and Clemens Tesch-Römer, 'The role of deliberate practice in the acquisition of expert performance', *Psychological Review*, 100 (1993), 363–406.

20 Sloboda et al., 'The role of practice'.

21 Linda M. Gruson, 'Rehearsal skill and musical competence: does practice make perfect?', in John A. Sloboda (ed.), *Generative Processes in Music: The Psychology of Performance, Improvisation, and Composition* (Oxford: Clarendon Press, 1988), 91–112.

22 Kacper Miklaszewski, 'A case study of a pianist preparing a musical performance', *Psychology of Music*, 17 (1989), 95–109.

23 Susan Hallam, 'Professional musicians' orientations to practice: implications for teaching', *British Journal of Music Education*, 12 (1995), 3–19.

24 See Susan Hallam, *Instrumental Teaching: A Practical Guide to Better Teaching and Learning* (Oxford: Heinemann, 1998).

25 See Norman Feather (ed.), *Expectations and Actions* (Hillsdale, NJ: Erlbaum, 1982).

26 Hallam, *Instrumental Teaching*, 104–6.

27 For example, details can be found in Sloboda, Davidson and Howe, 'Is everyone musical?'.

28 Jane W. Davidson, Michael J. A. Howe, Derek G. Moore and John A. Sloboda, 'The role of parental influences in the development of musical ability', *British Journal of Developmental Psychology*, 14 (1996), 399–412.

29 Jane W. Davidson, Michael J. A. Howe, Derek G. Moore and John A. Sloboda, 'The role of teachers in the development of musical ability', *Journal of Research in Music Education*, 46 (1998), 141–60.

30 See Jane W. Davidson, John A. Sloboda and Michael J. A. Howe, 'The role of parents and teachers in the success and failure of instrumental learners', *Council for the Bulletin of Research in Music Education*, 127 (Winter 1995–96), 40–4.

31 Jane W. Davidson, 'Self and desire: a preliminary exploration of why students start and continue with music learning', *Research Studies in Music Education*, 12 (1999), 30–7.

32 See Daniel Cavicchi, *Tramps Like Us: Music and Meaning among Bruce Springsteen Fans* (New York: Oxford University Press, 1998).

33 Hallam, *Instrumental Teaching*, 17.

34 See Desmond Sergeant, 'Experimental investigation of absolute pitch', *Journal of Research in Music Education*, 17 (1969), 135–43, and John A. Sloboda, *The Musical Mind: The Cognitive Psychology of Music* (Oxford: Oxford University Press, 1985).

35 John A. Sloboda and Jane W. Davidson, 'The young performing musician', in Deliège and Sloboda (eds.), *Musical Beginnings*, 171–90.

36 Jane W. Davidson, 'The social in musical performance', in David J. Hargreaves and Adrian C. North (eds.), *The Social Psychology of Music* (Oxford: Oxford University Press, 1997), 209–28.

37 Andrew Evans, *The Secrets of Musical Confidence* (London: Thorson, 1994), 79–133.

Further reading

Deliège, Irène and John A. Sloboda (eds.), *Musical Beginnings: Origins and Development of Musical Competence* (Oxford: Oxford University Press, 1996)

Evans, Andrew, *The Secrets of Musical Confidence* (London: Thorson, 1994)

Hallam, Susan, *Instrumental Teaching: A Practical Guide to Better Teaching and Learning* (Oxford: Heinemann, 1998)

Hargreaves, David J., *The Developmental Psychology of Music* (Cambridge: Cambridge University Press, 1986)

Hargreaves, David J. and Adrian C. North (eds.), *The Social Psychology of Music* (Oxford: Oxford University Press, 1997)

7   Preparing for performance

STEFAN REID

Introduction

Although musical performance is an extremely public experience, the preparation for a performance usually takes place privately, and often in complete isolation. Most performances are one-off events, rarely lasting more than a couple of hours at most, but they are cultivated during days, weeks or even years of intense work. The starting point for performances of Western music is normally a score, which consists of a series of instructions of varying degrees of indeterminacy that the performer must then translate into sound. The indeterminacy inherent in Western musical notation means that the decoding of the score requires considerable interpretative input and insight from the performer. Consequently, no two performances of a work will be the same.

The term most commonly used to describe the process of preparing for a performance is of course 'practice' – but this can mean many things. While the psychologist might define practice as 'learning skills through repetition',[1] musical practice in fact consists of a variety of different but interrelated activities including memorisation, the development of technical expertise and, ultimately, the formulation of interpretations. This chapter focuses on both the quantity and the quality of practice activities undertaken in preparing for a performance. The first section examines how much practice musicians require in order to develop their skills. The second section discusses how musicians practise effectively, looking specifically at the development of technical facility, the formulation of interpretations and the relationship between these two elements. The final section provides a summary, suggesting ways in which musicians might improve the efficiency and effectiveness of their practising.

In discussing these issues, the chapter refers to two main sources of information on practice: pedagogical literature on music from the eighteenth century to the present day, and psychological literature on skill acquisition both in general and in the field of musical expertise. Although largely subjective and anecdotal in nature, the pedagogical literature nevertheless forms the basis of Western musical education. Its subjectivity is balanced by the psychological literature which, through the use of experimental methods, attempts to provide more objective insights into how skills are acquired and how musicians practise.

How much is enough?

Most music students are told by their teachers at some point that they 'have not done enough practice'. References to practice in pedagogical works from the eighteenth century onwards include a range of prescriptive comments on how much practice is necessary in order to obtain musical success. For instance, the respected singing teacher Tosi proposed that 'an hour of application in a day is not sufficient, even for one of the quickest apprehension'.[2] In his *Klavierschule*, Türk suggested that 'he who learns to play the clavichord for his pleasure only, has done enough, if he practises two hours daily'.[3] Quantz, the flute teacher to Frederick the Great of Prussia, proposed four hours of practice per day, two in the morning and two in the afternoon,[4] while the celebrated pianist Hummel felt that at most three hours per day was sufficient 'to arrive at excellence'.[5] The lack of any clear unanimity between these suggestions might well lead musicians to ask themselves, 'How much practice is enough?'

Some researchers exploring the psychology of music have sought to address this question. K. Anders Ericsson, Ralf Krampe and Clemens Tesch-Römer conducted a study into the amount of 'deliberate practice'[6] carried out by three groups of student violinists during the course of their musical education. Their experiment was based on estimates of the amount of time each subject had spent practising since childhood and on practice diaries reflecting their current musical activities. The students were divided into three groups according to their teachers' assessment of their abilities and likely future careers: 'best violinists', 'good violinists' and prospective 'music teachers'. The results suggested that, by the time of the study, the 'best violinists' had acquired approximately 7,410 hours of practice, the 'good violinists' 5,301 hours and the eventual 'music teachers' 3,420 hours. Ericsson et al. then proposed that musical success and skill, rather than being the product of innate talent, resulted from a large amount of accumulated hours of deliberate practice. In terms of regular practice activity, they found that the 'best' and the 'good' violinists practised for an average of 24.3 hours per week, whereas the likely music teachers averaged 9.3 hours per week.[7]

Therefore, in answer to the question 'how much practice is enough?', the findings of Ericsson et al. would suggest that the amount of practice required depends on the ultimate goal of the musician. In order to achieve the highest levels of musical competence, a performer must engage in many more hours of practice than a musician who simply wishes to obtain a reasonable level of proficiency.

While this research appears to suggest that quantity of practice is the key to musical success, the term 'deliberate practice' highlights the importance of the quality and nature of practice activities. This emphasis on quality recurs throughout the pedagogical literature. Hummel refers to the need for '*attentive* study',[8] and in his widely respected *Versuch über die wahre Art das Clavier zu spielen*, C. P. E. Bach comments that with 'intelligent practice it is easy to achieve that which can never be attained through excessive straining of the muscles'.[9] If significant amounts of accumulated practice are an essential prerequisite for musical success, the effectiveness of these hours of practice will depend on the quality and nature of the practice activities undertaken. For musicians to obtain the optimal benefits from their practice time, they must therefore refine and develop their practice techniques.

How musicians practise

'Very few persons obtain from their practice all the benefit they hope for, because, in general, they practise badly.'[10] So commented the celebrated pianist Frédéric Kalkbrenner in his 1831 treatise, *Méthode pour apprendre le piano-forte*. It is probably the case that most musicians could improve their practice techniques and thus maximise the effects of the time they spend practising. As was stated in the introduction, the musician preparing for a performance has two primary objectives: first, the formulation of an interpretation of a musical work, and second, the development of sufficient technical expertise in order to realise this interpretation. While these two objectives are closely related – in fact, for a good performance they are wholly interdependent – they are nevertheless separate skills requiring separate methods of work. This is demonstrated by the fact that, as the psychologist John Sloboda points out,[11] a performer might be a superb technician but lack musical insight, and vice versa. An expert musician will be able to balance technical finesse with interpretative understanding.

Developing technical expertise

In *We Piano Teachers*, Victor Booth proposed that during practice, 'conscious or voluntary acts become subconscious or involuntary'.[12] In other words, an activity initially requiring conscious thought is rehearsed until it becomes automatic. The psychologists Paul Fitts and Michael Posner have suggested that the acquisition of a skill occurs in three stages:

(1) the *cognitive stage*, an initial phase when conscious attention is required

(2) the *associative stage*, characterised by refinement of the activity and elimination of errors

(3) the *autonomous stage*, where the skill no longer requires conscious attention as it has become automatic.[13]

Progression through the phases is gradual as the skill is transferred from short-term to long-term memory.

The primary method that musicians use to make an activity automatic is the repetition of that activity. In repeating an action or series of actions, the performer reinforces it in the memory until it no longer requires the conscious attention needed during the initial phases of learning. Research into skill acquisition in other domains of human expertise has demonstrated that short-term memory has a limited capacity, commonly judged to be about seven 'items'. In short-term storage such 'items' might be of varying size, but they will be lost unless they are transferred to long-term storage through repetition. The constraints of short-term memory impinge on a person's ability to perform a complex task such as learning a piece of music. If repetitive practice is to be effective, a complex task might have to be broken down into smaller, simpler tasks, a process referred to by psychologists as 'chunking'. In musical terms this might consist of practising only a small section of a work and then, when it is mastered, incorporating it into a larger 'chunk', and so on. In this way a piece is taken apart before being gradually rebuilt. This method of working was recommended by the English pianist James Ching among others.[14]

The size of the chunks chosen for repetition will depend on the complexity of the piece and the ability of the performer. This was shown by Linda Gruson in a study of the practice activities of a number of pianists with a wide range of abilities.[15] She found that the most experienced pianists divided the music into larger chunks than novice pianists. Detailed examination of chunking has been undertaken by Kacper Miklaszewski,[16] who observed an advanced Russian piano student practising Debussy's 'Feux d'artifice' (*Préludes*, Book II). During this process, the subject worked through the piece systematically, at first practising small chunks and then progressively larger chunks. Such an approach to learning often differentiates the work of experienced and novice musicians. Novices typically lack the systematic approach of more experienced performers who, as Robert Gerle advises, 'separate the problems and solve them one by one'.[17]

In later practice sessions, Miklaszewski's subject not only practised larger sections of the music but also performed them at a faster tempo. The use of slow practice is of course another means by which musicians can simplify a task. Dale Reubart recommends it in his *Anxiety and Musical Performance*, where he specifically suggests that slow practice in the early stages of learning can help prevent unnecessary errors, and that the motto for every performer should be 'do it right the first time'.[18]

Concentration, therefore, is an essential element of technical practice, not only to ensure accuracy but also to maintain efficiency. Experienced musicians systematically work through the problems presented by a musical work, using their powers of concentration to diagnose problems and implement ways of overcoming them. These goals will constantly change as learning progresses.

To summarise, the development of appropriate technical expertise for a performance requires the transfer of skill from short- to long-term memory. The most effective means of achieving this transfer is through the use of repetition, which is most successful when the musical material is divided into manageable chunks so that the performer masters one 'problem' at a time. As practice progresses, the chunks chosen for attention will become larger and the tempo might also be increased. Repetitive practice requires constant monitoring in order to assess its effectiveness and to maximise its benefits.

Formulating interpretations

An actor preparing a new role must not only learn the lines but also decide how they are to be delivered. The words themselves offer possibilities, but in order to realise their full significance, they have to be considered within the context of a scene, an act or the entire play. In performance, an actor's understanding and interpretation of the whole drama are communicated to the audience through the way he or she chooses to render the text. Parallels can be drawn with musicians preparing a performance, who must decide how each note will be played if its role within the immediate context as well as in the wider interpretation of the piece is to be properly conveyed.

Musical interpretations are communicated through the expressive parameters of timing, dynamics, articulation and timbre, among others. A score might contain a variety of expressive indications to aid the performer's interpretative choices, but, as mentioned earlier, expressive notation lacks precision. The performer will still have to decide how strongly to play a *forte*, how long to hold a fermata or how short to make a staccato.

Performers must tread the difficult path between the need to respect the score, which represents the composer's intentions, and the desire to exercise their own creative insights. In addition, aesthetic ideals vary from person to person and according to the fashions of the day. Interpreting music is therefore a highly subjective process and resistant to prescriptive recommendations. Whereas the advice offered in the pedagogical and psychological literature contains specific instructions for the development of technical expertise, interpretative advice is, not surprisingly, often more varied and less detailed.

Both the pedagogical and the psychological literature suggests that listening to the performance of others is the most effective means of developing interpretative skill. Tosi advises the student of singing to 'hear as much as he can the most celebrated singers and likewise the most excellent instrumental performers, because, from the attention in hearing them, one reaps more advantage than from any instruction whatsoever'.[19] Sloboda echoes this recommendation, explaining why listening to good performance might be beneficial:

Performing expertise first requires analytic listening powers of a developed kind so as to be able to 'latch on to' the minute timing and intensity [i.e. dynamic] variations that make a master performance and then *imitate* them. In my own experience, and that of many musicians, there is no really satisfactory way of *describing* expressive variations in a way which allows one to incorporate them into one's own performance. Expressive techniques are passed from one musician to another by demonstration. That is why master musicians are nearly always passionately interested in hearing the performances of other masters.[20]

However, it is not sufficient merely to imitate good performance. The expressive characteristics of good performance need to be absorbed in order to enrich a musician's own interpretative vocabulary. In this way, for example, musicians might use listening in order to become accustomed with an unfamiliar musical style, as was observed by Susan Hallam in interviews with twenty-two professional musicians.[21]

In particular, musicians are advised to listen to good singing in order to develop effective melodic performance. The Hungarian-born pianist György Sándor commented that 'we can learn much from listening to and watching good singers, who breathe and phrase music with more freedom and spontaneity than can any instrumentalist'.[22] Two hundred years earlier, C. P. E. Bach similarly proposed that instrumentalists should sing melodies, adding that 'this way of learning is of far greater value than the reading of voluminous tomes or listening to learned discourses'.[23] In singing a melodic line, the performer separates it from technique, allowing an expressive shape to emerge which can then be imitated on the instrument.

The singing of an instrumental line could be described as an analogical aid to interpretation. The vocalised melody acts as a mental construct connecting the individual notes of the melodic line into an expressive sequence.

This virtual performance then acts as the point of reference for the actual performance during practice. Another analogical procedure sometimes used by musicians is the creation of an extra-musical programme such as a story or a descriptive or emotional sequence. As with singing the melodic line, this programme instils relationships between the various elements of the musical work and allows the performer to bring out the significance of individual musical events within the context of the overall interpretation.

A further means by which musicians formulate their interpretations is through analysis, which often might take the form of a 'considered study of the score'[24] rather than a rigorous academic technique. Some performers analyse in order to gain a detailed knowledge and understanding of the work which will then inform their interpretative decision-making, while others use analysis as a means of solving specific interpretative problems.

Examples of how musicians analyse can be found in the pedagogical literature. Quantz makes interpretative suggestions which require the performer to undertake some form of harmonic analysis in order to generate expression; for example, he states that 'dissonances must be struck more strongly than consonances'.[25] Another example of how musicians might analyse is given by Fanny Waterman, piano teacher and founder of the Leeds International Piano Competition, who writes: 'Just as sentences contain key words, so each melody has a climax – though different artists will naturally have different views on where it should be. Pianists must learn to play rhythmically forward towards the climax, and never stand still, even in a rest or a pause.'[26] Therefore, in order to play 'towards the climax', musicians will have to engage in some form of analytical activity in order to decide where it lies.

Despite the subjective nature of interpretation, there are specific means by which musicians can develop their interpretative skills and enhance their ability to formulate interpretations. In interpreting a work the performer must somehow shape its disparate elements into a coherent performance, and listening to good performances, singing, analogy and analysis are useful methods of aiding that process of honing and refining.

The relationship between technique and interpretation

In preparing a work for performance, the musician has to negotiate between the processes required in formulating interpretations and in developing the appropriate technical skills. Research by Wicinski addressed how musicians organise their practising in order to accommodate these two requirements.[27] He based his findings on interviews with leading Russian pianists, who demonstrated two different working methods. One group suggested that their practising could be divided into three distinct phases:

(1) getting an overview of the work and developing initial interpretative ideas

(2) overcoming the technical demands of the work

(3) combining the first two phases and refining the interpretation.

The remaining pianists were unable to isolate stages in their practising and simply worked through a piece from beginning to end.

Gaining an overview of a work before detailed practice commences offers two main advantages to the musician. First, it provides a means of planning subsequent practice sessions so that technical difficulties can be isolated at an early stage, thereby allowing the performer to devise means of overcoming them. Second, the performer can formulate initial interpretative ideas before engaging in technical practising so that the latter will be informed by the interpretative requirements. Overview might take place at or away from the instrument depending on the abilities and the preferred working methods of the individual musician. But wherever it occurs, it requires conscious mental involvement in the process of practising and thereby encourages accuracy and efficiency, while in addition emphasising the importance of interpretation as the ultimate goal of musical performance.

The ways in which interpretations emerge during practice differ considerably from musician to musician. In her interview study, Hallam found three different practical approaches to the formulation of interpretations during practising: one group of musicians used analysis; another group used a mixture of analysis and intuition; and a third group worked purely on an intuitive basis,[28] that is, they did not consciously attend to interpretation during practice but instead let it emerge 'automatically' as a product of the technical practising. Rather than being some mystical force or natural ability, intuition could reflect a performer's automatised interpretative response to some aspect of a musical score or work; John Rink refers to this as 'informed intuition'.[29] An expert performer will have had years of experience playing and listening to a wide range of music, resulting in a highly developed 'intuitive' ability. Musicians might consciously employ analysis when intuition fails or to help develop overall interpretations, as opposed to expressive details of performance.

Given that a performer's working methods evolve over years of musical experience, it is not surprising that different musicians display a wide variety of working styles, especially in formulating interpretations. However, a common feature of the practice methods of the most experienced performers is a systematic approach to musical learning, demonstrated in an awareness of practice goals and the ability to call upon effective musical strategies which enable them to achieve these goals.

Summary: efficiency and effectiveness in practice

In preparing for a musical performance, the musician engages with a score and then translates it into sound via an instrument or the human voice. This requires the development of an appropriate technical facility in order to play or sing the notes and to realise the musician's own interpretation. Technical and interpretative practice require different but related practice techniques.

Student and amateur musicians can benefit from studying the working methods of experienced performers and teachers, and from recognising that practising is most productive when there is conscious mental involvement. Whether practice is intended to develop technique or formulate an interpretation, it will be most effective when the musician has clear, achievable goals and has decided on the means of realising them. The most common approach is to simplify the task through the division of the musical material into chunks of a small enough size to ensure a degree of progress.

In this sense, practising can be seen as a problem-solving activity whereby a musician identifies a problem and then finds a means of eliminating it. Performers must monitor their own actions in order to assess the effectiveness of their practice techniques and to avoid error. The efficiency of practice can be improved if performers constantly ask themselves three questions while practising:

(1) What am I hoping to achieve?
(2) What methods can I employ to achieve my goal?
(3) Have my methods been successful?

Notes

1 See Allen Newell and Paul Rosenbloom, 'Mechanisms of skill acquisition and the law of practice', in John R. Anderson (ed.), *Cognitive Skills and their Acquisition* (Hillsdale, NJ: Erlbaum, 1981), 1; compare the discussions of practice in chapters 9 and 10.

2 Pier Francesco Tosi, *Observations on the Florid Song*, trans. John Galliard, ed. Michael Pilkington (London: Stainer and Bell, [1723/1742] 1987), 27.

3 Daniel Gottlob Türk, *School of Clavier Playing*, trans. Raymond H. Haggh (Lincoln, Nebr.: University of Nebraska Press, [1789] 1982), 19.

4 Johann Joachim Quantz, *On Playing the Flute*, 2nd edn, trans. Edward R. Reilly (London: Faber and Faber, [1752] 1985), 118.

5 Johann Nepomuk Hummel, *A Complete Theoretical and Practical Course of Instructions on the Art of Playing the Piano Forte*, 3 vols. (London: T. Boosey & Co., [1828] 1830), I:iii.

6 They define 'deliberate practice' as 'a highly structured activity with the explicit goal of improving some aspect of performance'; see Ralf Th. Krampe and K. Anders Ericsson, 'Deliberate practice and elite musical performance', in John Rink (ed.), *The Practice of Performance: Studies in Musical Interpretation* (Cambridge: Cambridge University Press, 1995), 86.

7 Ibid., 93.

8 Hummel, *Complete*, I:iv.

9 Carl Philipp Emanuel Bach, *Essay on the True Art of Playing Keyboard Instruments* [*Versuch über die wahre Art das Clavier zu spielen*], trans. and ed. William Mitchell (London: Eulenburg, [1753, 1762] 1949), 101.

10 Frédéric Kalkbrenner, *Learning the Pianoforte*, trans. Sabilla Novello (London: J. Alfred Novello, 1866), 19.

11 John A. Sloboda, *The Musical Mind: The Cognitive Psychology of Music* (Oxford: Oxford University Press, 1985), 90.

12 Victor Booth, *We Piano Teachers* (London: Hutchinson, [1946] 1971), 77.

13 Paul M. Fitts and Michael I. Posner, *Human Performance* (Belmont, Calif.: Brooks/Cole, 1967), 11–15.

14 James Ching, *The Amateur Pianist's Companion* (Oxford: Hall, 1950), 102.

15 Linda M. Gruson, 'Rehearsal skill and musical competence: does practice make perfect?', in John A. Sloboda (ed.), *Generative Processes in Music: The Psychology of Performance, Improvisation, and Composition* (Oxford: Clarendon Press, 1988), 91–112.

16 Kacper Miklaszewski, 'A case study of a pianist preparing a musical performance', *Psychology of Music*, 17 (1989), 95–109.

17 Robert Gerle, *The Art of Practising the Violin* (London: Stainer Books, 1987), 17; cf. chapter 8 in this volume.

18 Dale Reubart, *Anxiety and Musical Performance: On Playing the Piano from Memory* (New York: Da Capo Press, 1985), 79; see also chapter 9 in this book.

19 Tosi, *Observations*, 37.

20 Sloboda, *Musical Mind*, 88.

21 Susan Hallam, 'Professional musicians' approaches to the learning and interpretation of music', *Psychology of Music*, 23 (1995), 111–28.

22 György Sándor, *On Piano Playing* (New York: Collier Macmillan, 1981), 211.

23 Bach, *Essay*, 152.

24 See John Rink, review of Wallace Berry, *Musical Structure and Performance*, in *Music Analysis*, 9 (1990), 323; see also chapter 3 in this volume.

25 Quantz, *On Playing*, 254.

26 Fanny Waterman, *On Piano Teaching and Performance* (London: Faber and Faber, 1983), 34; cf. Rachmaninoff's comments quoted on page 232 in this volume.

27 A. A. Wicinski, 'Psichologiceskii analiz processa raboty pianista-ispolnitiela nad muzykalnym proizviedieniem [A psychological analysis of how the pianist-performer works on a musical composition]', *Izviestia Akademii Piedagogiceskich Nauk Vyp*, 25 (1950), 171–215, cited in Miklaszewski, 'Case study', 96.

28 Hallam, 'Professional', 117–21.
29 Rink, review of Berry, 328; see also chapter 3 in this volume.

Further reading

Gruson, Linda M., 'Rehearsal skill and musical competence: does practice make perfect?', in John A. Sloboda (ed.), *Generative Processes in Music: The Psychology of Performance, Improvisation, and Composition* (Oxford: Clarendon Press, 1988), 91–112

Jørgensen, Harald and Andreas C. Lehmann (eds.), *Does Practice Make Perfect? Current Theory and Research on Instrumental Music Practice* (Oslo: Norges Musikkhøgskole, 1997)

Krampe, Ralf Th. and K. Anders Ericsson, 'Deliberate practice and elite musical performance', in John Rink (ed.), *The Practice of Performance: Studies in Musical Interpretation* (Cambridge: Cambridge University Press, 1995), 84–102

Miklaszewski, Kacper, 'A case study of a pianist preparing a musical performance', *Psychology of Music*, 17 (1989), 95–109

Reubart, Dale, *Anxiety and Musical Performance: On Playing the Piano from Memory* (New York: Da Capo Press, 1985)

Sloboda, John A., *The Musical Mind: The Cognitive Psychology of Music* (Oxford: Oxford University Press, 1985)

8   Memorising music

AARON WILLIAMON

Performing music from memory can be extremely demanding. Not only is there the initial challenge of retaining thousands of notes and complex musical structures, but also the equally formidable task of remembering and executing them in stressful performance situations. All too often, such demands have caused performers to accrue hours of mere repetitive practice, trying to develop multiple ways of recalling music so that their performance will continue come what may.[1] Such strategies, however, can be inefficient and can fail to guarantee perfect recall. As a result, musicians, teachers and researchers have sought to answer two questions: why should performers memorise music, and how can this be done most efficiently and effectively? Answers to these questions have traditionally been drawn from a large corpus of inconsistent, anecdotal evidence. This chapter will re-address these two questions in the light of recent studies which have examined musical memory more systematically.

Exploring why musicians perform from memory

In 1828, Clara Schumann set a precedent for musical performers by playing in public without a score. Shortly afterwards, Franz Liszt, with his 'predilection for showmanship, seized the opportunity to turn this new development into a dramatic ritual'.[2] He caused a veritable uproar at one performance by flinging not only his white gloves into the first few rows of the audience – a gesture for which he was renowned – but also his score. Such theatrics were not well received by critics. In fact, memorised performances were considered to be in bad taste and ostentatious even towards the end of the nineteenth century. In his book *With Your Own Two Hands*, Seymour Bernstein succinctly portrays how the perception and acceptance of performing from memory have changed since the nineteenth century:

In 1861, Sir Charles Hallé, the British virtuoso, began the first in a series of concerts devoted to all the Sonatas of Beethoven. He played from memory. By the third concert, he capitulated to the London critics and appeared on stage with the music. But . . . he continued to play from memory nonetheless. As late as 1870, Dr Hans von Bülow, whose feats of memory were legendary, found the London critics to be as resistant as ever to performances from memory. In this case, however, the audience came in for a greater share of censure from the Daily Telegraph than von Bülow: it was his memory and not his musicality that seemed to make the greatest impression, the critics complained. It was not until the end of the nineteenth century that playing from memory came to be regarded as a serious practice and not mere sensationalism. Certainly today it is far more unusual for a soloist to play with a score than without it.[3]

Indeed, performing from memory has become a measure of professional competence for concert soloists of all types – pianists, violinists, singers and trumpeters alike. Doing so, however, can be arduous and anxiety-provoking. Why, then, do performers insist on playing from memory? Is it only to impress and dazzle their audiences, or is there a more fulfilling musical justification for this tradition? A number of authors have argued for the latter reason. Edwin Hughes, for instance, suggested in 1915 that 'performing with a bundle of notes' obstructs 'absolute freedom of expression and the most direct psychological connection with the audience'.[4] Many performers have openly agreed with this view, claiming that performing from memory frees them to create and communicate novel musical interpretations and allows them to cast aside the unnecessary mental crutch and musical security blanket of the printed page. Not all performers, however, have felt so strongly about memorising music; notable exceptions include the famous French pianist Raoul Pugno, Béla Bartók and Dame Myra Hess, all of whom performed publicly with their scores.

A recent study has systematically investigated the value of performing from memory by examining four questions:

(1) does performing from memory actually offer 'absolute freedom of expression'?
(2) do memorised performances yield the 'most direct psychological connection with the audience'?
(3) if performing from memory does offer 'absolute freedom of expression' and the 'most direct psychological connection', do these advantages outweigh the hours of extra practice required to accomplish such feats?
(4) does musical training affect the ability to distinguish memorised from non-memorised performances?[5]

To answer these questions, audiences were asked to watch several video-taped performances of a cellist playing the Preludes from Bach's Cello Suites Nos. 1, 2 and 3. They rated these according to the performers' musical

Table 8.1. *Characteristics of the performances, including a description of each of the five performance types and indications of whether a music stand was visible to the audience and whether the cellist performed with the score*

Performance type	Description	Stand visible	Score
1	The cellist performed each Prelude as soon as she felt able to produce a satisfactory public performance. For these initial performances, she was asked not to have memorised the pieces. The view of the cellist was partially obstructed by a music stand (see Figure 8.1a).	✓	✓
2	The Preludes were video-taped again as soon as the cellist was able to perform them from memory (approximately one month after performances of type 1). Though empty, the music stand in front of the cellist gave the appearance that she was reading from the score (see Figure 8.1a).	✓	×
3	Performance type 3 was the same as type 2, except that the music stand was absent (see Figure 8.1b).	×	×
4	The cellist was asked to practise and play the Preludes once again using the score. The view of the performer was similar to that of performance types 1 and 2, in that a stand partially obstructed the audience's view (see Figure 8.1a).	✓	✓
5	Performance type 5 was the same as type 4, except that the camera was positioned facing the cellist's right side, resulting in the exclusion of the stand from the picture (see Figure 8.1c).	×	✓

understanding, communicative ability, technical proficiency and overall performance quality. The performances, however, were of five distinct types, with each differing in terms of memorisation, the visual information available to audience members and the amount of time spent preparing for performance. Also, audience members were classified as musicians and non-musicians so that some indication could be obtained as to whether musical background affected ratings of the performances. Specific characteristics of the five performance types are detailed in Table 8.1, and the visual information available to audience members is displayed in Figure 8.1.

The ratings of the performances were examined and compared in order to explore possible answers to the four questions posed above. Do memorised performances offer 'absolute freedom of expression'? Freedom, yes; absolute freedom, no. The analyses revealed that audiences rated the memorised

(a)

(b)

(c)

Figure 8.1 The view of the cellist during performances of the three Preludes from Cello Suites Nos. 1, 2 and 3 by J. S. Bach. Audiences were shown video-taped performances of each Prelude. In some of the performances (those of performance types 1, 2 and 4), the view of the performer was obstructed by a music stand (Figure 8.1a). In other performances (those of performance type 3), the view of the cellist was as in a memorised performance, in that it was not obstructed by a music stand (Figure 8.1b). Finally, the view of the performer in performance type 5 was from the cellist's right side, resulting in the exclusion of the stand from the picture (Figure 8.1c).

performances higher than the non-memorised performances, regardless of whether or not a stand obstructed the view of the cellist. Moreover, individuals with musical training scored the memorised performances even higher than non-musicians in terms of the cellist's communicative ability, thus indicating that listeners who were musicians may have been better equipped to pick up subtle communication cues embedded in the performances from memory. These findings suggest that, to some extent, performers can express themselves more freely when playing without a score. However, for this freedom of expression to be 'absolute', as Hughes proposed, it would need to be identified equally well by all listeners, independent of musical training.

Do memorised performances yield the 'most direct psychological connection with the audience'? Yes, especially for audience members who are musicians. Listeners rated performances without the music stand higher than those with the stand, regardless of whether they were from memory. This finding was even stronger for listeners who were musicians, suggesting that their musical training may have instilled a bias in favour of performances without a stand. Future research may clarify the nature of this bias, for instance by asking musicians to rate performances after having been correctly or incorrectly informed that the observed performances were from memory.

Is the extra time spent preparing for a memorised performance worthwhile? Yes. This answer was obtained by comparing ratings of the non-memorised performances before the extra month of practice (that is, performance type 1) to those afterwards (performance types 4 and 5). All audience members – musicians and non-musicians alike – rated the performances after this extra practice higher, especially with respect to ratings of musical understanding and communicative ability. Whether this finding would apply to other performers needs further exploration. The performer in this study felt that technical proficiency was a strong asset in her playing, and it is not surprising that she performed the pieces as soon as the technical demands had been satisfactorily addressed. Yet performers who have not attained the same standard of technical proficiency may improve across all performance aspects during an additional month of practice. Conversely, those who have stronger musical or communicative skills may show no improvement. To identify these individual differences, the practice leading up to both memorised and non-memorised performances should be systematically investigated and compared in future research.

This study provides an initial, empirical test of the view that memorised performances are more expressive and communicative than those that are non-memorised. Its findings may be applied, though with discretion, to both musical performance and pedagogy. For example, performers can be reassured that memorised performances offer enhanced experiences for audiences, whether through aural or visual means. Consequently, teachers should prepare their students for the demanding expectations of audiences – especially those composed of musicians – by offering them more opportunities to prepare for memorised performances. Also, once subsequent research has identified the precise role of visual information in determining audiences' evaluations of memorised performances, performers and teachers may gain enough information to decide whether music stands should be entirely absent from the stage or whether smaller, less imposing stands would produce an equally satisfying experience for audiences.

Despite such implications, this study has several limitations that must be noted. First, the performer, while having high performance standards, was not an eminent concert soloist. The advantages of performing from memory may be even greater for experts. Second, performing from memory may prove more advantageous for performances of certain pieces of music. The works chosen for this study were selected for consistency of composer, style, difficulty and length. Examining pieces that differ in these respects may more accurately demonstrate the value of performing from memory. Memorising an atonal composition, for example, may prove cumbersome and overwhelming if the performer is forced to do so note by note. Such a procedure would inevitably increase the demands on mental processes during performance and thereby reduce – or possibly eliminate – the advantages of performing from memory. Third, video-taped performances do not offer optimal viewing conditions for audiences. Some communicative aspects (for example, subtle eye movements, facial expressions and intensity of breathing) may have been diminished or eliminated in the video-taping process. By addressing the above limitations, future research may reveal precisely how audiences evaluate and measure performance, providing further information to help performers decide whether to memorise.

Exploring how musicians perform from memory
Methods of memorising music

Edwin Hughes and Tobias Matthay were two of the first musicians and pedagogues to write extensively on how musicians memorise compositions.[6] Hughes, for example, highlighted three principal ways in which performers can learn music when preparing for a memorised performance: aural, visual and kinaesthetic. *Aural memory* (sometimes referred to as auditory memory) enables individuals to hear compositions in the 'mind's ear', anticipate upcoming events in the score and make concurrent evaluations of a performance's progress. *Visual memory* consists of images

of the written page and other performance features that have been impressed upon the 'mind's eye'. Pianists and other keyboard players, for instance, may remember positions 'of the hand and fingers, the look of the
chords as they are struck and the pattern which the various figures make
upon the keyboard as they are played'.[7] *Kinaesthetic memory* (that is, finger,
muscular or tactile memory) enables performers to execute notes automatically. For pianists, it is facilitated by extended training of the fingers,
wrists and arms and can exist in two forms: (1) position and movement
from note to note, and (2) sense of key resistance. In addition, Hughes
and Matthay insisted that 'no really intelligent memorising is possible without a knowledge of harmony and musical form, and, for the stricter polyphonic forms of composition, of counterpoint and fugue as well'.[8] Neither
Hughes nor Matthay categorised this as a separate method for memorising music. Rather, they simply insisted that aural, visual and kinaesthetic
memory could not function properly without it. Subsequent performers
and pedagogues, however, have explicitly referred to this as *conceptual
memory* in order to accentuate its importance for making 'sureness more
sure'.[9]

Clearly, performances from memory can only result from complex interactions between all of the above methods of memorising music. Almost no
musician can execute note-for-note performances of a composition without
once – consciously or unconsciously – hearing the music, seeing the notes
on the printed page, seeing and feeling muscular movements that result
from playing, and studying the score to some extent. Therefore, Hughes
and Matthay recommended that each individual focus on the method or
combination of methods that he or she finds easiest and most reliable.

Interviews with musicians

Two recent investigations illustrate how musicians employ these
methods when performing. Susan Hallam interviewed twenty-two professional and fifty-five novice musicians.[10] The interviews revealed considerable individual diversity in the use of aural, visual and kinaesthetic memory.
One musician, for example, declared that 'visual memory I find very useful
sometimes, how the page looks . . . My visual memory is not all that good,
except for music.' Another reported that 'once you are into a moving passage
that runs at speed or is a continuous flow of music then the ear tends to take
over'.[11]

Hallam found that all of the professional musicians adopted some sort of
conscious, 'analytical' strategy which involved developing an understanding
of the structure of the music. One conductor remarked: 'I don't think that
the method that I use for learning scores . . . would be of any use at all

to an instrumentalist because I do it entirely by analysis, which is to me infallible.'[12] They also reported using a multiple coding of information (that is, a combination of aural, visual and kinaesthetic memory in conjunction with analytical strategies) to provide greater security during performance. For example, one of the professional musicians commented that

I have to understand what is happening harmonically, or if it's a melody with a definite sequence. But I wouldn't do it just hoping it comes . . . There are some things, which I have played so many times over the course of the years that I just know how they go and can play them. That's not analytical, but I would hate to stand up in public and play them because I think probably the automatic memory would fail.[13]

Regardless of whether musicians were classified as professional or novice, Hallam found that their strategies often depended on the nature of the task to be completed. She reported that some musicians felt confident in relying on automated processes when memorising short pieces, but for longer, more complex works such as a concerto, many adopted a more analytical approach. One musician remarked that

it depends what it is. If it has 'set' tunes, then I can learn it in a day. But if the music is modern, I start at the beginning, work through and then that's where the practice comes in because I'd make sure I can actually play it. Then I'd go over and over it . . . Then I'd picture it in my mind.[14]

In a similar study, Rita Aiello also examined the methods used by professional musicians to memorise music.[15] She interviewed seven concert pianists to explore their use of aural, visual and kinaesthetic memory and their approaches to memorising various types of music (for example, polyphonic and atonal compositions). In addition, she examined the role of fingering, mnemonic aids, improvisation and knowledge of musical structure in memorisation. She discovered several themes in the participants' responses. First, the musicians reported relying on aural memory much more than on kinaesthetic memory, although they all agreed on the importance of knowing the kinaesthetic components of a piece (for instance, the fingerings). Second, all of the pianists emphasised that having a clear idea of the musical structure and analysing the score were the most important and reliable methods for memorisation. Third, five of the seven pianists commented that they memorised in a 'holistic' manner by dividing the piece into short sections, in order to obtain a 'more solid memory of the entire work'.[16] Fourth, knowledge of improvisation was deemed an important asset for memorising music; even the one pianist who did not know how to improvise considered it to be a valuable tool. On the basis of her findings,

Aiello concluded that, in general, teachers should assist their students in memorising music by fostering a detailed knowledge of musical structure and helping them to carry out analyses of the score.

The research by Hallam and Aiello, in conjunction with the writings of Hughes and Matthay, provide insight into how musicians perform from memory. In sum, these investigations reveal that musicians tend to use a wide variety of methods to memorise music. Unfortunately, no prevailing evidence exists to suggest whether aural, visual or kinaesthetic memory or a combination of these is the most efficient or produces the most secure memorised performances. The amount of ambiguity concerning the importance of these – even among concert soloists – is very surprising. Some musicians contend that their way of memorising music is superior to others. Undoubtedly, each person's method will be one of the best for that individual simply because it has been chosen and developed over years of practice.

Nevertheless, the work by Hallam and Aiello – supported by the anecdotal claims of Hughes and Matthay – suggests that the most highly skilled musicians in their studies relied heavily on analytical strategies when memorising. Music teachers and analysts have long stressed the importance to performers of studying the structure of musical compositions. Nicholas Cook, for example, has argued that

the ability to set aside details and see large-scale connections appropriate to the particular musical context, which is what analysis encourages, is an essential part of the musician's way of perceiving musical sound. For the performer, it is obvious that analysis has a role to play in the memorization of extended scores, and to some extent in the judgement of large-scale dynamic and rhythmic relationships (although some of the claims that Schenkerian analysis, in particular, is indispensable for performers and conductors have surely been overstated).[17]

Still, further exploration is needed to determine whether studying the structure of music will provide the most reliable means for memorisation and should always serve as the foundation upon which works are aurally, visually and kinaesthetically learned. Valuable insight into this issue can be gained by considering the findings of research on exceptional memory abilities in other kinds of performance.

The principles of expert memory

Researchers have examined exceptional memory in many different types of activity, including chess, physics, medicine, writing and athletics. From this work, several theories have been proposed to explain how individuals are able to develop and maintain the extraordinary abilities that are often displayed by eminent and expert performers in those fields.[18] Before any theory of expert memory can be applied to music, we must first determine whether musical memory is comparable to other types of expert memory. Although the nature of musical performance may fundamentally differ from that of activities like chess or athletics, skilled musicians share some of the same demands on memory as other experts. For example, memory plays an important role in sports such as gymnastics and figure skating because individuals must memorise sequences of the movements that constitute a given performance and execute those movements with reference to defined, technical standards. Since technical skills are judged according to ideal forms, performers must make comparisons between 'actual' and 'ideal' techniques while performing. The bases for these comparisons are drawn from long-term memory, acquired over many years of training.[19] Concert soloists, like experts of those sports, train extensively in order to recall series of actions that constitute a performance; refer to defined, technical standards expected by audiences and judges; and monitor their performance as it happens in order to gauge its quality.

Having broached the issue of comparability, we can now begin to apply aspects of existing theories to musical memory. In general, research has shown that superior memory abilities are underpinned by a vast knowledge base specific to the activity. Information in this knowledge base is continually collected and stored into meaningful groups (or 'chunks'), often becoming associated with specific physical actions and commands.[20] Basic examples of such chunks in music include scales and arpeggios. Musicians spend hours practising these so that they can easily recognise and execute them when sight-reading or committing a piece to memory.

Once a large database of meaningful knowledge has been acquired, an individual can then use it to create a mental representation of any complex information that must be memorised.[21] Simply put, a mental representation is a kind of internal map that can be reliably used to recall specific material. As with any map, important landmarks (or 'cues') within the information must be identified in practice and then used to guide retrieval so that a resulting performance can stay on track.[22]

In musical terms, a composition may be represented in a hierarchy ranging from the highest level of global understanding (the piece as a whole) down to the lowest level (the piece as individual notes). Moreover, the representation may be based on aural, visual or kinaesthetic memory as well as various analytical strategies, depending on the preferences of the performer and the piece being learned. Limits in human information processing and attention, however, make it unlikely that an entire representation will be activated during performance, even for a piece of only moderate length.

Instead, just part of it is activated at any one time, with the active region shifting as the performer progresses through the music.[23] In the middle of a deeply embedded musical phrase, for instance, a musician may be primarily concerned with connections within the phrase itself. In that case, only low-level aural, visual and kinaesthetic cues would be active. Conversely, at a phrase boundary, a performer may need to know how the previous and subsequent phrases relate to one another and to the overall structure of the piece. At such a moment, higher-level cues specifying larger-scale relationships would be active – although some low-level cues may be needed for the immediate succession of events to be played.[24]

Obviously, there is a vast potential for individual differences to emerge in the specific content of musicians' representations. Such differences are clearly shown in the interview studies of Hallam and Aiello. Nevertheless, existing research has revealed that a representation can potentially be reliable and durable as long as it is highly organised and extensively rehearsed.[25] One of the most effective methods for organising memorised music – as indicated by the professional musicians in the studies of Hallam and Aiello – is to incorporate analytical strategies into practice. By doing so, performers can indeed establish a solid foundation upon which compositions are aurally, visually and kinaesthetically learned.

Further clarification of the importance of analytical strategies for organising practice and retrieval has been provided by Roger Chaffin and Gabriela Imreh.[26] They systematically observed the practice of a concert pianist – Imreh herself – to determine how she formed a representation of the third movement of Bach's *Italian Concerto*. They found that the composition's formal structure served as the tool by which she organised her representation. In fact, she integrated her knowledge of the formal structure into the early stages of practice and then relied heavily on it to retrieve the music during performance. Moreover, she reported that her cues were of three types – 'basic', 'interpretative' and 'expressive' – and that she had associated them with the note-to-note detail of the music by means of a combination of aural, visual and kinaesthetic memory. 'Basic' cues included fingerings, technical difficulties and groups of notes that formed identifiable units of information. 'Interpretative' cues included phrasing, dynamics, tempo and pedalling. 'Expressive' cues were places in the score where the pianist tried to elicit changes in the expression or mood of the music.

Not every performer will be as familiar with the formal structure of a composition as Imreh; nor will they all categorise the most memorable and important components of a composition into basic, interpretative and expressive cues. Nevertheless, this study confirms the importance of using analytical strategies for establishing a dependable mental representation of a composition by providing observational evidence for their use throughout the memorisation process. Other musicians can draw upon the analytical strategies preferred and known specifically to them, thus learning and storing important landmarks accordingly. Regardless of what those preferences may be, existing research suggests that, for the landmarks to be reliable and stable during performance, they should be organised in meaningful ways and used to direct practice.[27]

Conclusions

Recent investigations have shed light on the ways in which musicians memorise music. Musicians should be aware that generating and using internal representations to recall specific information is a salient characteristic of the process of memorising and that professionals have clearly been shown to use analytical strategies in doing so. Although advocating that all musicians carry out in-depth formal analyses of every composition they perform would be unrealistic, musicians should be encouraged to develop their own analytical strategies and to integrate them into the early stages of learning. This will enable them to recognise and rely with assurance on important landmarks within a piece, to which they can refer as a performance progresses or which will help them resume a performance that has unexpectedly halted.

One issue that must be addressed by subsequent research is the extent to which certain analytical strategies are the most effective and efficient. One could naturally suggest that the more ways in which music is encoded, the more associations and connections will be formed to that information and, therefore, the more likely an individual will be to remember it. In that sense, those performers who strive to learn compositions aurally, visually and kinaesthetically and who rehearse with analytical and other strategies (for example, improvisation and mnemonic techniques) should have the most secure and effective memory for performance. Still, such overencoding and over-practice may not be the most efficient approach to memorisation. Performers ideally should strike a balance between effectiveness and efficiency if they are to succeed in meeting the intense and wide-ranging demands of a career in music. Future research may well provide insight into where this balance lies.

Notes

1 See Roger Chaffin and Gabriela Imreh, ' "Pulling teeth and torture": musical memory and problem solving', *Thinking and Reasoning*, 3 (1997), 315–36.
2 Seymour Bernstein, *With Your Own Two Hands: Self-Discovery through Music* (New York: Schirmer, 1981), 220.

3 Ibid., 220.

4 Edwin Hughes, 'Musical memory in piano playing and piano study', *Musical Quarterly*, 1 (1915), 595.

5 Aaron Williamon, 'The value of performing from memory', *Psychology of Music*, 27 (1999), 84–95.

6 Respectively, Hughes, 'Musical memory', and Tobias Matthay, *On Memorizing and Playing from Memory and On the Laws of Practice Generally* (London: Oxford University Press, 1926).

7 Hughes, 'Musical memory', 598.

8 Ibid., 599.

9 Ibid., 599; see Gabriela Imreh and Roger Chaffin, 'Understanding and developing musical memory: the views of a concert pianist and a cognitive psychologist', *The American Music Teacher* (December 1996/January 1997), 20–4.

10 Susan Hallam, 'The development of memorisation strategies in musicians', paper presented at the Seventh Conference on Developmental Psychology (Cracow, Poland, 1995).

11 Ibid., 8.

12 Ibid., 6.

13 Ibid., 5.

14 Ibid., 7.

15 Rita Aiello, 'Strategies for memorizing piano music: pedagogical implications', poster presented at the Eastern Division of the Music Educators National Conference (New York, NY, 1999).

16 Ibid., 1.

17 Nicholas Cook, *A Guide to Musical Analysis* (London: Dent, 1989), 232; see also chapter 3 in this volume.

18 See William G. Chase and Herbert A. Simon, 'Perception in chess', *Cognitive Psychology*, 4 (1973), 55–81; K. Anders Ericsson and Walter Kintsch, 'Long-term working memory', *Psychological Review*, 102 (1995), 211–45; Eric F. Clarke, 'Generative principles in music performance', in John A. Sloboda (ed.), *Generative Processes in Music: The Psychology of Performance, Improvisation, and Composition* (Oxford: Clarendon Press, 1988), 1–26; and Andreas C. Lehmann and K. Anders Ericsson, 'Expert pianists' mental representation of memorized music', poster presented at the Thirty-sixth Annual Meeting of the Psychonomic Society (Los Angeles, 1995). The first two of these studies use the term 'retrieval structure' to describe the representations by which experts in many different fields retrieve stored information for performance. For the purposes of this chapter, the more general term 'mental representation' is used in order to remain consistent with the latter two studies, which address the representations used by musicians in particular.

19 See Fran Allard and Janet L. Starkes, 'Motor-skill experts in sports and other domains', in K. Anders Ericsson and Jacqui Smith (eds.), *Toward a General Theory of Expertise: Prospects and Limits* (Cambridge: Cambridge University Press, 1991), 126–52.

20 See Chase and Simon, 'Perception in chess'; Ericsson and Kintsch, 'Long-term working memory'; and Ericsson and Smith, *Toward a General Theory*.

21 See Ericsson and Kintsch, 'Long-term working memory'; see also chapter 7 in this volume.

22 See Endel Tulving and Z. Pearlstone, 'Availability versus accessibility of information in memory for words', *Journal of Verbal Learning and Verbal Behavior*, 5 (1966), 381–91; Alan D. Baddeley, *Human Memory: Theory and Practice* (Boston: Allyn & Bacon, 1990); and Ericsson and Kintsch, 'Long-term working memory'.

23 See Clarke, 'Generative principles'.

24 See ibid., 4.

25 See William G. Chase and K. Anders Ericsson, 'Skilled memory', in John R. Anderson (ed.), *Cognitive Skills and Their Acquisition* (Hillsdale, NJ: Erlbaum, 1981), 141–89.

26 See Chaffin and Imreh, '"Pulling teeth"', and Roger Chaffin and Gabriela Imreh, 'A comparison of practice and self-report as sources of information about the goals of expert practice', *Psychology of Music*, 29 (2001), 39–69; see also Roger Chaffin, Gabriela Imreh and Mary Crawford, *Practicing Perfection: Memory and Piano Performance* (Mahwah, NJ: Erlbaum, 2002).

27 See Aaron Williamon and Elizabeth Valentine, 'The role of retrieval structures in memorizing music', *Cognitive Psychology*, 44 (2002), 1–32, and Aaron Williamon, Elizabeth Valentine and John Valentine, 'Shifting the focus of attention between levels of musical structure', *European Journal of Cognitive Psychology* (forthcoming).

Further reading

Bernstein, Seymour, *With Your Own Two Hands: Self-Discovery through Music* (New York: Schirmer, 1981)

Chaffin, Roger, Gabriela Imreh and Mary Crawford, *Practicing Perfection: Memory and Piano Performance* (Mahwah, NJ: Erlbaum, 2002)

Matthay, Tobias, *On Memorizing and Playing from Memory and On the Laws of Practice Generally* (London: Oxford University Press, 1926)

Williamon, Aaron, 'The value of performing from memory', *Psychology of Music*, 27 (1999), 84–95

PART THREE

Making music

9   From score to sound

PETER HILL

Many performers refer to scores as 'the music'. This is wrong, of course. Scores set down musical information, some of it exact, some of it approximate, together with indications of how this information may be interpreted. But the *music* itself is something imagined, first by the composer, then in partnership wth the performer, and ultimately communicated in sound.

The moment when music as sound is born, along with the attendant joys and frustrations, has been beautifully described by the great accompanist Gerald Moore. In the passage that follows, Moore subjects to microscopic analysis the introductory bars, or *Vorspiel*, of Schubert's 'Wandrers Nachtlied' (see Example 9.1). Moore's choice of such an 'easy' song is revealing, emphasising that technique is not simply a matter of accurately reproducing the score – in this instance the notes are simple enough to read at sight – but one of bringing the score to life in sound. Moore takes a delight in showing how elusive this can be:

Dynamically this little *Vorspiel* is all *pianissimo* but within the bounds of that *pianissimo* there must be a slight increase or swelling of tone and a subsequent reduction of tone. It is a curve – rising then falling; the smoothest of curves with one chord joined to the next. So restricted in range is it, so narrow the margin between your softest chord and your least soft chord that if you go one fraction over the limit at the top of the curve all is ruined. Each chord though related and joined to its neighbour is a different weight, differing by no more than a feather. You listen self-critically as you practise it. You experiment. You play it giving each chord a uniform and gentle pressure so that there is no rise and fall of tone – all *pianissimo*. You then try to give it that infinitesimal *crescendo* and *diminuendo* that is really wanted to give shape and meaning to the phrase: but it is out of proportion – you have overdone it – so you start again. Now you find that your chords are muddy, your pedalling is faulty, one chord trespasses on another's preserves instead of gently merging into it without blurring. You work at this. But despite the *pianissimo* you are achieving, you begin to realise that your chords are

Example 9.1 Schubert, 'Wandrers Nachtlied' D. 768, bars 1–2

without character – they are leaden, and the whole phrase is lifeless. So now very delicately you experiment by giving a fraction more weight to the top finger of your right hand . . . All this is the most fascinating pursuit imaginable. In your search for light and shade you are as happy and absorbed as a painter mixing the colours on his palette, and the satisfaction to the player when he does succeed in producing that perfect undulation, that clean line, when he feels at last that the whole design is shapely and fine, is immense. But this satisfaction or self-satisfaction is experienced but rarely. Just as surely as you are aware you *have* brought it off, so surely does your ever sharpening sensibility tell you how elusive is the prize and how many times you fail to attain it.[1]

Moore's masterclass is highly instructive. We have noted already his elegant reversal of the normal view of what makes music difficult. Moore's argument is that, precisely because there are so few notes, each requires super-fine artistry and control. A split note in the finale of a Beethoven sonata will make little or no difference to the musical result; but in 'Wandrers Nachtlied' even a tiny miscalculation spells disaster. Next there is the sequence of events, with conception – Moore's initial image of how the phrase should sound – leading to experiment at the piano, then reflection and self-criticism followed by further experiment. A key point is that the work progresses in a mood of serenity: the search for the ideal is its own reward, however rarely that ideal is actually achieved. The balance between an extreme care and patience on the one hand and the fierce desire to make music is one of the hardest of the many such balances the performer has to strike. In one sense we need to be impatient; but if impatience spills over into the work itself, the results are damaging as we cut corners and lower standards. Moreover we may build in doubts and tensions which resurface destructively in performance, and which in the long term may be difficult or impossible to eradicate.

Moore ends his account by addressing the drawback of his method: 'It may be argued that by working and experimenting in the repetitive way I advocate, the spirit, inspiration, freshness of the music may be lost. Indeed this is the greatest danger.'[2] This central difficulty, which Moore leaves un-resolved, occurs because the perfection he seeks is built up from layer upon layer of ingrained habit. The question then arises as to how we may cement such habits without at the same time cementing our musical conception. 'Drilling' the performance must, as Moore acknowledges, dull the player's creativity. Moreover it weakens or destroys our ability to adapt, whether to the vicissitudes which are part and parcel of a live performance, or to the different ideas of others. Moore as much as anyone must have suffered from working with musicians locked into their own interpretation, unwilling or unable to respond to the pianist's point of view.

This, then, is the central dilemma of the performing musician. How can we work and work, without losing enthusiasm or the open-mindedness that enables our ideas to develop? How, indeed, can we *perform* at all – in the sense of creating a unique event, with insights which arise from the inspiration of the moment? Clearly if repetition is at the heart of the problem, we need to find a way of working which minimises its role, or at least build into our method a means of mitigating its disadvantages.

The first step is to review the way we begin learning. The earliest stage is the most crucial: not only are we setting the standards for all subsequent work, but our decisions – taken rapidly and perhaps thoughtlessly – may come to govern how we play the piece for the rest of our lives. What as-sumptions are we making about a piece's style? What does the composer's notation mean? What indeed is our role as performers in relation to the composer? This last question is so fundamental that it calls for a digres-sion. In the example we have discussed – Moore and Schubert – the attitude is typical of the mid twentieth-century performer: deferential towards the composer's text and intentions, and seeing interpretation as the art of read-ing between the lines. Move to music written a century after Schubert, however, and we may find that the space 'between the lines' is apparently already filled, as in the works of the Second Viennese School, by markings which seem to specify every shade of nuance. The general increase over the past two centuries of the amount of information specified by the composer suggests either a mistrust of the performer's ability to understand, or an anxiety to control, attitudes for which Stravinsky, in his diatribes against 'interpretation', was a spokesman. In the circumstances it is no wonder that performers have become literal-minded. This is especially true of the most recent music. At rehearsals even of elite specialist ensembles, one gets the impression that the score *is* the music: absolute precedence is given to getting the facts of the score right, while what the score might *mean* goes by default.

The trouble with literal-mindedness is that it may get things hopelessly wrong. A classic and well-documented example comes with the Variations Op. 27 for piano by Webern. A study of the work's performance history shows that for years pianists took the score's austere appearance at face value: performances were rigorously impersonal, adding nothing to the very few marks of expression on the page. In due course it emerged, thanks to the efforts of Webern's pupils,[3] that this was the opposite of his intentions, and that what he really had in mind involved a constant interplay of rubato and light-and-shade. Why, then, did Webern not write down these nuances? Perhaps they were too subtle to specify, or perhaps too dependent on the instincts of individual pianists (Webern included) to make mandatory. Whatever the reason, the mistake of pianists had been to ignore the change in approach to notation between Webern's early and later works.

Another example comes from personal experience. When I first began to learn the music of Messiaen, the often hair's-breadth distinctions in his rhythms led me to strive for an extreme precision; but when I eventually went to study with him, he found this aspect of my playing mechanical. Messiaen wanted rhythm and phrasing to be supple, and no matter how complex the notation the music should never sound 'like an étude'. For Messiaen, the performer's job was to infer meaning and 'character' from what was written in the score – as in Schubert's 'Nachtlied'.[4]

Assuming that these wider issues – on style, notation and the performer's role – have received thought, how do we begin with the score itself? When I put this to my students I get a variety of answers. One suggestion is to start by organising the technique: fingering, bowing etc. The trouble with this is that it treats the score 'like an étude' and not as a piece of music. Since fingering and bowing alter, often radically, the way music sounds, we cannot devise these in a vacuum, without knowing what end they are to serve. Another school of thought prefers to make first contact with the score by sight-reading it through. This too has drawbacks. Corrections, modifications and improvements will be made piecemeal; and without a fundamental view of how the piece works, the result will be haphazard. Performers form habits with astonishing facility. It is only too easy for this facility to be misused rather than exploited. Lacking a vision of how the music ought to sound, we are liable subconsciously to become accustomed to defects in our playing – defects which are inevitable at this early stage – and so build in bad habits which, as everyone knows, are easy to acquire but much more troublesome to unlearn.

A further objection to both approaches is that they are throwbacks to childhood: the dutiful pupil who first learns the notes and then, as a reward, is allowed to 'put in the music'. If, important as they are, 'the notes' come first, the danger is that 'the music' will follow rather than lead our technique, conditioned by our level of skill and, it should be said, by our shortcomings.

In answer to these objections, my students often suggest listening to a recording, as a model performance. However, though a step in the right direction – in that the music is put first – this is a lazy shortcut, the musical equivalent of looking up the answer in the back of the book. Simply copying the way others play is an admission that what we have to offer is second rate. Again it is a misuse of the first stage: lacking our own ideas, we cannot avoid being overly influenced.[5]

What then? Discounting the possibilities already mentioned, the inescapable conclusion is that the first job is to begin by developing our own view of the work: the ideal is to exploit the precious time when the piece is unfamiliar, when we are most able to bring fresh insights to bear. We need, however, to do this without becoming unconsciously influenced by our inevitable limitations of skill. The answer is to work intensely at the score, but heard in our heads *away from the instrument*. The musical payoff is that we can develop our understanding free from all considerations of technique, focusing entirely on the musical issues that need to be decided in advance of practising at the instrument. Obvious though it may be, we have to be clear, in outline at least, about what we are trying to do before looking for the means to achieve it.

Here are two examples which show ways in which one might begin to think about a score. Debussy's 'L'ombre des arbres' sets Verlaine's poem as two four-line verses. The setting evokes the misty river, whose surface acts as a mirror dividing reality from illusion, real objects from their reflections:

L'ombre des arbres dans la rivière embrumée	The reflection of the trees in the misty river
Meurt comme de la fumée,	Dies like smoke,
Tandis qu'en l'air, parmi les ramures réelles	While above, among the real branches,
Se plaignent les tourterelles.	The turtledoves complain.
Combien ô voyageur, ce paysage blême	How much, O traveller, this pale landscape
Te mira blême toi-même	Mirrored your own pallor
Et que tristes pleuraient dans les hautes feuillées,	And how sadly in the high foliage wept
Tes espérances noyées.	Your drowned hopes.

The main musical motif is the pair of opening harmonies, rocking between seventh chords a tritone apart, on C♯ and G♮ (see Example 9.2). This is a musical counterpart, perhaps, to Verlaine's image, with the E♯ (common to both chords) a sort of 'horizon', analogous to the water's surface, further emphasised (as F♮) in bar 5 as the harmony shifts to a minor ninth on E, imparting a bitter twist to 'Meurt comme de la fumée'. So far the relationship between poem and music is clear. But in the second half, puzzlingly, the two go their separate ways. Verlaine uses his image from nature as a metaphor for the human condition, in the 'traveller' whose pallor matches that of the landscape, and whose highest aspirations – like the topmost branches – are lost in the water's depths. This resignation is not supported by the piano part,

Example 9.2 Debussy, 'L'ombre des arbres', *Ariettes oubliées*

Example 9.2 (*cont.*)

which surges forward via eloquent chromatic sequences, and as the voice falls silent ('Tes espérances noyées'), breaks out into a hugely magnified version of the G^7 harmony. Finally, and even more puzzlingly, this harmonic impasse is gently resolved (onto a harmony of C♯ major), the 'horizon' (E♯) pulsating quietly in the treble. Thus the despair of the poem is seemingly contradicted by the apparent serenity and acceptance of the postlude.

This is of course only an outline of how one's thoughts might begin to develop when coming to understand poem and music and their relationship. The point is that there is clearly much for singer and pianist to discuss – not least the paradox of the second verse – before they will be in a position to take any specific musical decisions.

From the distilled concentration of Debussy and Verlaine to a large-scale movement from one of Beethoven's last piano sonatas – Sonata in A♭ major Op. 110, first movement – is a step into another world. Yet, similarly, the process of thinking about the music begins with considering a curiosity. The development section (bars 40–55; Example 9.3) is strikingly at odds with

Example 9.3 Beethoven, Sonata in A♭ major Op. 110, i, bars 40–56

the expansive nature of the rest of the movement: both brief and oddly formal, it simply passes the theme through a series of sequential phrases. This observation suggested at first glance an understated, 'objective' style of playing, at once confirmed by Beethoven's way of engineering the recapitulation. The line breaks out into trills (bar 55) – an urgent variant of the cadential trill of the movement's opening phrase (bar 4; Example 9.4) – introducing the return of the main theme in bar 56, now in an impassioned version propelled by the left hand's demisemiquavers. The even flow of the development can be understood, with hindsight, as a prelude to the movement's decisive transformation. The extent of this transformation can be seen by turning back to the first page of the score (Example 9.4). Now one can understand that the start of the recapitulation is a compression of what at the opening

Example 9.4 Beethoven, Sonata in A♭ major Op. 110, i, bars 1–12

was a series of gentle gradations, from the hymn-like statement of the theme via a semiquaver accompaniment (from bar 5) to the demisemiquavers that begin at bar 12. Given that the harmonic pace remains constant, the effect of these gradations is of a series of variations, emphasised by the fact that in each case the first harmonic move is the same. Viewing the music in this way suggests that the pianist should make the gear changes smooth and inexorable, without the sudden rush in tempo often given to the start of the demisemiquavers. This line of enquiry, noting the differences between recapitulation and exposition, can be extended. There is, for example, the excursion to the remote key of E major for the reprise of the demisemi-quaver arpeggios (from bar 70; Example 9.5) and balancing of this (in A♭ major) in the lengthy coda (bars 105ff.). Even more significant is the final chord of the exposition, with its descant of upwardly spiralling semiquavers (from bar 36; Example 9.6), which in the recapitulation blossom into a new variant – poised in the heights of the keyboard – in a passage (bars 97–104; Example 9.7) which seems to be the emotional heart of the movement.

Gradually in this way one begins to discover not only what the music is saying, but how each phrase or section belongs to the whole, a sense of Beethoven's dramatic logic as the pieces of the jigsaw slip into place. The great advantage of working away from the instrument becomes apparent, as

Example 9.5 Beethoven, Sonata in A♭ major Op. 110, i, bars 70–2

Example 9.6 Beethoven, Sonata in A♭ major Op. 110, i, bars 36–7

Example 9.7 Beethoven, Sonata in A♭ major Op. 110, i, bars 95–105

one can experiment and reflect at will, unencumbered by details of technique which at this stage would be an irrelevant distraction.

All this mental work is analogous to the preparation done by a conductor in advance of the first rehearsal with orchestra. Like the conductor I can now approach the first 'rehearsal' – the first practice session – with the essential foundations in place: an outline of a conception; an understanding of context, of what the music does and why; and, most important, the ability to hear the music in every dimension. Even detailed technical problems will have been anticipated and at least partially solved. Notice also that the piece will already largely, if not entirely, be memorised: this is 'active' memory, springing from understanding the music's logic rather than from repetitive note-learning. In this way one hopes to address the central dilemma outlined earlier, so that one can *know* the music through and through without being trapped into a single set of habits.

Only now are we in a position to begin the sort of painstaking experiment at the instrument described earlier by Moore. By listening intently to the sound we produce, and comparing it with our inner conception, the two can gradually be brought into alignment. Yet all the time there is a fine line between trying to make an idea work and being prepared to revise our strategy.

At this point we reach the second phase of attacking our problem. Too often performers, myself included, tackle technical problems with a sticking-plaster approach. Errors must be corrected, of course, but merely to do this is to treat the symptom without addressing the cause. A simple example would be wayward intonation: before adjusting the fingers on the string, are we certain that we can *hear* (or sing) the passage correctly? If not, to 'blame' the fingers is useless.

This truth was impressed on me, as a raw and largely self-taught nineteen-year-old, at my first lesson with the pianist Cyril Smith. I was playing the first movement of Mozart's A major Piano Concerto K. 488, and my fingers became momentarily confused in the transition before the second subject (see Example 9.8). I at once began to repeat the passage and correct my slip; Smith, however, stopped me, and instead told me to practise the passage by playing the right-hand semiquavers slowly (without the score) but using only one finger. This bizarre instruction was instantly revealing. By removing the *physical* memory (of my fingering) I was forced to reconstruct the passage by ear, which (embarrassingly) I was unable to do. Smith then left me to relearn the passage aurally; when he returned, I played him the whole section as a 'concert performance' – uninhibitedly at full tempo – and miraculously found it clean and secure. By discovering where the fault lay, in this case in my ear, not my fingers, I was able to cure it – permanently so – and I would stress without any conventional repetitive practice.

Example 9.8 Mozart, Piano Concerto in A major K. 488, i, bars 86–93 (piano part only)

More recalcitrant difficulties can be approached by extending this principle, again with a view to tackling a problem at its root. The key to this is 'indirect' practice, a concept familiar to pianists in particular thanks to the famous editions of Alfred Cortot. For example, Cortot precedes each of the Chopin Etudes with pages of preliminary exercises, in line with his precept that one should practise 'not the difficult passage, but the difficulty contained in it, by starting such practice from its very root'.[6] Smith, who in his own playing was a master of Rachmaninoff concertos and similarly virtuoso repertoire, went further. He advocated a ferocious regime whereby as well as approaching the difficulty in stages (as Cortot did) one also exaggerated the problem, stretching the level of skill beyond what was called for. To take a simple example: if the problem was one of keyboard 'geography' – securely finding the right notes – the answer was to learn to play the passage with equal facility 'blind', without using the eyesight to direct the hands. For even and brilliant passagework, figuration was learned in different keys, made more awkward by using the original fingering – which has the incidental benefit of checking one's aural grasp and understanding of the music's harmony. As I write this, I have been working in a similarly 'indirect' way on the Bourrée from Bach's French Suite No. 6 in E major. In order to improve the tricky balancing and coordination of the two voices I have relearned the piece with hands crossed, the left-hand part transposed two octaves higher than written and the right hand down an octave (see Example 9.9). This helps counteract the fault inherent in pianists of 'right-handedness', whereby we listen to the upper line at the expense of the left hand. Also helpful, particularly in contrapuntal music of this sort, is to learn to sing the lower voice while playing the upper. Quite apart from the immediate benefit, such techniques have valuable side effects. One of these is that the act of relearning the music in

Example 9.9 Bach, French Suite No. 6 in E major BWV 817, Bourrée, bars 1–12 (left hand transposed up two octaves; right hand transposed down one octave)

Example 9.10 Stockhausen, *Klavierstück VII*, page 1, system 2 (© 1965 by Universal Edition (London) Ltd., London)

different ways exposes any lingering uncertainties in our basic knowledge – aural, intellectual, musical – of the music; and knowing that one can cope with a challenge beyond what is strictly needed is a great boost to confidence. Finally, notice that all these strategies bypass much repetitive practice of the music itself.

The value of preceding practice by mental study was confirmed for me through the experience of learning avant-garde music. In the scores discussed so far, the performer could bring a large measure of pre-existing skill or 'technique' to the music: indeed, as Moore argued, the fact that one can readily sight-read 'Wandrers Nachtlied' disguises how difficult the music really is. However, in Example 9.10, from Stockhausen's *Klavierstück VII*, the techniques of playing are so unusual that the attempt to sightread is largely futile. As this excerpt shows, *Klavierstück VII* is based on isolating and combining the piano's resonances. These 'shadow' sounds are produced in two ways. The pianist may release specified strings by holding down keys silently (indicated in the score by diamond noteheads), their harmonics then being touched off by sharp staccato attacks. Alternatively, attacks may be prolonged as echoes, the still vibrating string being re-released either by the pedal or by a silent retake with the finger. An additional difficulty for the pianist is the intricate way in which the groups of resonating 'shadow' sounds are gradually filtered out, as note by note the keys are released.

Studying music of this 'experimental' kind, where the techniques of playing owe little or nothing to the techniques of traditional repertoire, forces one to rethink one's approach to learning and practice. In *Klavierstück VII*, my first attempts at the piano were preceded by hours marking up the score, mentally absorbing and 'testing' the details, as a way of understanding their musical implications. The reward for painstaking preparation is that at the piano one can concentrate on the essential problem, the balance between the loudness of the attacks and the resonances. (Incidentally, this varies markedly from one piano or acoustic to another, and so has to be replanned for every performance.) The work of recreating the score in sound is fascinating, as one explores often super-fine distinctions of sonority. This new awareness of the potential of the instrument undoubtedly influences one's attitude to sound in classical playing. Similarly, one begins to see 'technique' in a more creative light: rather than applying standard formulae, playing contemporary music encourages one to seek the solution that works, no matter how unorthodox.

It would be wrong to imply that learning a piece is a simple progression from mental work to practice at the instrument, from silence to sound. Practice needs to be interspersed with rest, during which the piece is 'forgotten'. Equally, periods of further reflection may be needed: practice may have revealed weaknesses in our grasp of the score, or a need to rethink the conception. This is particularly true when tackling outstandingly challenging repertoire. In works which push pianistic possibilities to the limit, if not beyond – Stockhausen's *Klavierstück X*, Xenakis's *Evryali*, Messiaen's *La Fauvette des jardins* or the fugal sixth movement from *Vingt regards* – each difficulty has to be dissected with infinite care. Absolute mental clarity is a prerequisite, of course. Equally, regular study away from the instrument helps refresh and deepen our vision, helps remind us where we are going. This is a necessary counterbalance to what may be weeks of careful study, during which one can easily become discouraged or bogged down in the musical foothills.

In this essay I have emphasised the mental side of a performer's work, both because it holds the key to the central problem outlined earlier, and also because it is the side most often neglected. In musicians of student age, it may simply be a matter of ignorance, with performers still using the methods of childhood and still reliant on teachers for decisions. Sheer pressure of time may cause mature performers to cut the early stages of learning and go straight to the instrument, especially in later life when more effort may have to be devoted to the physical aspects of technique. In education, the fragmented nature of the curriculum is a factor, with aural skills, harmony and analysis taught in separate compartments and their direct relevance to performance seldom explained. And as a teacher I know how tempting it is to go for the quick fix, adjusting the sound itself rather than investigating its motivation.

However, a more common reason for neglect is a legitimate suspicion of what might be seen as an overly intellectual approach. For musicians, the argument runs, it is enough that they are 'musical'. The performer's job is to master the technical challenge of a score; once that is done one's instincts will supply the interpretation. Indeed too much thought may actually impede the natural working of these instincts.

Of course we should listen carefully to 'what comes naturally'; but the idea that one can understand the Beethoven sonata discussed earlier purely by the light of nature seems dangerously self-deluded. Moreover, mental study, far from stifling instinctive reactions to music, is designed to put instinct to the best use. The problem, as I have argued, is the nature of practice. We have to practise, of course, but we need to recognise that practice may blunt our creative intelligence and leave us locked into habits which, as we become accustomed to our deficiencies, may leave us unable to hear ourselves as we really are. One solution is to ensure that as much as possible is learned before we take a work to the instrument. But the main aim of mental study is to liberate our musicality, to make sure that musical goals – not technical constraints – come first. The ideal is that music should be driven not by what we can (or cannot) do, but by what we want and need to do.

Notes

1 Gerald Moore, *Am I too Loud? Memoirs of an Accompanist* (London: Hamish Hamilton, 1962), 197–8.

2 Ibid., 198–9.

3 See Peter Stadlen, 'Webern's ideas on the work's interpretation', preface to Anton Webern, *Variationen für Klavier* Op. 27 (Vienna: Universal Edition, 1979), v–vii; see also the liner notes to Peter Hill, *Schoenberg, Berg, Webern Piano Music* (Naxos CD 8.553870, 1999), 4.

4 See Peter Hill (ed.), *The Messiaen Companion* (London: Faber and Faber, 1994), 277–8.

5 This is not to deny the great value of studying recordings; however, that should be kept to a later stage of study when one is better placed to make an independent critical assessment. Chapters 13 and 14 in this book discuss further what recordings can mean to the performer.

6 Frédéric Chopin, *Douze Etudes Op. 10*, ed. Alfred Cortot (Paris: Editions Maurice Senart, 1915), 5; my translation.

Further reading

Cone, Edward T., *Musical Form and Musical Performance* (New York: Norton, 1968)

Menuhin, Yehudi, *Unfinished Journey* (London: Macdonald and Janes, 1977)

Moore, Gerald, *Am I too Loud? Memoirs of an Accompanist* (London: Hamish Hamilton, 1962)

Neuhaus, Heinrich, *The Art of Piano Playing*, trans. K. A. Leibovitch (London: Barrie and Jenkins, [1958] 1973)

Solti, Georg, *Solti on Solti* (London: Chatto and Windus, 1997)

Stein, Erwin, *Form and Performance* (New York: Knopf, 1962)

10 Communicating with the body in performance

JANE DAVIDSON

Introduction

This chapter describes the important role of 'presentation' in solo performances within the classical tradition. As a starting point it acknowledges the huge transition between the isolation of individual practice and the social interactions experienced on the concert platform. It will argue that the work that takes place in rehearsal must anticipate the social context of the performance and the inevitable physiological and psychological arousal that situation will bring; it will also consider the need for performance to be both spontaneous and alive to the social dynamic of the performing experience. Central to this discussion is the visual aspect of presentation. It is critical to note the manifold assessments that occur between performer and audience, on the basis of information from such visual cues as dress code, general mannerisms and other non-verbal behaviours like the direction of gaze and the physical gestures made when playing.[1]

The role of practice

Research has shown that musical expertise involves high-level refinement of both mental and physical activity to such a degree that the relationship between the information stored in memory, the mental plans and schemes which organise these memories, and associated thoughts and physical actions becomes completely automatic and fluent.[2] Practice is central to achieving this fluency. In the early stages of learning, thoughts and actions are initially clumsy, deliberate and difficult to coordinate, but with large amounts of practice and experience, a musician can play without conscious attention to the thoughts and actions used in the production of the performance. However, several curious phenomena characterise the interplay of automaticity, conscious thought and action. For example, many performers suddenly direct conscious thought to the automatic process of playing and become aware that they are in the middle of a piece but have no idea where. The effects of arousal caused by the presence of other people can also disrupt attention and the balance between automatic versus conscious mental systems used in playing. One way to develop and learn to coordinate automatic and conscious thought and action is to rehearse in front of others in an attempt to become familiar with these arousal effects, and to train conscious mechanisms to stay focused on the task, rather than be distracted by the audience.

Music, of course, contains a strong emotional content: it can inspire a happy or contemplative feeling or make a listener move in response, whether slowly or energetically. These potentials should be fully explored in the preparation of a piece so that an individualised interpretation can be consolidated. Manuals and texts on teaching musical skills often advise students to find an optimum articulation of their expressive ideas by using their bodies. For instance, a singer may make a slow, upward arm gesture to help convey the idea of getting louder though a musical phrase.[3] During the nineteenth century, many performance treatises referred to the essential interplay of musical structure, expression and the body. For instance, in his *L'Art du violon* of 1834, Baillot suggested that different types of movement both arise from and create the effects associated with different musical tempos. He noted that an Adagio requires 'more ample' playing than an Allegro, in which trills should be 'tossed off' more rapidly, whereas lightness and vivacity should be retained in a Presto and in passages of 'greatest abandon'.[4] A century later, Alexander Truslit,[5] a German psychologist, discovered that performers produced measurably different musical performances in response to different kinds of movement instruction or movement image. Furthermore, information about structural features of the music played and the expressive intentions of the performer are communicated to observers through body movements.[6] For example, performances of the same piece of music with three different expressive intentions – to perform with no expression, with normal expression or with exaggerated expression – can be clearly differentiated by viewers who watch a video of performers' movements alone.

Focusing on the body as the source of musical expression implies that musical expression is a means of communicating basic qualities of human nature to one another, qualities which emerge out of movement and which are translated and abstracted into musical forms. Indeed, the rhetoric surrounding music reveals that musical expression draws heavily on the body as a metaphor – for instance, 'it was a moving performance', or 'her singing really uplifted me'. Additionally, writers such as Ray Jackendoff[7] have suggested that the experience of motion we often give to music ('the music ran along') may either have an actual bodily origin (for example, it activates our movement and balance physiology) or be associated with sounds or sights that convey a sense of bodily movement. According to this line of argument, musical expression is intertwined with who and what we are. Roger Scruton reflects as follows on what listeners do:

in hearing rhythm we hear the music as active; it seems to be doing something (namely, dancing) which no sounds can do . . . at the same time, we do not believe that any such thing is happening in the realm of sound: in a crucial sense, we are aware of the movement as ours.[8]

Thus, in preparing for a performance, exploring the role of the body in the production of the expressive as well as the technical features seems to be of critical importance.

Viewing the performer

Having established that the body is vital in generating the technical and expressive qualities of a musical interpretation, it is necessary to explore what the body movements of a performer comprise. A lengthy case study of a single pianist by Jane Davidson[9] attempted to decode the movements used in performance and determine what information these movements might be transmitting from the performer to the audience. In summary, it was discovered that for the pianist, an expressively intentioned performance always involved an overall, circular and swaying movement on his part. Generally, these cyclical movements were expressive, but there were certain moments within them that were more expressive than others. Indeed, there seemed to be a correlation between expressivity ratings made by audiences and the specific kind of movement being used at that moment. Several identifiable gestures were found: hand and arm lifts and depressions of varying degrees ranging from lavish, circular gestures to small wrist rotations; a 'wiggling' of the shoulder blades; and forward and backward head nods and shakes. All movements, including the all-encompassing swaying, were found to emanate from the hip region. Given the pianist's sitting position, it was theorised that the hips represented the fulcrum for his centre of gravity, therefore providing the pivotal point for all upper torso movements. This centre of gravity seemed to be the central location for the generation of physical expression.

One-to-one correspondences were sought between the gestures used by the pianist and specific moments in the musical structure, but it was discovered that these gestures were employed in a fairly flexible way, so on repeat performances with similar expressive intentions, a head nod might have appeared where a shoulder 'wiggle' previously existed. However, it was also discovered that such gestures always appeared at the same points in the music, suggesting a strong link between the physical production of expression and its correlated expressive sound effect. For instance, there would always be a gesture at a phrase boundary or climax, though it would vary from performance to performance.

Research on physical expression is scant, but a parallel can be drawn between the findings of the case study and the work of James Cutting and his co-workers.[10] The nature of physical expression was examined by looking at walkers; in this case, the 'expression' was each walker's identity and gender. The studies showed that any body joint (for example, hip or ankle) in the walking movement cycle provided similarly expressive information. The researchers demonstrated that there is a point within the walker's body which acts as a reference for movements in all other parts. In piano playing the body is not engaged to equal degrees in producing a performance; thus, a point for expressive movements at the piano will inevitably be related to the sitting position and the centre of gravity, and given Davidson's findings, it may well be revealed in the swaying movement.

Cutting's description clearly provides a basis on which an understanding of the importance of the swaying movement in the pianist's performances can be built. Moreover, his description has been refined[11] to explain the discovery that different parts of the body convey similar expressive information, and it is proposed that some areas of the body are global indicators of expression while other local parts of the body provide more specific information. This accounts for the continuously available expressive information (swaying motion) and much more local information (for instance, a specific hand gesture) found in the piano playing. It could be that the local indicators occur where the potential to express through the body is greatest. Indeed, many of these most pronounced movements took place when the body was 'free' at that moment: for example, a high arm lift would often occur when the arm was free of technical requirements, like during a sustained chord at a cadence point.

As implied, the movement information is fully available and used by audience members in their assessment and understanding of a performance. Therefore, it would seem that such movements are to be acknowledged and encouraged, rather than discouraged. In fact, a small-scale study[12] has shown that pianists could not play with optimal expression if their bodies were in any way constrained during the learning or performing process. Thus, finding the right mental and physical intention and allowing that to be freely communicated through the body seems essential in the production of a fluent and meaningful performance.

Of course, movements and gestures need to be appropriate to the social and cultural context in which they exist. For instance, a classical pianist is far more likely to sit relatively still when playing, whereas a rock keyboard player will probably stand, dance on the spot and make lavish gesticulations while playing. These are just two examples of the specific ways performers learn to present their performances.

Social factors

The social etiquette of performance, including such behaviour as bowing and wearing appropriate dress, is significant to performers and audiences.[13] Indeed, a recent study of assessment processes in music[14] shows that assessors of vocal performance regarded physical appeal to be one of the most significant criteria in their assessments of soloists' performances. Intriguingly, the assessors felt that achieving a balance between self-disclosure and a 'larger than life' presentation of the personality was necessary in order to communicate the intimacy of the musical content and to cope with the public nature of a performance. Thus, the florid arm gestures of Luciano Pavarotti as he waves his handkerchief when singing represent an exaggerated public act of emotional expression, while the subtle movements of his eyes and mouth as he sings a plaintive line simultaneously seem to embody his innermost thoughts and feelings, and so become acts of intense emotional and personal disclosure.

Of course, all kinds of movement behaviours are learned from other people, and in musical performance, it is often possible to recognise a student's teacher in the way in which the student approaches the instrument. For instance, one highly regarded violin teacher trains all her students to bend their knees in a particular manner to add weight and relaxation to their playing. The teacher is immediately visible in each student's movements.

Martin Gellrich[15] has investigated imposed surface gestures like Pavarotti's arm waving and how these interact with essential and intrinsic expressive movements such as the eye and mouth inflections Pavarotti can also be seen to make. Gellrich suggests that specifically learned movements and gestures furnish a performance with expressive intention, and that these gestures can have both negative and positive effects on the production of the performance. They can provide the observer with information which assists in understanding the performance since the gestures can clarify meaning, even when the movement itself is 'superfluous' to the production of the musical whole. There can be a 'surface' level of movement which the performer adds to the performance. Conversely, if these gestures are not consistent with the intentions of the performer, they can create physical tensions in the performer, inhibiting fluency and causing incongruity between the gesture used and the performance aim.

The negative consequences of incongruous gesture are accounted for in work by Sverkar Runeson and Gunnar Frykholm,[16] who demonstrated that mental dispositions become specified in movement. Using the simple task of lifting a box, they asked observers to report what they could see, and discovered that the box weight, and how much that weight differed from the lifter's expectation about the weight, could be detected. Most relevantly, attempts to give false information about the box weight were detected by the onlookers. Therefore, the deceitful attempt and the real weight of the box are co-specified.

'Surface' gestures may contribute to the production and perception of a musical performance in an important way. Indeed, a further interpretation of the finding that certain two-second excerpts of the performances by the pianist discussed above were more richly informative than others could be that mimetic gestures are used at points during the performance, and that these movements heighten the expressive impact of the moment in question. For instance, a large head-shaking gesture might have its own distinguishable form, yet be part of the all-pervasive swaying movement. The literature on physical gesture in spoken language[17] indicates that gestural repertoires emerge which are associated with specific meanings; for example, a 'thumbs up' is an emblematic gesture in Western culture to mean 'good'. It could be that the pianist had developed specific gestures for particular musical expression – in other words, a gestural movement repertoire.

Presenting a performance

It is evident that an audience discerns all kinds of subtle information about performers from their body movements and general appearance and of course from the musical sounds made. The performer also picks up many different cues from the audience: the general degree of enthusiasm and concentration as well as what people are wearing, how they are sitting and so on. Thus there is two-way communication. But in presenting a performance, a musician is not simply coming to a public space and offering a well-rehearsed model of a musical work, taking some credit for the arousal induced by the presence of the audience. Far more is going on: the performer and the audience are continually exchanging information through visual and aural cues. In such circumstances, the performer 'goes with the flow' of the moment.[18] Researchers have noted that if the performer senses the many cues of the live performance context and interprets them positively, a new state of psychological awareness can be achieved which allows the individual to become both highly task-focused and able to explore spontaneous thoughts and feelings in a creative manner.[19]

So, in live performance new decisions can occur about interpretation and interaction with co-performers and audience. As mentioned in the section on learning, psychological and physiological arousal is the inevitable consequence of social interactions.[20] At optimum levels, the faster heart rate and associated increase in oxygen supplies brought about through the production of adrenaline can lead to the enhancing circumstances referred to above as 'flow'. However, over-arousal can cause thoughts of self-doubt and worry about matters such as one's ability to remember the task to become critical to success or failure. Indeed, adrenaline experienced in association with these thoughts can create a chain-reaction of devastating physiological consequences on the performance: physical tremor leading to mistakes, confusion of thoughts leading to memory slips and so on.

Summary

In conclusion, musical performance is a highly expressive and abstracted activity which emanates from a grounded bodily origin. For the performer, a careful balance is needed between control and abandon, between obeying some rules and rebelling against others. Performance assumes a profound knowledge of music, the instrument and the self in the music. It is not an easy task to become a performer, least of all a soloist, because of all the preparation required, but presenting a performance seems to be a rare opportunity for performers to share with others who and what they are precisely at that moment.

Notes

1 For more details on these issues, see Jane W. Davidson, 'The social in musical performance', in David J. Hargreaves and Adrian C. North (eds.), *The Social Psychology of Music* (Oxford: Oxford University Press, 1997), 209–28. Chapter 11 in this volume discusses the nature of visual and aural communication between ensemble players.

2 For a general discussion of skill see John A. Sloboda, *The Musical Mind: The Cognitive Psychology of Music* (Oxford: Oxford University Press, 1985), 215–36; see also chapter 7 in this volume.

3 See for instance the directions given in Esther Salaman, *Unlocking Your Voice* (London: Victor Gollancz, 1990) and Eloise Ristad, *A Soprano on Her Head: Right-side Up Reflections on Life and Other Performances* (Moan, Ut.: Real People Press, 1982).

4 Quoted from Robin Stowell, *Violin Technique and Performance Practice in the Late Eighteenth and Early Nineteenth Centuries* (Cambridge: Cambridge University Press, 1985), 271.

5 For a translation and summary see Bruno H. Repp, 'Music as motion: a synopsis of Alexander Truslit's (1938) *Gestaltung und Bewegung in der Musik*', *Psychology of Music*, 21 (1993), 48–73.

6 See Jane W. Davidson, 'Visual perception of performance manner in the movements of solo musicians', *Psychology of Music*, 21 (1993), 103–13, and Davidson, 'What type of information is conveyed in the body movements of solo musician performers?', *Journal of Human Movement Studies*, 6 (1994), 279–301.

7 Ray Jackendoff, *Consciousness and the Computational Mind* (Cambridge, Mass.: MIT Press, 1988), 131.

8 Roger Scruton, *The Aesthetic Understanding: Essays in the Philosophy of Art and Culture* (London: Methuen, 1983), 84.

9 See Jane W. Davidson, 'The perception of expressive movement in music performance' (Ph.D. thesis, City University, London, 1991); Davidson, 'What type'; and Davidson, 'Understanding the expressive movements of a solo pianist', *Deutsches Jahrbuch für Musikpsychologie* (forthcoming).

10 James E. Cutting and Lynne T. Kozlowski, 'Recognising friends by their walk: gait perception without familiarity cues', *Bulletin of the Psychonomic Society*, 9 (1977), 353–6, and James E. Cutting, Dennis R. Proffitt and Lynne T. Kozlowski, 'A biomechanical invariant for gait perception', *Journal of Experimental Psychology: Human Perception and Performance*, 4 (1978), 357–72.

11 See James E. Cutting and Dennis R. Proffitt, 'Gait perception as an example of how we may perceive events', in Robert D. Walk and Herbert L. Pick (eds.), *Intersensory Perception and Sensory Integration* (New York: Plenum Press, 1981), 37–59.

12 Jane W. Davidson and Jeremy C. Dawson, 'The development of expression in body movement during learning in piano performance', in David Wessel (ed.), *Conference Proceedings of Music Perception and Cognition Conference* (Berkeley: University of California Press, 1995), 31.

13 Outlined in detail in Davidson, 'The social'.

14 Jane W. Davidson and Daniela C. C. Coimbra, 'Investigating performance evaluation by assessors of singers in a music college setting', *Musicae Scientiae*, 5 (2001), 33–54.

15 Martin Gellrich, 'Concentration and tension', *British Journal of Music Education*, 8 (1991), 167–79.

16 Sverkar Runeson and Gunnar Frykholm, 'Kinematic specification of dynamics as an informational basis for person-and-action perception: expectations, gender, recognition and deceptive intention', *Journal of Experimental Psychology: General*, 112 (1983), 585–615.

17 See the work of Paul Ekman and Wallace V. Friesen, 'The repertory of nonverbal behaviour: categories, origins, usage, and coding', *Semiotica*, 1 (1969), 49–204, and Andrew Ellis and Geoffrey Beattie, *The Psychology of Language and Communication* (London: Weidenfeld and Nicolson, 1986).

18 See Mihalyi Csikszentmihalyi, *Finding Flow: The Psychology of Engagement with Everyday Life* (New York: Basic Books, 1997).

19 For more detail, see Jane W. Davidson, Stephanie E. Pitts and Jorge S. Correia, 'Reconciling technical and expressive elements in young children's musical instrument learning', *Journal of Aesthetic Education* (forthcoming).
20 A detailed overview can be found in Glenn D. Wilson, 'Performance anxiety', in Hargreaves and North, *Social Psychology*, 229–48; see also chapter 12 in this volume.

Further reading

Clarke, Eric and Jane Davidson, 'The body in performance', in Wyndham Thomas (ed.), *Composition, Performance, Reception: Studies in the Creative Process in Music* (Aldershot: Ashgate, 1998), 74–92

Evans, Andrew, *The Secrets of Musical Confidence* (London: Thorson, 1994)

Hargreaves, David J. and Adrian C. North (eds.), *The Social Psychology of Music* (Oxford: Oxford University Press, 1997)

Sloboda, John A., *The Musical Mind: The Cognitive Psychology of Music* (Oxford: Oxford University Press, 1985)

11   Ensemble performance

ELAINE GOODMAN

Ensemble performance involves musical and social interaction between a group of performers. The term 'ensemble' derives from the French
for 'together', and it defines the seemingly infinite array of musical performances involving more than one person, ranging from a duo to a symphony
orchestra. At the same time, 'ensemble' refers to the precision with which
musicians perform together: a good group is often praised for its 'tight'
ensemble work, whereas an inferior one might have 'sloppy' ensemble.

Our experience of ensemble performance can be enhanced by realising
some of the processes involved in making music together. This chapter
considers four aspects in particular: coordination, communication, the role
of the individual and social factors. Most of the observations refer to small
chamber groups within the Western art tradition, but reference will also be
made to larger ensembles on occasion.

Coordination: keeping time

The most fundamental requirement of any ensemble is that the
individual parts fit together. It is necessary, therefore, for each musician to
be able to perform in time with the rest of the group; indeed, the coordination
of an ensemble is all about timing. Any accomplished ensemble performer
knows that counting is vital in order to keep time, at least to realise which beat
is being performed and when to enter or exit. There are, however, further
matters to consider with regard to the coordination of timing, and three
will be discussed in this section: the ensemble's clock, timekeeping skills
and the illusion of synchrony.

The ensemble's clock

The starting point of a rehearsal by a small ensemble without a
conductor is to establish the overall tempo of a piece, and this might involve assessing different speeds through trial and error until a tempo is
agreed upon. Alternatively, the conductor of a large ensemble will indicate

the speed of the main beat for the performers. In either case, the music's main beat (i.e. the overall tempo) provides a benchmark for keeping time. Indeed, each musician will generate an internal pulse according to the main beat (sometimes this is shown outwardly when a musician taps his or her foot to maintain the pulse, but such movement is probably best confined to a wiggle of the toe inside the shoe). The overall tempo therefore functions as the ensemble's clock, for it provides a source of coordination and controls the beat ticking inside each musician. In other words, ensemble performers possess a 'shared common timekeeper' in the overall tempo of the music.[1]

While the main beat is an important yardstick for keeping time, local considerations might inspire individual musicians in an ensemble to subdivide or lengthen the beat in different places. Here, the bar acts as an important structure for coordination, since it is a unit of time around which the main pulse can be individually organised.

Timekeeping skills

Performing in time with other people requires more than just the ability to count and to realise the overall tempo, for the execution of each beat in performance needs to be carefully administered. This involves two main skills: *anticipation* and *reaction*. Ensemble performers carry out complex predictions that are intimately bound to reactions gained through feedback: on the basis of the previous note, when is the next note of a fellow performer going to sound? Michael Tree from the Guarneri String Quartet states that 'every moment of our playing is conditioned by what has just occurred or by what we think is about to occur'.[2] The anticipation of each beat and the reaction to the production of each beat are virtually defined by the nature of interaction manifest between the performers.

Ensemble performers interact with one another in various different ways in order to keep time. One kind of interaction can be likened to the process of *hunting*, in the sense that one musician follows another just as the hunter tracks its prey by anticipating and reacting to its movements. 'Hunting', which might also be regarded as following or tracking, is a one-way process because the individual musician responds to the timing produced by the other performer(s).[3]

A second kind of interaction involves mutual adjustment, or *cooperation*, between performers. Cooperation is a dynamic (as opposed to one-way) process, although elements of 'hunting' might be exhibited at the same time as performers 'exchange roles . . . to allow one or other to lead'.[4] In effect, there is a fine line between cooperating and hunting, and such skills might be affected by dominant personalities in the ensemble as well as the nature of the music itself (for instance, an accompanist might follow the performer who has the melody).

Musical interaction can be planned to a certain extent in rehearsal: performers might wish to work out who will follow whom during a particular passage, or who will take the lead in the ensuing passage. This type of conscious planning can usefully assist coordination, but it does not account for the moment-to-moment hunting and cooperating that necessarily go on throughout performance.

The illusion of synchrony

Successful timekeeping ideally results in the coordination of notes between individual musicians in an ensemble, but the reality of performing together is not so simple. In fact, the execution of notes at exactly the same time by a group of musicians is beyond the limits of human skill and perception: there will always be minute discrepancies in timing – that is, asynchronisation – between the notes intended to be performed simultaneously.[5] Figure 11.1 exemplifies the asynchronisation that could arise in a string trio, showing that the notes from the violin might sound, on average, fractionally earlier than the notes from the cello and viola respectively. In effect, therefore, the art of performing together is to create the *illusion* of perfect ensemble.[6]

There are several factors to be taken into account when trying to achieve coordination in an ensemble, not least the physical differences between instruments (including the human voice). Musicians need to be aware of the amount of time it takes for a note to 'speak' on a particular instrument. For example, one would expect a wind instrument to 'speak' sooner than a stringed instrument because its *rise time* – the length of time it takes for a

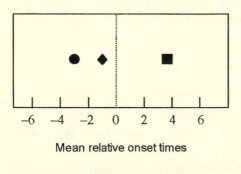

Mean relative onset times

KEY: Violin ■   Cello ◆   Viola ●

Figure 11.1 Hypothetical example of average onset times in milliseconds for a string trio (adapted from Rasch, 'Timing'); note that the violin leads, the cello follows and the viola lags further behind.

note to be heard after it is played – is shorter. The challenge for ensemble performers is to control the perception of notes from each instrument and each musician, particularly when different combinations of instruments are used. Moreover, problems can arise when performers are placed at different distances from the audience: the orchestral conductor, for example, must consider the amount of time it takes for sound to be perceived by the audience when it comes from musicians at the back of the performing arena.

The difficulty of achieving coordination in an ensemble might also be affected by the speed of the music: evidence shows that it is harder to synchronise notes at slower tempos because of the need for individual musicians to subdivide the main beat.[7] In addition, passages of the music involving tempo changes and entrances that follow pauses or rests are less easy to get together. In the case of the latter, the absence of sound during a rest means that performers might rely on visual communication – as well as the ensemble's clock – to help coordinate an entry.

Communication: aural and visual signals

The information communicated between ensemble performers is primarily aural and visual: signals (or cues) are constantly relayed in sound and through eye contact, gestures and body movement. Ensemble performers watch and listen to each other not merely to coordinate actions, but also to communicate ideas about the expression or interpretation of the music. However, aural communication (being able to hear each other) is more important than visual communication (being able to see each other). The simplest way to relate to this point is that we hear music – we don't see it.[8] The ensuing sections will respectively concentrate on these two aspects of communication, and consideration will be given to the extent of planning aural and visual signals.

Aural communication

Ensemble performers need to be able to hear each other for the purposes of coordination, that is, to ensure that the individual parts sound together in the right places. At a more critical level, however, each performer continually listens to the expressive nuances of sound emanating from fellow performers, such as fluctuations in timing, gradations in dynamics and changes in articulation, timbre and intonation. In effect, the individual's concentration is divided between monitoring the sound produced from his or her own part and attending to the sound produced from the rest of the group. As a result, fine adjustments are made either consciously or unconsciously to the balance and resolution of the ensemble's sound throughout performance.

Regardless of the size of the ensemble, all the tiny nuances emerging from the individual parts will have a greater or lesser effect on the way in which the music is expressed. The two skills mentioned previously – anticipation and reaction – come into play as ensemble performers try to predict and respond to signals or cues relayed by fellow musicians. At the same time, they also contribute to the sound by giving out their own signals. For instance, if a performer in a small group starts to crescendo, the other musicians might adjust their volumes accordingly, perhaps by matching the increase in dynamic or by playing quieter to allow the individual crescendo to dominate the overall sound. In addition, ensemble performers might be able to predict each other's physical actions on the basis of aural awareness, so when the level of the oboist's tone begins to decrease, the co-performers in a wind quintet might accelerate the tempo towards the end of the phrase in order to ensure that the oboist does not run out of breath. Similarly, the ensemble might react to changes in sound by compensating for each other's actions: in the case of the breathless oboist, the fellow performers might increase their dynamic levels in order to maintain the volume of the overall sound, or alternatively decrease them to ensure that the oboe part projects above the ensemble.

Some expressive nuances might be planned in rehearsal so performers can at least understand (if not respond to) each other's intentions, although paradoxically, the strategic planning of expressive nuances is viewed with caution by some performers.[9] Moreover, research shows that extensive practice can reduce the ability to control the expression of sound in performance, for ideas become fixed and harder to adjust. Caroline Palmer writes that 'lack of extensive practice with a particular piece should result in more control of expressive features than in well-practiced performances . . . Extensive practice of particular performances may make expressive gestures more difficult to suppress.'[10]

This point has far-reaching implications for ensemble performers because it suggests that individuals should be wary of the amount of practice they do on their own in preparation for ensemble work. After individual practice, performers might find it harder to 'suppress' their individual expressive ideas in order to blend with the overall sound. This observation contradicts the cherished beliefs of some ensemble performers, for instance Abram Loft, who advises: 'develop as much of your own idea about the piece and its special world as you can . . . then measure and modify that concept in the light of the viewpoints expressed by other musicians'.[11] In contrast, William Pleeth reminds his readers to practise 'with the whole canvas in view' and to develop the sound 'with the total concept in mind'.[12]

Similarly, strategies developed in ensemble rehearsal might become less easy to adjust during performance because musicians are unable to deviate from their plans. Some performers, such as skilled piano accompanists, show remarkable flexibility in ensemble work and might (quite rightly) reject the above paradox: they are readily able to adapt their own expressive intentions to accommodate or blend with another part after little or extensive practice.

Visual communication

Ensemble performers can also communicate ideas about expression to one another using body language, hence through visual channels. Jane Davidson observes that 'physical expressions of musical structure provide a means of understanding and sharing musical intentions'.[13] For example, the performers in a string quartet are unlikely to move around wildly during a quiet, slow passage of music; instead, they might retain a still body posture, or at most allow a gentle sway of the upper torso.

The coordination of sound can be assisted by the planning of visual signals – for instance, by determining who gives the lead at the beginning of the piece, or who makes eye contact with whom following a large pause. As suggested above, however, such choreography might be detrimental to the spontaneity of the performance. Interestingly, the members of the Guarneri String Quartet state that their physical movements are mutually absorbed at an unconscious level over a period of time, so they are hardly aware of visual signals relayed in performance: 'There's a certain body language that each of us has when he plays. You get to know that about your colleagues and react accordingly. Over the years a great deal of it becomes intuitive.'[14] In that sense, they remind us that ensemble performers do not necessarily have to look pointedly at each other throughout performance, for peripheral vision is always at work.

As stated above, ensemble performers rely more heavily on aural communication (information expressed in sound from fellow performers) than visual communication to make music together. Nevertheless, research shows that visual feedback 'contributes significantly to both the accuracy and the expressive freedom of cooperative performances'.[15] A conductor, whose mode of communication is purely visual, can assist and improve the coordination of timing in ensemble performance. Orchestral performers constantly monitor a conductor's baton movement in order to learn to anticipate and react to it. For a conductor, however, visual signals are only partially conveyed by the baton. The baton movement of Simon Rattle on the podium, for example, is absorbed within his overall body movement – including seemingly capricious gestures, changing postures and different facial expressions – which conveys information about the mood and character of the music. In effect, therefore, the conductor communicates much more than just a beat, for the members of an orchestra might read visual signals about expression through a conductor's entire body language in the same way that the co-performers of a string quartet might project interpretative ideas by watching each other's physical movements.

The role of the individual

The performer in a music ensemble plays a role similar to that of the actor in a drama. An actor develops a sense of character on his or her own, but when the character comes into contact with others in the play, it changes, not least through the pacing and delivery of lines. Just as actors mould and adjust their characters to one another by playing up to and playing off each other's parts, so do musicians in ensemble performance. However, actors never lose sight of their own character, so the drama is at once defined by each actor as well as the combination of actors. The same is true in ensemble music, for each musician stamps the ensemble with his or her own identity, but also tries to blend in with the group. This relationship between the individual and the ensemble will be explored below.

In 1996, Mitch Waterman investigated the kinds of emotional responses experienced by performers. He asked musicians in a piano duet and a cello–piano duo to comment on their feelings after performance according to moments 'when the music caused something to happen'.[16] Waterman observed that each performer had different emotional responses to the music, and this led him to conclude that 'performers do not agree about emotionally loaded events within a shared performance'.[17] This suggests that individuals do not necessarily experience similar things when performing together or possess shared ideas about a performance; instead, they retain quite separate identities.

There are many truisms surrounding the notion of an ensemble that undermine the role of the individual: for example, the ideal ensemble has been described as 'an integrated musical organism, reflecting the collective insight of all members'.[18] An ensemble is in fact far more complex and almost certainly less 'integrated' than this description suggests, for the ensemble is about individual characters as much as the blending of characters. So, what happens to the individual when performing in an ensemble?

The ensuing discussion focuses on the case of a professional pianist performing the third movement (Largo) of Chopin's Cello Sonata in G minor

Op. 65. Research by the present author compared expressive features – specifically, timing and dynamics – of two performances made prior to an ensemble rehearsal: the first was given individually, so the pianist performed her part in a solo context, and the second was given with the cellist, thus in an ensemble context. The pianist had prepared her part without consulting the cellist, so the ensemble performance was the first time the two players had met and performed the work together. The data therefore expose the ways in which the pianist's 'solo' realisation of the music changed when she performed with the cellist.

Figure 11.2 shows the beat-by-beat timing fluctuations of the pianist's solo and ensemble performances.[19] In the first place, it is evident that the overall tempo of the ensemble performance was slower than that of the solo performance (this can be seen on the graph because the ensemble timing profile lies beneath the solo timing profile). This shows that the pianist was immediately affected by playing with the cellist, for she negotiated her 'solo' tempo to comply with the cellist. Nevertheless, the peaks and troughs of the profiles are very similar, which suggests that some of the pianist's 'solo' tendencies were retained in the ensemble. The degrees of rubato, however, differed in each performance: in general, there was more rubato in the pianist's solo performance than in the ensemble performance (compare, for instance, the extent of the fluctuations in bars 7–11 and the amount of ritardando at the end of bars 15 and 23). It seems, therefore, that the pianist's rubato was constrained in the ensemble performance.

The opening six bars (see the score and the circled area on the graph in Figure 11.2) merit close attention, for the ebb and flow of the pianist's timing differed markedly here between the two performances. (This reflects what happened in the first few moments of the pianist's encounter with the cellist.) In the solo performance, the pianist slowed down at the end of bar 2, whereas in the ensemble performance, the tempo subsided throughout bars 1–2, particularly towards the middle of the second bar (the point at which the cellist executes a turn figure in the melodic line). The slowing down in the ensemble performance hints at the way in which the pianist gradually adopted the cellist's overall tempo, and how she accommodated the cellist's ornamentation of the melodic line. Moreover, the pianist's realisation of the second phrase (bars 3–4) altered in the ensemble context, for the tempo increased over the phrase boundary at bars 2–3, but then remained relatively stable. In effect, as soon as the pianist came into contact with the cellist, she both played up to and played off the other part, which meant that the timing fluctuations differed in the two contexts.

Figure 11.3 shows the pianist's beat-by-beat dynamic fluctuations in the same solo and ensemble performances.[20] While the peaks and troughs of the

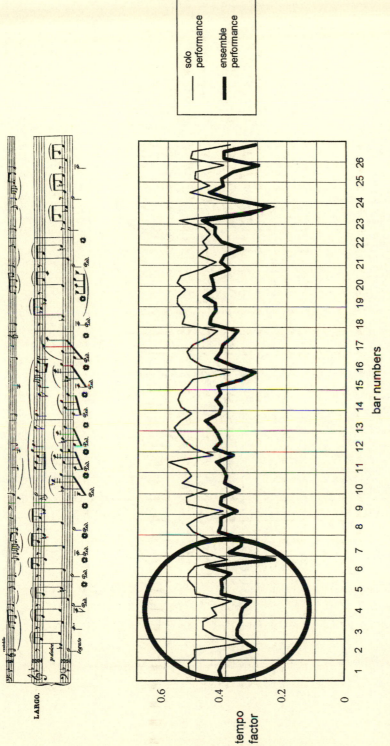

Figure 11.2 Profiles of the timing fluctuations in the pianist's solo and ensemble performances of Chopin's Cello Sonata Op. 65, iii, bars 1–26; an extract of the score (bars 1–6 of the German first edition; Leipzig: Breitkopf & Härtel, 1846) is provided to facilitate reference to the circled area of the graph in the discussion.

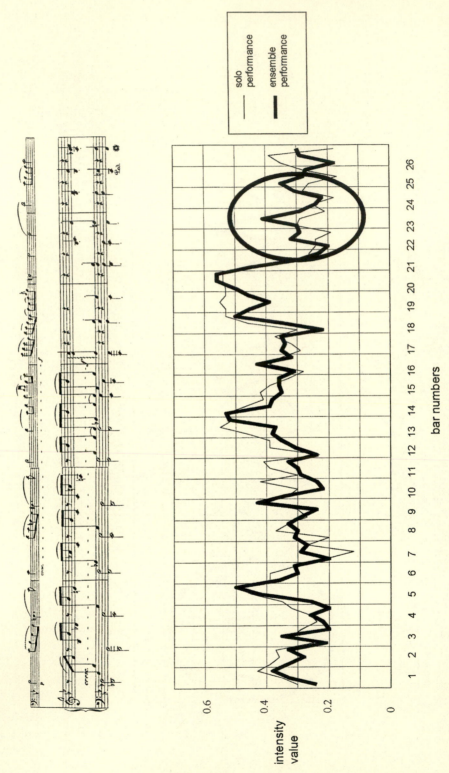

Figure 11.3 Profiles of the dynamic fluctuations in the pianist's solo and ensemble performances of Chopin's Cello Sonata Op. 65, iii, bars 1–26; an extract of the score (bars 18–23 of the German first edition; Leipzig: Breitkopf & Härtel, 1846) is provided to facilitate reference to the circled area of the graph in the discussion.

two profiles generally coincide, it is evident that the pianist tended to play slightly quieter in the ensemble (compare, for instance, the dynamic levels in bars 1–6 and 10–15). Once again, therefore, some element of constraint appears to underlie the pianist's ensemble playing, although within the same overall dynamic range.

The passage in bars 21–3 (see the circled area on the graph in Figure 11.3) is particularly interesting because the pianist actually played louder in the ensemble than in the solo performance. This passage is the main climax of the movement and is marked by a change of texture (as shown in the score above the graph): the quaver momentum in the piano part ceases at bar 21 and is replaced by offbeat chords that occur under a recitative-like declamation in the cello part (the dynamic marking is *forte* in both parts). Curiously, the pianist responded to the change of texture by playing relatively quietly in bars 21–3 in the solo performance, apparently having overlooked the *forte* marking in the score. By contrast, her dynamics in the ensemble performance increased in bars 22–3. Here she quickly altered her previous approach by gradually producing a louder sound, so giving more support to the cellist (this exemplifies the importance of aural communication, for the pianist undoubtedly responded to the cellist's dynamic signals). Interestingly, the pianist subsequently commented in rehearsal that her part was marked *forte*.

The individual performer's realisation of the music can be affected in different ways by interaction with co-performers: expressive features might become constrained or enhanced (i.e. exaggerated) or might simply be maintained at a similar level. At the same time, the individual musician can preserve patterns of expression. In the above example, expressive aspects of the pianist's solo performance were constrained in the ensemble context, and while some timing or dynamic fluctuations were altered, others were retained. This suggests that musicians do not necessarily forfeit their own ideas when performing in an ensemble: the individual's role is one of negotiation, or give and take.[21]

Social factors: staying together

A musical ensemble is . . . an unusual kind of social group whose mode of interaction involves a degree of intimacy and subtlety possibly not equalled by any other kind of group.[22]

Ensemble performance is about teamwork: half the battle of making music together (and ultimately staying together as an ensemble) is fought on social grounds. The most important issue to consider is leadership, for every group needs at least one leader. Some are appointed (such as the conductors of orchestras), while others emerge without being elected as such (for instance, a bossy member of a string quartet). Factors influencing the choice of leader in an ensemble include the performers' personalities, the music and social stereotyping.

A dominant person might lead an ensemble by directing the course of a rehearsal and by dictating interpretative aspects of a performance. The way in which the music is composed can also affect the relationship between performers[23] (thus the composer has a certain impact on the social interaction between musicians). Furthermore, ensemble performers aware of social stereotypes attached to specific instrumental groups (such as the supposedly inferior role assumed by the second violinist in a quartet or the subservient piano 'accompanist') might be affected by them either consciously or unconsciously.

The style of leadership generated in an ensemble will determine its social climate. On the one hand, the members of a string quartet might endeavour to work together democratically, thus possibly ensuring that 'a reasonable amount of work is willingly engaged in by the group members not only during rehearsals and performances (when the leader is present) but also when practising individual parts at home'.[24] On the other hand, the orchestral conductor might strive towards a less dictatorial approach by gradually relinquishing control 'for the good of the collective effort'.[25]

While the role of the leader is vital in determining the group dynamic within an ensemble, the interaction between co-performers is also important. It goes without saying that positive feedback between musicians will inspire high levels of confidence and ultimately help the group perform well together. The social interaction between performers is like a 'constant working-out process',[26] which can be realised most effectively during ensemble rehearsal when musicians openly negotiate ideas, handle conflicts and try to reach compromises.

An ensemble will flourish as long as 'each individual feels that he or she is contributing to their full artistic capacity and yet collaborating with their colleagues to produce something more beautiful than could be produced individually'.[27] In team sports, emphasis is placed on 'synergy' (group potential, which is greater than the sum of the members' individual potentials) and 'confluence' (the sense of belonging to a team). Musicians can also endeavour to generate the same kind of spirit when performing together.[28]

Finally, why do some ensembles stay together longer than others? Aside from practical reasons (such as one member of an ensemble relocating), successful groups try to recognise the influence of social stereotypes and the paradoxes of leadership and democracy, as well as the need for confrontation and compromise.[29] While it is impossible to predict how compatible individuals will be, and therefore the likely lifespan of an ensemble, it is clear that relationships will continually develop and change. After all, professional ensemble performers not only make music together, but also spend a great deal of extramusical time with each other – for instance, travelling. Social and musical relationships have to be nurtured, and personality clashes might well arise over a period of time.

Conclusion

To summarise, four aspects of ensemble performance have been discussed in this chapter, specifically coordination (keeping time), communication (aural and visual signals), the role of the individual and social factors. We can now begin to realise the demands of performing together and to appreciate the sheer achievement implicit in such an activity. Indeed, an ensemble performer displays numerous different skills at both musical and social levels. To attain coordination in timing, co-performers anticipate and react to each other's actions by following or cooperating with fellow musicians. At the same time, expressive ideas are communicated through sound and visual channels, so performers watch and listen to each other as musical signals are constantly relayed and monitored. An ensemble performer exhibits individual, 'solo' tendencies in performance at the same time as he or she tries to blend with the rest of the group. The social and musical relationships between co-performers are always developing, so that every group continually generates a new spirit, which is perhaps why ensemble performance can be so refreshing and exciting.

Notes

1 See L. Henry Shaffer, 'Timing in solo and duet piano performances', *Quarterly Journal of Experimental Psychology*, 36A (1984), 592.

2 Quoted from David Blum, *The Art of Quartet Playing: The Guarneri Quartet in Conversation with David Blum* (Ithaca: Cornell University Press, 1986), 20.

3 See Shaffer, 'Timing', 587.

4 Lucy J. Appleton, W. Luke Windsor and Eric F. Clarke, 'Cooperation in piano duet performance', in Alf Gabrielsson (ed.), *Proceedings of the Third Triennial European Society for the Cognitive Sciences of Music (ESCOM) Conference* (Uppsala: Uppsala University Press, 1997), 471–4.

5 See Rudolf A. Rasch, 'Timing and synchronisation in ensemble performance', in John A. Sloboda (ed.), *Generative Processes in Music: The Psychology of*

Performance, Improvisation, and Composition (Oxford: Clarendon Press, 1988), 70–90.

6　Ibid., 71; see also Jonathan Dunsby, *Performing Music: Shared Concerns* (Oxford: Clarendon Press, 1995), 64–5.

7　See Rasch, 'Timing', 80–1.

8　See Anthony Clayton, 'Coordination between players in musical performance' (Ph.D. thesis, University of Edinburgh, 1985), and Elaine C. Goodman, 'Analysing the ensemble in music rehearsal and performance: the nature and effects of interaction in cello–piano duos' (Ph.D. thesis, University of London, 2000).

9　According to Blum (*Art*, 16), 'too much planned rubato can restrict true freedom'; see also chapter 9 in this volume.

10　Caroline Palmer, 'On the assignment of structure in music performance', *Music Perception*, 14 (1996), 54.

11　Abram Loft, *Ensemble! A Rehearsal Guide to Thirty Great Works of Chamber Music* (Portland, Ore.: Amadeus Press, 1992), 17.

12　William Pleeth, *Cello*, compiled and ed. Nona Pyron (London: Kahn and Averill, [1982] 1992), 113, 119.

13　Jane W. Davidson, 'The social in musical performance', in David J. Hargreaves and Adrian C. North (eds.), *The Social Psychology of Music* (Oxford: Oxford University Press, 1997), 222.

14　John Dalley, quoted from Blum, *Art*, 14.

15　Appleton et al., 'Cooperation', 474; see also Clayton, 'Coordination', 72–108.

16　Mitch Waterman, 'Emotional responses to music: implicit and explicit effects in listeners and performers', *Psychology of Music*, 24 (1996), 56.

17　Ibid., 65; in contrast, Goodman's recent study of ensemble rehearsal showed that performers often discussed emotional ideas as a means of reconciling conflicting points of view over the interpretation of the music (see Goodman, 'Analysing', 105–52).

18　Loft, *Ensemble*, 18.

19　The 'tempo factor' in Figure 11.2 expresses the difference between note values executed by the performer in real time and their 'normal' metronomic value (so the higher the tempo factor, the faster the actual tempo in performance). The pianist played on a Yamaha Disklavier which enabled her performances to be retrieved in MIDI format. MIDI data were subsequently analysed using advanced software programs such as POCO.

20　The 'intensity value' in Figure 11.3 reflects the dynamic or volume of a note on an arbitrary scale of 0 to 1, starting from a true zero. The higher the value, the louder the dynamic.

21　For further discussion, see Goodman, 'Analysing', 165–225.

22　Vivienne M. Young and Andrew M. Colman, 'Some psychological processes in string quartets', *Psychology of Music*, 7 (1979), 12–13.

23　As Loft claims (*Ensemble*, 18), 'the prominent, topmost voice sets an inescapable stamp on the temper of the group'.

24 Young and Colman, 'Some psychological', 16.

25 Yaakov Atik, 'The conductor and the orchestra: interactive aspects of the leadership process', *Leadership and Organisation Development Journal*, 13 (1994), 27.

26 John Dalley, quoted from Blum, *Art*, 7.

27 John Harvey-Jones, *All Together Now* (London: Heinemann, 1994), 137.

28 See John Syer, 'Team building: the development of team spirit', in Stephen J. Bull (ed.), *Sports Psychology: A Self-Help Guide* (Marlborough: Crowood Press, 1991), 123–43.

29 See J. K. Murningham and D. E. Conlon, 'The dynamics of intense work groups: a study of British string quartets', *Administrative Science Quarterly*, 36 (1991), 165–86.

Further reading

Appleton, Lucy J., W. Luke Windsor and Eric F. Clarke, 'Cooperation in piano duet performance', in Alf Gabrielsson (ed.), *Proceedings of the Third Triennial European Society for the Cognitive Sciences of Music (ESCOM) Conference* (Uppsala: Uppsala University Press, 1997), 471–4

Atik, Yaakov, 'The conductor and the orchestra: interactive aspects of the leadership process', *Leadership and Organisation Development Journal*, 13 (1994), 22–8

Blum, David, *The Art of Quartet Playing: The Guarneri Quartet in Conversation with David Blum* (Ithaca: Cornell University Press, 1986)

Rasch, Rudolf A., 'Timing and synchronisation in ensemble performance', in John A. Sloboda (ed.), *Generative Processes in Music: The Psychology of Performance, Improvisation, and Composition* (Oxford: Clarendon Press, 1988), 70–90

Shaffer, L. Henry, 'Timing in solo and duet piano performances', *Quarterly Journal of Experimental Psychology*, 36A (1984), 577–95

12   The fear of performance

ELIZABETH VALENTINE

The analysis of performance anxiety

Performance anxiety, commonly known as 'stage fright', is an age-old problem, but interest in its nature, causes and cures has intensified over the last fifteen years with the burgeoning of clinics, conferences and journals devoted to performing arts medicine. Music performance anxiety has been defined as 'the experience of persisting, distressful apprehension about[,] and/or actual impairment of, performance skills in a public context, to a degree unwarranted given the individual's musical aptitude, training, and level of preparation'.[1] Notable sufferers have included Maria Callas, Enrico Caruso, Pablo Casals, Leopold Godowsky, Vladimir Horowitz, Ignacy Paderewski and Sergei Rachmaninoff. A number of surveys have indicated that performance anxiety is a serious problem for a substantial proportion of musicians. In one large-scale study of American orchestras,[2] stage fright was the most frequently reported performance problem, with 24 per cent of players claiming to be affected by it, and 15 per cent finding it severe. It is ameliorated by age and experience,[3] though whether this is due to the beneficial effects of exposure or to 'survival of the fittest' is not clear.

The symptoms of performance anxiety are well known and are of three kinds: physiological, behavioural and mental. The *physiological symptoms* of increased heart rate, palpitations, shortness of breath, hyperventilation, dry mouth, sweating, nausea, diarrhoea and dizziness are the result of over-arousal of the autonomic nervous system. This flight–fight response, which assisted our hunter–gatherer forebears in fleeing large animals, is highly detrimental to musicians requiring dexterity and fine muscular control over their instruments. Trembling limbs and slippery fingers are likely to hinder rather than help the performer. In addition, this autonomic arousal may have become associated with fear as a result of past experience. Increased arousal generally leads to a narrowing of the focus of attention, which may also be deleterious. The *behavioural symptoms* of performance anxiety may take the form either of signs of anxiety, such as shaking, trembling, stiffness and dead-pan expression, or of impairment of the performance itself. The *mental symptoms* are subjective feelings of anxiety and negative thoughts about performing. Rather than fear of performance per se, it is fear of public performance that is at issue, with the risk of negative evaluation and consequent loss of self-esteem. This fear may be the result of too close an identification of self-esteem with performance perfection, even the belief that self-worth is conditional upon success. Negative thinking has a bad effect on performance quality. Worry leads to poor concentration, diverting attention and wasting valuable resources, possibly also acting as a cue to increase anxiety further.

One variant of negative thinking is 'catastrophising', the irrational exaggeration of the likelihood of disaster – for example, 'I am almost sure to make a dreadful mistake and that will ruin everything'. It is more likely to be associated with high levels of performance anxiety in professionals, students and amateurs, whereas realistic appraisal – recognising the inevitablity of mistakes, the generally tolerant nature of audiences and the need to concentrate on technical and interpretative aspects of music – is associated with moderate levels of stage fright.[4]

Another variant is 'self-handicapping',[5] where a performer deliberately sets up situations to serve as excuses for poor performance, such as failure to practise, staying up late the night before, damaging equipment and so on. These can become self-fulfilling prophecies and run the risk of actually sabotaging performance. They are intended to locate the blame for bad performance on external factors but to claim extra credit for good performance, which occurred despite the adverse circumstances. However, these strategies are essentially destructive since they avoid the situation, which often makes matters worse. They may arise where there is over-concern with competence, perhaps because it has been made a condition of deserving parental love, or where perceived self-competence is fragile, perhaps where a level of performance which has previously been achieved cannot be maintained.

A comprehensive account of performance anxiety thus needs to include physiological factors (such as heart rate and blood pressure), behavioural measures (of anxiety and the quality of performance) and self-reports (of thoughts and feelings). The reactions of these three systems may not be correlated.[6] In particular, it is common to have physiological symptoms without either of the others. Correlation is more likely to occur in states of high anxiety. Craske and Craig[7] found that relatively anxious pianists performing in a stressful situation before an audience showed anxiety in all three systems, whereas relatively non-anxious pianists exhibited only physiological symptoms. This also raises the question of whether treatment should match symptoms, for example, drug treatment for physiological symptoms and psychological treatment for mental ones. The evidence is not clear-cut on this.

Several questionnaire studies have identified different components of music performance anxiety, not all of which may be negative. A survey of about 200 musicians, mainly professionals, isolated four factors: nervousness/apprehension; confidence/competence; self-consciousness/distractibility; and an arousal/intensity factor.[8] A similar-sized but more wide-ranging sample distinguished five independent components: worry about anxiety and its effects; fear of evaluation, that is, concern with the reactions of others to performance; judgemental attitudes about performing abilities; distraction and memory problems; and the deliberate cultivation of techniques to cope with anxiety. Of these, worry was most closely associated with debilitating performance anxiety, but all except the last have negative consequences for performance.[9]

It is important to distinguish between beneficial and detrimental kinds of anxiety – or to be more precise, between reactive, maladaptive and adaptive anxiety. Reactive anxiety, the result of inadequate preparation, is realistic and is best dealt with by music analysis and rehearsal. Anxiety is widely regarded as deleterious, but every performer knows that a certain amount of arousal is beneficial to performance. Performance is generally best at moderate levels of arousal: if arousal is too low, the performance will be dull and lifeless; if it is too high, the performer and the performance may come to pieces. This can be represented in the shape of an inverted U (plotting quality of performance as a function of arousal) and is known as the Yerkes–Dodson law (see Figure 12.1).[10] Steptoe[11] confirmed this pattern for student and professional singers by asking them to rate their emotional tension and performance quality in different situations. For both groups, performance quality was judged to peak at an intermediate level of emotional tension, after which it plummeted. For students the optimal situation was a lesson; for professionals (happily) it was a public performance. Fazey and Hardy[12] have argued that it is necessary to distinguish the mental, or cognitive, component of anxiety (fear of failure and its consequences) from the bodily, or somatic, component (physiological responses to stress). This requires a three-dimensional model of the relation between anxiety and performance (see Figure 12.2). They go on to argue that when cognitive anxiety is low, the relation between arousal and performance follows the Yerkes–Dodson function (represented at the back of Figure 12.2), but when it is high it follows the catastrophe model: as arousal increases, performance is liable to a catastrophic decline, from which it is difficult to recover. The reason is that worries and ruminations lead to a vicious spiral

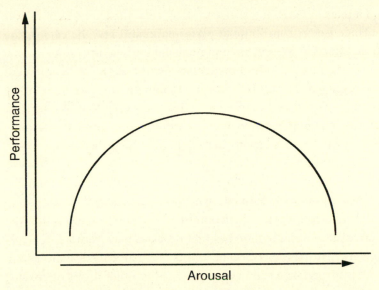

Figure 12.1 The Yerkes–Dodson function, showing the hypothesised relation between arousal and performance quality

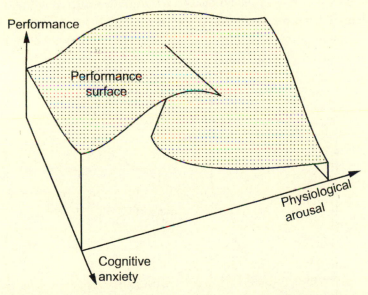

Figure 12.2 Catastrophe model of the relation between anxiety and performance (© 1996 John Wiley & Sons Limited; reproduced with permission from Lew Hardy, Graham Jones and Daniel Gould, *Understanding Psychological Preparation for Sport: Theory and Practice of Elite Performers* (Chichester: John Wiley & Sons Limited, 1996), 151)

of negative thoughts, causing the performer to go 'over the top' and collapse. Hardy and Parfitt[13] have provided evidence for this model from work with athletes. Wilson[14] has suggested that it may apply equally well to music performance.

Causes

Three factors contribute to performance anxiety: the person, the task and the situation. Wilson has represented these in a three-dimensional extension of the Yerkes–Dodson model (see Figure 12.3).[15] A high level of one can be compensated for by a low level of another. Hence, a naturally anxious person would do best to select a relatively easy or well-rehearsed piece for a demanding occasion such as an audition; conversely, experienced performers may need more challenging situations than do novices to perform at their best.[16]

People differ substantially in the responsiveness of their autonomic systems and their sensitivity to both internal types of arousal and critical judgement by others. There is evidence that musicians are more anxious than the general population[17] and that orchestral musicians may be more susceptible to anxiety than other performing artists (such as singers, dancers and actors).[18] Music performance anxiety is related to other forms of anxiety, particularly neuroticism and social phobia.[19]

The more difficult the task, the more anxious the performer is likely to be. With increasing levels of skill and task mastery, it will take a correspondingly more difficult task to produce the same level of anxiety, as noted above.

A number of studies have demonstrated the effect of the situation. LeBlanc et al.[20] found that self-reported anxiety in high school band players increased

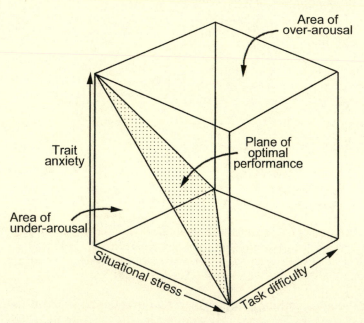

Figure 12.3 Wilson's (1994) extension of the Yerkes–Dodson model, illustrating three factors contributing to performance anxiety (reproduced by permission of Glenn Wilson and Jessica Kingsley; all rights reserved)

significantly across three performance situations: playing a solo alone in a practice room; in a practice room with one researcher present; and in a rehearsal room with four researchers and fifteen to nineteen peers present. Leglar[21] found that playing from memory to a large audience generally produced the most debilitating effect on performance and the maximum autonomic response in organists. Abel and Larkin[22] observed increases in heart rate, blood pressure and self-reported anxiety when college music students played before a jury. Interestingly, males showed greater increases in blood pressure, whereas females showed greater increases in feelings of anxiety, illustrating both gender differences and the fact that different manifestations of anxiety often do not correspond. Brotons[23] found it did not matter whether the jury was open, where performers and judges are in full view of each other (as is common in college auditions for performance courses), or blind, where the performer is behind a screen so that performers and judges are unaware of each other's identity (as is common in job auditions).

These three factors – the person, the task and the situation – mutually interact: the effect of one depends on the level of the others. A study by Cox and Kenardy[24] demonstrates the interaction between personality characteristics and the situation. Performers with social phobias were much more anxious than non-socially phobic ones in a solo setting, whereas there was little difference between them in group or practice situations. The interaction between task and situation can be illustrated by reference to a study carried out by Hamann and Sobaje.[25] The improvement in performance in an enhanced anxiety condition (where a jury evaluated performance) over a reduced anxiety condition (where performance took place in a room with only tape recording equipment present) was greater for more experienced performers, that is, those with more years of formal study and presumably greater levels of skill. Anxiety facilitated performance more for those with a greater degree of task mastery.

Cures

Brodsky and Sloboda[26] list the following methods of dealing with performance anxiety: Alexander and Feldenkreis techniques, aerobic exercise, anxiety management training, attention focusing, autogenic training, cognitive systematic desensitisation, development of interests and hobbies outside music, exposure to performance situations, mental rehearsal, muscle tension and finger temperature feedback, nutrition therapy, positive self-statements, prayer, relaxation training, self-hypnosis, stress inoculation therapy, systematic rehearsal and yoga. This offers a wide range of possibilities, to say the least. Hanser[27] draws a useful distinction between 'instrumental' techniques aimed at changing the environment or the self, and palliative measures which aim to regulate emotions and responses to stress.

Eighty-four per cent of a sample of professional and amateur musicians, asked to describe effective coping stategies for performance anxiety, reported using at least one each. Of the 478 strategies suggested, two-thirds focused on emotions, for example, 'I try to sit quietly and pray for calmness before I sing'; one-third focused on problems, for instance, 'be well-prepared – have no unmastered technical difficulties in the music'. Musicians whose predominant coping style was emotion-focused reported feeling greater confidence and competence and less self-consciousness and distractibility than those employing balanced or predominantly problem-focused styles. On the other hand, the problem-focused group recalled experiencing fewer disruptive thoughts during their most recent performance.[28] This supports the idea that different strategies may deal with different aspects of performance anxiety.

The following evaluation of the efficacy of treatments for performance anxiety will begin with the more physical and proceed to the more psychological. Of course, many techniques combine elements of both.[29]

Physical techniques

Relaxation, induced by deep breathing or by Jacobson's technique of progressive relaxation whereby muscles are alternately tensed and relaxed, is the most commonly used technique.[30] In one study, six sessions of progressive relaxation training proved effective in reducing heart rate and self-reported anxiety in anxious instrumentalists.[31]

Biofeedback is sometimes used to provide information about tension and to aid training in relaxation. Violinists were trained to reduce unnecessary left-hand tension by having electrodes attached to the muscles in their hand that controlled the thumb movement. The electrodes were connected to a machine which emitted a sound when the level of tension exceeded a given level. This level was systematically decreased as individuals learned to relax.[32] Similar techniques have been used to reduce tension in the forearms of violinists and clarinettists, the laryngeal muscles of singers and the facial muscles of wind players. One drawback with biofeedback is that performers cannot take the apparatus with them onto the concert platform.

Twenty-two per cent of a sample of London orchestral players reported taking *alcohol* and 12 per cent *sedatives* to deal with performance anxiety. These figures are likely to underestimate actual consumption, although other studies[33] have reported minimal usage. The problems with these general depressants are that they impair function and judgement, possibly leading players to believe their performance is better than it is, and that they may have undesirable side effects and can be addictive if taken habitually in high doses, leading to a downward spiral and deterioration in general health. Sedatives may appear beneficial in the short term but prevent the development of more adequate long-term coping strategies.[34]

However, '*beta-blockers*' (beta-adrenoceptor blocking agents), which act on the peripheral autonomic nervous system without pronounced effects on the central nervous system, have attracted much attention. A large-scale American survey indicated that they were taken by over 20 per cent of professional players, in many cases without medical supervision.[35] Inderal (propanolol) has become the drug that many musicians turn to. A European survey indicated occasional use by 15 per cent of orchestral players. A number of carefully controlled studies[36] have demonstrated the effectiveness of beta-blockers in relieving physiological symptoms of anxiety (increased heart rate and blood pressure), behavioural symptoms (tremor) and self-rated anxiety, as well as improving performance quality. The most marked benefits are in reducing tremor in string players, with improved evenness of vibrato and regularity of fast trills.[37] However, there have also been reports of deterioration in rhythmic control and more monotonous dynamics,[38] feeling unnerved, memory slips and impaired concentration.[39] It is important to stress that these drugs can have potentially dangerous side effects and therefore should only be taken under medical supervision. The consensus is that they are suitable for occasional rather than habitual use.

Physical and mental techniques

Many of the techniques that can be applied to combating performance anxiety *combine physical relaxation with mental alertness*, especially those derived from the East, such as yoga and tai chi, or the effortless concentration of the 'Inner Game'.[40] A therapeutic package incorporating hypnotic relaxation suggestions, breathing induction, visual imagery and verbal suggestions linking the images to increased mental control decreased performance anxiety in music conservatoire students with stage fright immediately after treatment and at a six-month follow-up, whereas discussion sessions had no effect.[41]

The *Alexander technique* is employed by many musicians and others to maintain an appropriate balance between different parts of the body and to reduce unnecessary tension. In one study,[42] it was shown to be almost as effective as, and preferable to, beta-blockers in reducing blood pressure in orchestral players prior to performance. In another,[43] music students who had undergone a course of lessons in the technique showed improvements, relative to those who had not, on overall musical and technical quality, heart-rate variance, self-reported anxiety and positive attitude towards performance. However, these benefits were generally confined to relatively less stressful class contexts and did not generalise to the high-stress recital situation. Nor were the effects associated with improvements in bodily 'use' as rated by Alexander experts; thus their locus remains unclear. However, all students who had lessons reported an increase in their awareness of tension and ability to relax, and most said they would recommend lessons to others.

Psychological techniques

Behaviour therapy is based on principles drawn from the psychology of learning. In *systematic desensitisation*, a person is taught to maintain a calm, relaxed state during progressive exposure to a feared stimulus, relaxation being incompatible with fear. This has been demonstrated to be an effective treatment for performance anxiety as shown by physiological, performance and self-report measures in many studies. In one,[44] systematic desensitisation combined with practice in 'live' situations was found to be more effective in reducing subjective anxiety than either score analysis or no training; it also reduced heart rate. In another,[45] systematic desensitisation led to a greater reduction in technical errors and anxious verbal responses than either training in improvisation and cognitive skills or no treatment.

Positive thinking is a frequently recommended[46] and well-tried method. Research has demonstrated that its modern counterpart, *cognitive behaviour therapy*, is the most effective technique for performance anxiety, but it is the least used by musicians who tend to prefer more physical methods such as relaxation and drugs.

It is therapeutically beneficial to accept anticipatory anxiety as a natural element of performing and to use the consequent tension to mobilise one's preparation. The idea behind *stress inoculation*[47] is to accept but re-appraise anxiety symptoms, turning them to positive account. An anxiety-provoking event is imagined, followed by preparatory activity or effective coping behaviour.

Benefits can also be gained by judicious *timing of anxiety* and worrying in advance. Work with parachutists has shown that experienced practitioners time their anxiety to occur prior to rather than during the activity. The same has been shown for music students asked to rate their anxiety at various times prior to a jury performance. More experienced performers showed peak anxiety prior to performance whereas less experienced performers peaked during the performance itself.[48]

As for the efficacy of some of these psychological techniques, Sweeney and Horan[49] found that training in either relaxing to a self-instructed word such as 'calm' or analysing self-defeating statements and substituting more positive coping statements for them – for instance, shifting attention from the anxiety to the task – reduced heart rate and self-reported anxiety in music-major pianists. The former technique also improved performing competence while the latter reduced behavioural manifestations of anxiety, such as trembling. A comparison group which received training in music analysis did no better than a 'wait-list' group – that is, pianists waiting to undergo training.

In a study of pianists with debilitating performance anxiety, Kendrick et al.[50] compared the relative efficacy of cognitive behaviour therapy (which involved self-instruction, attention focusing and replacing negative task-irrelevant thoughts with positive task-oriented self-talk) and behaviour rehearsal (practising performing in front of friendly, supportive audiences). Immediately following treatment there were no differences between the three groups within the study, but five weeks later the two treatment groups were superior to a wait-list control on almost all measures of performance anxiety (negative thoughts, visible signs of anxiety, expected efficacy and the actual quality of performance). However, neither treatment reduced *feelings* of anxiety. Cognitive behaviour therapy was superior to behaviour rehearsal in reducing visible signs of anxiety and increasing self-efficacy. Furthermore, measures of positive thinking and self-efficacy immediately following treatment predicted improvement in visible signs of anxiety and/or the quality of performance at follow-up.

Treatment package

Frequently a treatment package, combining different techniques, is employed. Two examples must suffice here. A six-week programme of group therapy, involving a combination of progressive muscle relaxation, cognitive therapy (identifying negative thoughts, replacing them with positive ones and challenging irrational thoughts) and temperature biofeedback training, proved effective in reducing self-rated performance anxiety in twelve competent pianists who complained of debilitating performance anxiety, in comparison with a wait-list group.[51] Clark and Agras[52] achieved success with the following package: identifying negative self-statements and distorted thinking, homework assignments to modify them, providing coping models on slides and audiotapes, relaxation training, and encouragement to face feared performance situations. Together these significantly reduced subjective anxiety and improved both confidence and the quality of musical performance in performers who suffered from social phobia. In comparison, taking buspirone (an anxiety-reducing drug) was not an effective treatment. These studies clearly demonstrate that there are effective treatments for performance anxiety. What they do not demonstrate is precisely what these are. Much careful research is needed in order to isolate the critical ingredients and to determine optimal combinations.

Recommendations

On the basis of what has been argued above, the following advice may be offered to readers who suffer from performance anxiety. First, distinguish carefully between the different types of performance anxiety – reactive, maladaptive and adaptive. Consider whether your anxiety is really detrimental to your performance. Remember that a certain amount of anxiety is normal and indeed beneficial, turning a dull performance into a lively and exciting one. If your anxiety is excessive, consider whether there are practical steps you can take to reduce it (bearing in mind the three-dimensional model discussed above), such as selecting an easier piece or rehearsing it more thoroughly. Drugs such as beta-blockers may be considered in exceptional circumstances but only as a temporary measure and with medical supervision: they have undesirable side-effects and can become addictive. Your aim should be to become self-reliant. If you tend to be an anxious person prone to over-react in stressful situations, consider one or more of the following: (a) physical techniques of various kinds, involving relaxation – for example autosuggestion or Alexander technique; (b) behavioural techniques, such as systematic desensitisation and behaviour rehearsal; (c) positive thinking and 'self-talk', focusing on the task itself rather than performance evaluation, and on your own and the audience's enjoyment rather than adopting a judgemental attitude. Combinations of these are also possible, such as visualising successful performances. If, despite all these precautions, the costs still outweigh the benefits, then perhaps public performance is not for you.

Notes

1 Paul G. Salmon, 'A psychological perspective on music performance anxiety: a review of the literature', *Medical Problems of Performing Artists*, 5 (1990), 3.

2 Martin Fishbein, Susan E. Middelstadt, Victor Ottati, Susan Strauss and Alan Ellis, 'Medical problems among ICSOM musicians: overview of a national survey', *Medical Problems of Performing Artists*, 3 (1988), 1–8.

3 See ibid.; Mary L. Wolfe, 'Correlates of adaptive and maladaptive musical performance anxiety', *Medical Problems of Performing Artists*, 4 (1989), 49–56; and Andrew Steptoe and Helen Fidler, 'Stage fright in musicians: a study of cognitive and behavioural strategies in performance anxiety', *British Journal of Psychology*, 78 (1987), 241–9.

4 See Steptoe and Fidler, 'Stage fright'.

5 See Edward E. Jones and Steven Berglas, 'Control of attributions about self through self-handicapping strategies: the appeal of alcohol and the role of underachievement', *Personality and Social Psychology Bulletin*, 4 (1978), 200–6.

6 See Peter J. Lang, *The Application of Psychophysiological Methods to the Study of Psychotherapy and Behavior Change: An Empirical Analysis* (New York: Wiley, 1971).

7 Michelle G. Craske and Kenneth D. Craig, 'Music performance anxiety: the three-systems model and self-efficacy theory', *Behavior Research & Therapy*, 22 (1984), 267–80.

8 See Wolfe, 'Correlates'.

9 See ibid.

10 See Robert M. Yerkes and J. D. Dodson, 'The relation of strength of stimulus to rapidity of habit-formation', *Journal of Comparative Neurology and Psychology*, 18 (1908), 459–82.

11 Andrew Steptoe, 'The relationship between tension and the quality of musical performance', *Journal of the International Society for the Study of Tension in Performance*, 1 (1983), 12–22.

12 John A. Fazey and Lew Hardy, *The Inverted-U Hypothesis: A Catastrophe for Sport Psychology* (Leeds: The National Coaching Foundation, 1988).

13 Lew Hardy and Gaynor Parfitt, 'A catastrophe model of anxiety and performance', *British Journal of Psychology*, 82 (1991), 163–78.

14 Glenn D. Wilson, *Psychology for Performing Artists: Butterflies and Bouquets* (London: Jessica Kingsley, 1994).

15 Ibid. 'Trait anxiety' in Figure 12.3 refers to a stable (that is, permanent and persisting) personality characteristic.

16 See Steptoe, 'Relationship between tension'.

17 See Anthony Kemp, 'The personality structure of the musician: I. Identifying a profile of traits for the performer', *Psychology of Music*, 9 (1981), 3–14.

18 See Susan E. Marchant-Haycox and Glenn D. Wilson, 'Personality and stress in performing artists', *Personality and Individual Differences*, 13 (1992), 1061–8.

19 See Steptoe and Fidler, 'Stage fright'. For further discussion of personal factors in performance anxiety, see Jolanta Ossetin, 'Psychological aspects of performance anxiety. Part I: Personality characteristics', *Journal of the International Society for the Study of Tension in Performance*, 5 (1988), 26–30.

20 Albert LeBlanc, Young Chang Jin, Mary Obert and Carolyn Siivola, 'Effect of audience on music performance anxiety', *Journal of Research in Music Education*, 45 (1997), 480–6.

21 Mary A. Leglar, 'Measurement of indicators of anxiety levels under varying conditions of musical performance' (Ph.D. thesis, Indiana University, 1978).

22 Jennifer L. Abel and Kevin T. Larkin, 'Anticipation of performance among musicians: physiological arousal, confidence, and state anxiety', *Psychology of Music*, 18 (1990), 171–82.

23 Melissa Brotons, 'Effect of performing conditions on music performance, anxiety, and performance quality', *Journal of Music Therapy*, 31 (1994), 63–81.

24 Wendy J. Cox and Justin Kenardy, 'Performance anxiety, social phobia, and setting effects in instrumental music students', *Journal of Anxiety Disorders*, 7 (1993), 49–60.

25 Donald L. Hamann and Martha Sobaje, 'Anxiety and college musicians: study of performance conditions and subject variables', *Psychology of Music*, 11 (1983), 37–50.

26 Warren Brodsky and John A. Sloboda, 'Clinical trial of a music generated vibrotactile therapeutic environment for musicians: main effects and outcome differences between therapy subgroups', *Journal of Music Therapy*, 34 (1997), 2–32.

27 Suzanne B. Hanser, 'Music therapy in stress reduction research', *Journal of Music Therapy*, 22 (1985), 193–206.

28 See Mary L. Wolfe, 'Coping with musical performance anxiety: problem-focused and emotion-focused strategies', *Medical Problems of Performing Artists*, 5 (1990), 33–6.

29 There are many problems in designing studies to investigate the efficacy of different treatments. Basic requirements are random assignment of participants to treatment conditions and 'blind' judgements, i.e. assessors must not know who has had which treatment. Ideally, the treatment of interest should be compared with a plausible alternative (a 'treatment control') rather than nothing (a 'no-treatment control'), so as to be able to rule out expectancy effects – the belief that a treatment will work. In drug studies a non-active placebo is used. Since effects are often short-lived, long-term follow-ups need to be included.

30 See Wolfe, 'Coping', and Andrew Steptoe, 'Stress, coping and stage fright in professional musicians', *Psychology of Music*, 17 (1989), 3–11.

31 See Alan Grishman, 'Musicians' performance anxiety: the effectiveness of modified progressive muscle relaxation in reducing physiological, cognitive, and behavioral symptoms of anxiety' (Ph.D. thesis, University of Pittsburgh, 1989).

32 See William R. LeVine and Jeffrey K. Irvine, 'In vivo EMG biofeedback in violin and viola pedagogy', *Biofeedback and Self-regulation*, 9 (1984), 161–8, and Jeffrey K. Irvine and William R. Levine, 'The use of biofeedback to reduce left-hand tension for string players', *American String Teacher*, 31 (1981), 10–12.

33 Robert Wesner, Russell Noyes, Jr. and Thomas L. Davis, 'The occurrence of performance anxiety among musicians', *Journal of Affective Disorders*, 18 (1990), 177–85, and Geoffrey I. D. Wills and Gary Cooper, *Pressure Sensitive: Popular Musicians Under Stress* (London: Sage, 1988).

34 See Yvon-Jacques Lavallee, Yves Lamontagne, Gilbert Pinard, Lawrence Annable and Léon Tétreault, 'Effects on EMG feedback, diazepam and their combination on chronic anxiety', *Journal of Psychosomatic Research*, 21 (1977), 65–71.

35 Fishbein et al., 'Medical problems', 1–8.

36 For a review, see Paul M. Lehrer, Raymond C. Rosen, John B. Kostis and Daniel Greenfield, 'Treating stage fright in musicians: the use of beta blockers', *New Jersey Medicine*, 84 (1987), 27–34.

37 See Klaus A. Neftel, Rolf H. Adler, Louis Kappeli, Maria Ross, Martin Dolder and Hans E. Kaser, 'Stage fright in musicians: a model illustrating the effect of beta blockers', *Psychosomatic Medicine*, 44 (1982), 461–9.

38 See Ian James and Imogen Savage, 'Beneficial effect of nadolol on anxiety-induced disturbances of musical performance in musicians: a comparison with diazepam and placebo', *American Heart Journal*, 108 (1984), 1150–5.

39 See Michael Nielsen, 'A study of stress amongst professional musicians', in Christopher Stevens (ed.), *Medical and Physiological Aspects of the Alexander Technique* (Aalborg, Denmark: International School for the Alexander Technique, 1988), and C. O. Brantigan, T. A. Brantigan and N. Joseph, 'The effect of beta blockade on stage fright', *Rocky Mountain Medical Journal*, 76 (1979), 227–32.

40 See Barry Green with Timothy C. Gallwey, *The Inner Game of Music* (Garden City, NY: Doubleday, 1986).

41 See Harry E. Stanton, 'Reduction in performance anxiety in music students', *Australian Psychologist*, 29 (1994), 124–47.

42 Nielsen, 'Study of stress'.

43 Elizabeth R. Valentine, David F. P. Fitzgerald, Tessa L. Gorton, Jennifer A. Hudson and Elizabeth R. C. Symonds, 'The effect of lessons in the Alexander technique on music performance in high and low stress situations', *Psychology of Music*, 23 (1995), 486–97.

44 Sylvia S. Appel, 'Modifying solo performance anxiety in adult pianists', *Journal of Music Therapy*, 13 (1976), 1–16. Though less effective than systematic desensitisation in reducing subjective anxiety, music analysis did reduce performance errors.

45 Barbara A. McCune, 'Functional performance anxiety modification in adult pianists' (Ed.D. thesis, Columbia University Teachers' College, 1982).

46 See Robert Triplett, *Stage Fright: Letting it Work for You* (Chicago: Nelson-Hall, 1983); Eloise Ristad, *A Soprano on Her Head: Right-side Up Reflections on Life and Other Performances* (Moan, Ut.: Real People Press, 1982); and Kato Havas, *Stage Fright: Its Causes and Cures, with Special Reference to Violin Playing* (London: Bosworth, 1973).

47 See Donald Meichenbaum, *Stress Inoculation Training* (New York: Pergamon, 1985).

48 See Paul Salmon, R. Schrodt and J. Wright, 'A temporal gradient of anxiety in a stressful performance context', *Medical Problems of Performing Artists*, 4 (1989), 77–80.

49 Gladys Acevedo Sweeney and John J. Horan, 'Separate and combined effects of cue-controlled relaxation and cognitive restructuring in the treatment of musical performance anxiety', *Journal of Counseling Psychology*, 29 (1982), 486–97.

50 Margaret J. Kendrick, Kenneth D. Craig, David M. Lawson and Park O. Davidson, 'Cognitive and behavioral therapy for musical-performance anxiety', *Journal of Consulting and Clinical Psychology*, 50 (1982), 353–62.

51 See Julie J. Nagel, David P. Himle and James D. Papsdorf, 'Cognitive-behavioural treatment of musical performance anxiety', *Psychology of Music*, 17 (1989), 12–21.

52 Duncan B. Clark and W. Stewart Agras, 'The assessment and treatment of performance anxiety in musicians', *American Journal of Psychiatry*, 148 (1991), 598–605.

Further reading

Lehrer, Paul M., 'A review of the approaches to the management of tension and stage fright in music performance', *Journal for Research in Music Education*, 35 (1987), 143–52

Salmon, Paul G., 'A psychological perspective on music performance anxiety: a review of the literature', *Medical Problems of Performing Artists*, 5 (1990), 2–11

Steptoe, Andrew, 'Performance anxiety. Recent developments in its analysis and management', *Musical Times*, 23 (1982), 537–41

Wilson, Glenn D., 'Performance anxiety', in David J. Hargreaves and Adrian C. North (eds.), *The Social Psychology of Music* (Oxford: Oxford University Press, 1997), 229–48

Wilson, Glenn D., 'Stage fright and optimal performance', in Wilson, *Psychology for Performing Artists: Butterflies and Bouquets* (London: Jessica Kingsley, 1994), 185–203

PART FOUR

Interpreting performance

13 Listening to performance

ERIC CLARKE

Introduction

Listeners are exposed to a greater number and variety of musical performances today than at any other time in human history, and the rapid expansion that began with the advent of the recording industry in the early twentieth century shows no signs of abating. With the proliferation and diversification of performance through recording has come a renewed pre-occupation with performers themselves as interpreters and personalities. This chapter is concerned with the different circumstances of listening to performance and their implications, and with the perceptual processes involved in what listeners can and do hear in performance.

The title of this chapter suggests that it is possible to listen to the performance component of what might be called 'the total sound of music'. Is this a defensible view? To what extent and in what way are listeners aware of performance as a separable element of music – indeed, can anything *other* than performance be heard? For the score-based music of the Western concert tradition, a distinction between 'music' and 'performance' seems justified if only because the score stands as a representation of the music which is free of any *particular* performance. But what of the vast number of listeners who seldom if ever look at scores, or the overwhelming majority of other music for which no score exists? In short, do people ever listen to performance (as opposed to music), and if so, what do they hear?

Strong, informal evidence of the importance of performance to listeners can be seen in the enormous emphasis that our culture places on performance: performers have star status in contemporary musical culture, as the design of record and CD sleeves often demonstrates,[1] and as their fees and public profiles also illustrate. The recording industry depends for its survival on an almost insatiable appetite on the part of the CD-buying public for new, or re-released, performances of a largely static repertoire of music, and the industry in turn fosters the emphasis on performance for obvious commercial reasons. From this evidence alone there is clearly a case to be answered, just as the burgeoning of performance studies testifies to the rapidly growing academic interest in performance.

Circumstances and attitudes

Until about 1910 there was only live performance: listening to music took place in the presence of the performers, who were usually in full view. Under these circumstances it would be hard *not* to be aware of performance (or at least the performers) at the direct level of a physical presence. However, before the birth of a concert culture around 1800, performance and performers were deeply embedded within the social functions of which they were explicitly a part (church, court, secular celebration, domestic entertainment, military function). This social embeddedness might imply that musical performance would be difficult to separate from its function and circumstances, and thus unlikely to feature as an object of contemplation or a matter for discussion. This is manifestly not the case, however: even St Augustine, for example, writing of the tension between music for its own sake and music in the service of God, acknowledges the capacity for a suitably effective performance to 'beguile' him, and for aesthetic pleasure to overtake religious reason.[2]

Nevertheless, by comparison with the position of music within its secular and sacred contexts, concert culture brought a more intense focus on performance and placed it centre stage – literally. Performers were separated from their listeners, often raised up on a platform; they began to play only when an audience had assembled, whose members listened with a degree of focused attention and in conditions of comparative quiet. These physical and social arrangements are part of a historically specific attitude to performing and listening, and taken together all these factors – which still characterise the conventional conditions for live performances of the concert repertoire[3] – conspire to present music as autonomous (independent, self-sufficient) and occupying a special realm. It is therefore not surprising that great performers – the 'realisers' of music – have come to be regarded with the kind of awe that oracles or geniuses have also inspired.

But live performance has been eclipsed by recording (in quantitative terms, at least), and far more music is now heard on recorded or broadcast media of one sort or another, with important effects on listening attitudes. When records and gramophones started to become widely available in the first quarter of the twentieth century, they maintained something of the social character of listening to live performance. But the gramophone also provided for solitary 'acousmatic listening', in which the instrumental source of the sound is hidden, and which arguably encourages a concentration on sound itself of a kind barely possible before.[4] While it may not represent the greatest refinement of sound, the personal stereo in its various manifestations can be seen as the culmination of acousmatic listening, allowing a listener to carry around and control a virtual sound world seemingly located inside his or her own head.

The implications of recording for listening are paradoxical. On the one hand, the acousmatic nature of recordings – the physical absence of the performer – means that performance itself is more in the background, more implicit, than in live performance. On the other hand, the advent of recording, combined with a more or less fixed repertoire of constantly re-recorded music, means that performance itself has become the centre of attention. Furthermore, as the history of recording demonstrates, there is a deep-seated uncertainty about how recordings should be understood – whether as captured performances or as studio creations.[5] Recording companies such as Nimbus in the UK, specialising in 'single-take' recordings, testify to the view that recordings should be like performances, just as many performers will assert that in a studio they are trying to record a performance. In contrast, there are performers – of whom Glenn Gould was perhaps the most widely known representative – who insist that recording is quite different from performance, that editing allows the creation of something that cannot be achieved live, and that recordings must be understood as distinct manifestations of music. The highly edited multi-take recording is not a 'stitch-up': it is a deliberately and carefully constructed sounding of the music which has its own characteristics and invites unique evaluative criteria. Studio processes are completely intertwined with what are conventionally regarded as performance factors, and the result is simply a different kind of object/event as compared with a real performance. Other genres of music make this even more obvious: much pop and electroacoustic music involves a type of studio production that admits of no live performance in the usual sense of the term, and there are pieces in the concert music repertoire which arguably exist in different versions for recording and live performance. Steve Reich's *New York Counterpoint*, for example, can either be played by eleven clarinet players in live performance or created on a recording by one player using multitrack recording methods.[6]

In summary, recording introduces a number of considerations (such as recording and post-production studio techniques, editing, the playing approach that studio circumstances induce or require, the fidelity and acoustical character of the recording medium, and the physical and acoustical nature of the diffusion system on which the recording is reproduced) which mean that we should be cautious about equating recorded music with recorded performance. Some recordings clearly *are* intended to be like performances – most obviously so-called live recordings of concerts and operas. But even for these, their acousmatic character significantly changes a listener's relationship with the music, and the result has properties (among them repeatability, interruptibility and transformability at the moment of reproduction) which may profoundly change the way in which listeners react to and use these 'performances'. The failure to recognise that recordings are *not* just conveniently packaged performances, and that the listening practices and expectations associated with recordings are also quite different from those at concerts, may be two reasons why many people find the relationship between their experiences of recordings and concerts uncomfortable and perhaps disappointing. We should not expect to listen to both in the same way.

I have suggested that recordings may foreground performance factors. In live performance, are there particular musical circumstances which induce listeners to become aware of performance as such? Catastrophe and triumph can make performance particularly audible: when things go disastrously wrong or the performer is hopelessly incompetent, the gulf between what the music demands and the performer is able to supply becomes all too obvious. Conversely, when performers appear to be in complete control of technically demanding music, their technical prowess and 'athleticism' may be clearly audible, as the showpieces of gala performances and music competitions are intended to demonstrate. At the extremes, then, performance is audible as incompetence or virtuosity.

But the extremes are unusual, and it is less obvious what listeners hear under more normal circumstances. An important factor may be the kind of listener in question. On the one hand, there are those for whom distinguishing between levels of performance excellence is part of their profession, and who have cultivated an acute, if sometimes very particular, sensitivity to performance (for instance, the judges of music competitions and auditions). On the other hand, there are listeners who may be completely unfamiliar with a particular musical idiom and its performance conventions and traditions. Listeners learn to pick up and evaluate performance features in any idiom over a long period of continuous perceptual learning, and usually in an informal and unsupervised manner. Most of these listening skills develop from simple exposure and a constant trickle of irregular interactions with other listeners and their views and preferences, together with the influence of CD and concert reviews, radio programmes in which different recordings are evaluated, and the more indirect influence of representations of performance and listening in films, television programmes and literature. There is no systematic research on how these kinds of everyday listening skills develop, what the primary factors and influences are, and how consistent or reliable the evaluations of professional adjudicators might be. But informal evidence repeatedly confirms that listeners with different skills, interests and preoccupations hear and react to performances in sometimes radically divergent ways.

However, broader aesthetic attitudes can also play an important role, since listeners may want or expect different *kinds* of relationships between performer and material – and for different kinds of music. Within the Western concert tradition, two ends of a spectrum can be identified which have serious implications for listening, dubbed by Wilfrid Mellers as the distinction between performers as intermediaries and as interpreters.[7] Mellers identifies 'intermediaries' as performers who are a channel for the composer's intentions, and 'interpreters' as those for whom the composer's intentions (or more tangibly, the score) are a starting point for their own creative/interpretative work. Although there is a historical dimension to this issue, distinctions can also be drawn between different approaches at the same moment in history: in the 1940s and 1950s, for example, the conductors Toscanini and Furtwängler were respectively stereotyped as 'intermediary' and 'interpreter', Toscanini being revered (or pilloried) for his 'fidelity to the score', and Furtwängler for his creative insight and idiosyncrasy. If there are such fundamental disagreements about what performers should even *try* to do, it is not surprising that listeners may have radically divergent responses: what is wayward and indulgent to one (perhaps on the basis of its 'departure from the score') may be committed and inspired to another (because of the 'originality and idiosyncrasy of its interpretation').

For many musical traditions outside the concert music of the West, the situation is even more fluid. It is certainly not the case that the distinction between performer and material disappears for non-literate traditions, but the relationship changes. For example, in traditional jazz, which has a core of 'standard' tunes that are continually reinterpreted, it makes little sense to talk of a performer being more or less faithful to the original, if only because there is often a degree of uncertainty about what the 'original' actually is (or was), and a high level of indeterminacy in the specification of even the more fixed or well-defined examples. A 'standard' has an identity which is often little more than a harmonic/metrical framework and an associated melody, and represents a skeleton on the basis of which performers are expected to display their creative improvisatory skill. There may be a sense of the performer's fidelity to the 'spirit' of the original on the part of some listeners, and a consequent resistance to radical treatments by idiosyncratic performers, but considerable scope clearly exists for the performer's interpretative freedom – as well as the expectation by listeners that this will and should be the case.

Jazz listeners are more interested in performance and performers than in pieces and repertoires.

However, the primary concern of this chapter is the Western concert tradition, and what listeners do and can hear in the performance of that music. An ideal for performance that is often proposed or assumed is that the listener should be swept along by the force of the performance with little or no awareness of the performer as either intermediary or interpreter. For some listeners, then, concentrated and rewarding listening paradoxically renders the performance inaudible: they regard the music as speaking to them directly. Peter Johnson writes: 'The outstanding performance of a fine musical work is, I suggest, an invitation to transcendental listening in that, paradigmatically, it avoids drawing attention to itself *as* a performance (whether for positive or negative reasons).'[8] If the lack of awareness of performance is for some listeners a measure of its success, this suggests that the ideal would be for the performer to be so involved with the music, and so possessed by it, as to be identified with either the composer or the work. The contrasting outlook would be a fascination with performance itself – with the ways in which performers do what they do, and the limitless ways in which music is made in performance.

What do the sounds of performance specify?

While it is possible for an attentive and engaged listener to have little or no awareness of the specific features of a performance, such a listener can *become* conscious of performance attributes. Furthermore, since perception involves not only conscious awareness but also the continuous and unconscious attunement and response to the environment, listeners will also be influenced by performance features whether they realise it or not. The sounds of a performance have the potential to convey a wealth of information to a listener, ranging from physical characteristics related to the space in which the performance is taking place and the nature of the instrument, to less palpable properties such as the performance ideology of the performer. One way to tackle this great diversity is to ask, 'What do the sounds of performance specify?', and in so doing to encourage close attention to the characteristics of the sounds of performance, and their richness as a source of information.

Space/instrument/body

The most tangible and physical properties of performances are the spaces in which they take place, the instruments used and the performers' physical interactions with them. For some music (for instance, the antiphonal music of Andrea Gabrieli or Karlheinz Stockhausen's spatially distributed music in a work like *Gruppen*), the 'geometry' of space is important as a component of the music's structure. But for a great deal of music in the Western concert tradition, space is important not as an element of structure but in the way it conveys the 'aura' or character of the performance. Many listeners prefer to hear a work such as Bach's *St Matthew Passion*, for example, in a 'space' (either the real space of a performance or the virtual space of a recording) that is large and resonant, for at least two reasons. First, a large and resonant acoustic is consistent with the type of performance space for which this music was written (a church), and in conveying this space, the acoustic also conveys the materials (stone and wood), surroundings and ideology (Christian worship) that are associated with performances of this music. Second, the music was composed arguably to exploit the kind of acoustic for which it was intended, and thus works better with the long reverberation time (and consequent wash of sound) that such spaces provide. By contrast, the majority of the chamber music repertoire was composed for domestic performance, and the music may suffer when played in a very reverberant acoustic not only because the associations are wrong, but also because the musical textures are blurred.

Along with the spaces of performance go the instruments and the performers themselves, whose actions upon the instruments are specified in sound. The sound of a performance projects not only basic properties such as the particular instruments being played, but also the performer's physical interaction with the instrument. The ease or effort, energy, confidence and level of control of a performance are vividly conveyed in the sound of a performance, and provide the listener with information about the body of the performer and its relationship with the instrument.

Conventional attitudes towards the standard concert repertoire have tended to play down the physicality of performance, about which listeners are often ambivalent. Within a tradition that celebrates virtuosity, listeners generally want to remain unaware of performers' efforts to maintain technical control in challenging music, but do want a sense of their physical presence, involved in mind *and* body in the 'heroic struggle' to express and communicate. One of the failures of attempts to simulate human performance with computer systems (such as the CHANT system for vocal simulation developed at IRCAM in Paris in the 1980s) is the lack of any sense of physical commitment and 'effort' in the resulting performance.

Events and processes

Listening to performance has much in common with listening to speech, in that the challenge for a listener is to keep track of a stream of events in time and to find sense in them. Although a considerable amount of music theory has emphasised the importance of large-scale hierarchical structure in music,[9] there is also evidence that listeners are insensitive to these large-scale features in any directly perceptual fashion.[10] Jerrold Levinson[11] has argued that listeners do not construct elaborate and large-scale hierarchical structures, but are primarily focused on the continuously evolving detail of a small amount of 'current' music. This idea is consistent with work in the psychology of time perception which suggests that at any moment we are aware of a relatively brief 'patch' of time (around 6–10 seconds), referred to as the perceptual present.[12] Larger structures are a function of memory, and Levinson argues that listeners' memories for these structures are usually rather imprecise and do not support a large-scale 'architecture'. Listening, in other words, is like a wave in which the current and immediately surrounding events are vivid and immediate in their impact, leaving behind a wake of memories whose history of accumulated events and influences endows the wave with a particular shape.

In listening to performance, we are primarily sensitive to what is happening *now* in a continuous flow. This flow is not seamless, however: in the performance of most music, particular events segment the stream and periodically provide an opportunity to organise the events of the last few seconds and consign them to memory. Similarly, in listening to someone talking, we are aware at any moment of the active contents of the current phrase or sentence – a few seconds' worth of words. As a notional full-stop or semi-colon is reached, the contents of that phrase or sentence are condensed into the gist of what the speaker has just said – perhaps with the odd word or phrase literally remembered, but mostly in terms of what the passage means. And at the same time as this parcel of meaning is being registered, a new window of immediate perceptual awareness opens up which carries the listener on. In music, this segmentation of the flow of information is derived from a mixture of structural properties (long notes, discontinuities in pitch, tonal functions etc.) and performance characteristics (changes in tempo, dynamics, articulation etc.). The ways in which performers shape the events of performance are discussed in a number of chapters in this volume; the next section considers whether and how listeners pick up these features of performance, and how they interpret them.

Expression, emotion and style

How sensitive are listeners to the microvariations of performance, and in what ways do they make sense of them? A number of studies have shown that under controlled conditions, listeners can detect very small timing changes, of the order of 30 to 50 milliseconds,[13] and other studies have shown that listeners are similarly sensitive to changes in loudness and intonation.[14] Less is known about the detectability of articulation, timbre and vibrato, in part because each of these is a more complex attribute than duration, pitch or loudness. Equally, there has been little research on listeners' sensitivities to any of these features under normal listening conditions.

Bruno Repp, however, has shown that listeners' abilities to detect the detailed features of performance are dramatically affected by musical context. When listeners were played a short section from a Beethoven piano sonata (the opening of the Minuet from Op. 31 No. 3) with differing amounts of note-lengthening at various places, they showed considerable perceptual variation depending on the position of the change.[15] Where listeners would expect expressive timing changes (typically at phrase boundaries), they failed to detect timing changes – as if the predictability of such changes made them inconspicuous. Conversely, in the middle of a phrase, where expressive timing changes are less likely, listeners were particularly sensitive to their presence – as if they were made more noticeable by being incongruous.

Although Repp's study considered only one aspect of performance, it illustrates an important general principle – that listeners' abilities to detect the detailed features of performance are strongly dependent on context. This principle might affect both listeners' *awareness* of features of performance and how they interpret them – how they function as signs.[16] A decrease in tempo in the middle of a phrase might be interpreted as an expressive intensification, while the same tempo change at the end of a phrase might be understood as a decrease of tension, marking the conclusion of a passage of music. Different interpretations of notionally 'the same' performance feature are a product of the network of structural and expressive relationships in which every performance feature is embedded.

The expressive properties of performance specify emotional qualities as well as structural features. Patrik Juslin has shown that if a performer is asked to play a piece so as to convey one of a number of specific emotional states, listeners can reliably tell which state is being communicated.[17] This is a controlled (and somewhat artificial) version of the common experience that listeners hear emotions conveyed by performance which they often attribute to the performers – whether these are heard as the actual emotional states of the performers, or as the acted-out emotions of an adopted persona.

More than one hundred years of recorded performance, and developments in historical performance practices, have made available a fascinating diversity of performance styles and ideologies. The systematic study of how these are variously specified in sound has hardly begun (though Robert Philip's work is a starting point)[18] but is potentially fascinating. Hearing expression, emotion, style and ideology in performance requires the listener to identify properties of the performance which stand out against an implicit background of neutrality – a kind of theoretical 'norm' in relation to which expression, emotion, style and ideology are marked (as chapter 4 explains). In other words, performance is heard against the backdrop of previous performances and recordings. Continuous historical change means that the norms of one age become the idiosyncrasies or anachronisms of another, and it is for this reason that old recordings can strike a contemporary listener as mannered or peculiar. Here again the explosive growth of recorded and broadcast performances in the twentieth century led to profound changes for performers and listeners who now have access to unprecedented numbers and varieties of performances of an enormous repertoire of music. Some have regarded this as enriching and enabling, while others such as Hans Keller have seen it as contributing to a disastrous erosion of both listening and performance skills.[19]

Conclusion

One view of successful performance and of concentrated listening is that we as listeners should be unaware of performance – with the consequence that this chapter need never have been written. But this is an unnecessarily restricted view: it assumes a particular listening aesthetic which is far from universally shared, relates to particular listening circumstances, depends on idealised conditions and is concerned only with conscious awareness. As this chapter has shown, there are many situations in which listeners are undeniably – if sometimes unhappily – aware of performance, and arguably listeners *always* respond to performance even when they are unaware of it. However, a feature of concert music and its associated listening attitude, stemming from the whole concept of musical works and their (separable) performance, is a deep-seated uncertainty or ambivalence about what one is, or should be, listening to. The 'work concept' suggests that performance should be self-effacing, while the rise of the performer as artist results from and encourages a concern with performance itself. But whether listeners believe they are listening to performance or to 'the work itself', there is no escaping the reality that it is a performance (or recording) that they hear, and a second aim of this chapter has been to show how much, and of what diversity, is conveyed in the sounds of performance. Finally, in an age when far more music is heard via recorded and broadcast media than in live performance, we have still not arrived at a stable conception of what a recording is – 'captured' performance or studio construct – with all the consequences for our responses and attitudes to recordings that this entails. At a time when the dominance of the score in writing about music is increasingly questioned, and performances and recordings are becoming much more common as the objects of study, we know more about what can be *measured* in performances and recordings, but still very little about what listeners of all kinds actually *hear* in them.

Notes

1 See Nicholas Cook, 'The domestic *Gesamtkunstwerk*, or record sleeves and reception', in Wyndham Thomas (ed.), *Composition, Performance, Reception: Studies in the Creative Process in Music* (Aldershot: Ashgate, 1998), 105–17.

2 Oliver Strunk, *Source Readings in Music History: From Classical Antiquity through the Romantic Era* (New York: Norton, 1950), 74.

3 For an engaging account of the rituals and circumstances of twentieth-century concert listening, see Christopher Small, 'Performance as ritual: sketch for an enquiry into the true nature of a symphony concert', in Avron Levine White (ed.), *Lost in Music: Culture, Style and the Musical Event* (London: Routledge and Kegan Paul, 1987), 6–32.

4 See Denis Smalley, 'The listening imagination: listening in the electroacoustic era', in John Paynter, Tim Howell, Richard Orton and Peter Seymour (eds.), *Companion to Contemporary Musical Thought*, 2 vols. (London and New York: Routledge, 1992), I:514–54.

5 See Michael Chanan, *Repeated Takes: A Short History of Recording and its Effects on Music* (London: Verso, 1995).

6 Evan Ziporyn's recording on Nonesuch 7559-79451-2 is an example of the latter.

7 Wilfrid Mellers, 'Present and past: intermediaries and interpreters', in Paynter et al. (eds.), *Companion*, II:920–30.

8 Peter Johnson, 'Performance and the listening experience: Bach's "Erbarme dich"', in Nicholas Cook, Peter Johnson and Hans Zender (eds.), *Theory into Practice: Composition, Performance and the Listening Experience* (Leuven: Leuven University Press, 1999), 85.

9 E.g. Heinrich Schenker, *Free Composition (Der freie Satz)*, trans. and ed. Ernst Oster (New York: Longman, 1979), and Fred Lerdahl and Ray Jackendoff, *A Generative Theory of Tonal Music* (Cambridge, Mass.: MIT Press, 1983).

10 See for example Nicholas Cook, 'The perception of large-scale tonal closure', *Music Perception*, 5 (1987), 197–205.

11 Jerrold Levinson, *Music in the Moment* (Ithaca and London: Cornell University Press, 1997).

12 See John A. Michon, 'The making of the present: a tutorial review', in John Requin (ed.), *Attention and Performance VII* (Hillsdale, NJ: Erlbaum, 1978), 89–111, and Eric F. Clarke, 'Levels of structure in the organization of musical time', *Contemporary Music Review*, 2 (1987), 211–38.

13 See Eric F. Clarke, 'The perception of expressive timing in music', *Psychological Research*, 51 (1989), 2–9.

14 For an overview, see Brian Moore, *An Introduction to the Psychology of Hearing*, 4th edn (London: Academic Press, 1997).

15 Bruno H. Repp, 'Probing the cognitive representation of musical time: structural constraints on the perception of timing perturbations', *Cognition*, 44 (1992), 241–81.

16 See Eric F. Clarke, 'Expression in performance: generativity, perception and semiosis', in John Rink (ed.), *The Practice of Performance: Studies in Musical Interpretation* (Cambridge: Cambridge University Press, 1995), 21–54.

17 See for example Patrik Juslin, 'Emotional communication in music performance: a functionalist perspective and some data', *Music Perception*, 14 (1997), 383–418.

18 Robert Philip, *Early Recordings and Musical Style: Changing Tastes in Instrumental Performance, 1900–1950* (Cambridge: Cambridge University Press, 1992); see also chapter 14 in this volume.

19 Hans Keller, 'The gramophone record', in Robert Matthew-Walker (ed.), *The Keller Column: Essays by Hans Keller* (London: Alfred Lengnick, 1990), 22–5.

Further reading

Chanan, Michael, *Repeated Takes: A Short History of Recording and its Effects on Music* (London: Verso, 1995)

Day, Timothy, *A Century of Recorded Music* (New Haven: Yale University Press, 2000)

Francès, Robert, *The Perception of Music*, trans. W. Jay Dowling (Hillsdale, NJ: Erlbaum, 1988)

Gaver, William, 'What in the world do we hear? An ecological approach to auditory event perception', *Ecological Psychology*, 5 (1993), 1–29

Johnson, James H., *Listening in Paris: A Cultural History* (Berkeley: University of California Press, 1995)

Storr, Anthony, *Music and the Mind* (London: Harper Collins, 1992)

14 The legacy of recordings

PETER JOHNSON

The most enduring visual image in the entire history of recording is surely that of Nipper the dog, peering wistfully into the enormous horn of an old gramophone. The caption, of course, is 'His Master's Voice'. In some ways this was a curious choice for a record label, for it speaks of absence: the master has long departed. Music recordings speak more characteristically of presence, of performers' voices and of real, sounding music.

Perhaps it is because recordings are so much a part of our daily lives that we routinely accept them in lieu of the live performance. Somehow we manage without the visual contact between performer and listener or that intangible sense of the music taking shape before us. We accept that the virtuoso passage will always be executed in the same way, and that it probably took the performer a dozen takes to achieve its level of perfection. And we do not routinely hear a professional recording as less authentic than a live performance: on the contrary, it asserts its authority over the transient, soon-to-be-forgotten concert performance. Even so, recordings have not replaced the live event: they provide an alternative mode of musical production, of proven value for performers and their audiences and for scholars and composers.

Voice and persona

If recordings significantly differ from the live performance, what do they have in common? The performing voice of any major performer, be it Håkan Hardenberger or Heinz Holliger, Yo Yo Ma or Yuri Bashmet, is unmistakable once we have heard it, regardless of whether it is on CD or in a live performance. It is this performing voice that recordings capture so effectively and which becomes present every time we play a record or a CD. A recording is, literally, *of* the performer or the ensemble engaged in interpreting the work. To that extent, record companies are right to market their products by performer rather than by work.[1]

Each work, however, makes its own interpretative demands, and like the actor, the good performer adjusts his or her voice accordingly. I shall refer to this second level of presence as the performer's 'persona'.[2] In a live performance we see the performers moving in and out of role: the unassuming figure of Alfred Brendel is transformed into the magisterial pianist as his fingers touch the keys, but the man returns as he quietly acknowledges the applause. Recordings, like films, do not allow us to observe such transformations, and offer only the persona. But they do allow us to compare personae: Callas's Butterfly is very different from her Tosca, yet the voice is always that of Callas.

Recordings as evidence

It is often asked whether earlier artists such as Schnabel or Cortot really performed as their recordings suggest. At one level, this is an irrelevant question, for recordings are what they are rather than what they might have been. In post-war recordings, where the producer has probably exercised considerable control over the physical sound and even the interpretation, the product itself may still be of considerable musical and historical interest. Even so, recordings can reveal a remarkably clear picture of how performers actually sang or played since the beginning of the twentieth century. The question is how we analyse them.

There has as yet been very little serious musicological study of recordings, for twentieth-century musicology had other priorities. And so it is to the practising performer that I mainly address this chapter: what can the performer today expect to learn from the legacy of recordings? Three immediate problems are the sheer size of the archive, the complexity of the art of performance itself and the influence of the recording medium on what we hear. We could narrow the field by concentrating on our own voice type or instrument, or on one work or movement in multiple performances.[3] However, this chapter will adopt a thematic approach, marking some of the more promising areas and illustrating certain analytical techniques. All such approaches raise the much larger questions of interpretation and meaning, which I shall briefly consider in a concluding section. I would stress that this is merely an introduction, for the subject is vast; with so much uncharted territory, the journey promises to be exciting, if, at times, hazardous.

Recording methods

The first step is to understand the several recording technologies and how they might have influenced what we hear on a recording.[4] Since 1900, there have been five principal recording media: acoustically recorded shellac disc (1900–25); electrically recorded shellac disc (1925–54); monophonic vinyl LP (1950 to c. 1960); stereophonic vinyl LP (1958 to c. 1985); and modern digital recording, starting with the CD in the early 1980s. Pianists will also be interested in the piano roll, which enjoyed a brief but important history from its invention in 1904 to its demise around 1930. It is worth noting that the '78' shellac disc survived for more than fifty years, but that its pre-1925 phase was strikingly different from its later form. The single most important development in the entire history of recording was probably the introduction of electrical recording in 1925.

Broadly speaking, the earlier the recording, the more distortion there will be from the recording process, but the less intentional manipulation by the producer. The early '78' records could not be edited at all, for once the zinc master was made, it had to be sent to the processing plant and a record pressed before the recording could be heard. But the recording and playback mechanisms had their own limitations, including an uneven response across the recorded spectrum and an extremely limited frequency range and duration.

The introduction of electrical recording in 1925 had several immediate consequences. First, the frequency range was broadened from an upper limit of 3 kHz (see Figure 14.3, discussed below) to about 5 kHz, the latter being sufficient for most of the essential acoustical information contained in mainstream classical music. Second, large ensembles could be recorded with something approaching a realistic balance, although for many years to come, microphones were to impose their own noticeable characteristics on the recorded sound. As electric recording developed, the possibilities of artificial balancing began to be exploited, most importantly by Leopold Stokowski, who tried all kinds of experiments with the seating of the orchestra and the control of balance in the search for an ideal sound.[5]

By the 1930s, several recording turntables were used so that a continuous performance could be captured without having to stop the performers every few minutes, and by 1940, the problem of timing had finally been solved by the use of tape for the masters.[6] The length of the tape was theoretically unlimited, and it could be spliced and edited in ways that were impossible with the '78' record. The age of the studio-manufactured recording began from this time. Since the 1960s, editing and recording have become so sophisticated that there is now little guarantee that any recording derives from a single performance, except for the explicitly 'live' recording. John Culshaw, the Decca producer responsible for the first complete *Ring* cycle (1959–65), celebrated the power of stereophonic recording to create performances impossible by any other means. Assembling the world's best singers and orchestras (for instance, the Vienna Philharmonic for his *Ring*), he achieved aural effects that would have been quite unobtainable in the theatre.[7] The problem, of course, is that live performances of the *Ring* tend to pale in comparison to the extraordinary presence of Culshaw's recording.

Post-war recordings display several different ideals of recorded sound. For a time in the 1960s, a very dry, 'close' acoustic was favoured; then came the fashion for an intrusive and artificial reverberation. In both cases, the dynamic levels and timbral qualities of the original performance were almost certainly manipulated in the recording process. More recently, some producers have sought a natural recorded sound, using a single pair of microphones placed at an appropriate distance from the ensemble. It is only in such recordings that the balance of the performance, as distinct from that of the recording, can sensibly be discussed.

A notorious problem in dealing with any recording is that the label may name different performers from those actually recorded. There is a piano roll purportedly of Ravel playing his *Miroirs* and other pieces, several of which are now known to have been performed by Robert Casadesus.[8] A more trivial example from the early 1950s was the dubbing of Kirsten Flagstad's top Cs in Act II of an EMI recording of *Tristan und Isolde* with Wilhelm Furtwängler. The Cs were actually sung by Elisabeth Schwarzkopf.[9]

Instruments and technique

One of the most interesting features of early recordings is the sound of the instruments then in use and the ways in which they were played. For instance, wooden flutes, with their mellow, boxy tone, were widely used by the senior British players up to the late 1950s but fell out of fashion in the next decades. Today they are returning to our orchestras, no doubt a response to period performance practices, but also, perhaps, to the dissemination of CD transcripts of LP recordings. The distinctive sound of French woodwinds can be heard in innumerable early records, such as Roger Désormière's wonderful discs of Debussy's *Pelléas et Mélisande*, made in Paris in 1941.[10] The sonorities are very different from those of today's instruments, yet poignantly beautiful; the oboe, associated with Mélisande throughout the opera, has a particular frailty that seems entirely appropriate to this role. In pre-war orchestral recordings we can still hear narrow-bore trombones and gut-stringed violins. Perhaps it will one day be common practice for mainstream performers to select their instruments according to the character of the composition, as many trumpeters do today; or by reverting to locally made instruments, orchestras might once again find a characteristic voice.

Early piano recordings are perhaps the most offensive to contemporary tastes. Most pianists prior to about 1925 seem perverse in the licence they take with the composer's notation, yet it is fascinating to hear the multiplicity of ways in which a chord can be arpeggiated,[11] or to observe the improvisatory nature of much of the playing, with middle voices brought out or cadenzas added with no cue from the score.[12] It is easy to condemn such practices, but much more interesting to try to understand and even emulate them. Our modern rule that we should play only what is written in the score becomes irrelevant when the composer's notation was not intended to be so restrictive. Of course, this does not mean that today's performer can safely ignore the composer's indications.

Case study 1: tempo and timing

Tempo poses a special set of problems, particularly in dealing with earlier recordings. It is often claimed that, because of the short duration of the shellac record, no reliable conclusions can be drawn concerning the original tempo from recordings before about 1950. Yet there is very little evidence that performers actually hurried their performances. What, then, can reliably be deduced about tempo from the evidence of recordings?

First, we need to differentiate between recordings made prior to about 1922, when the limit was roughly three minutes, and the later '78s', when the limit was well over four minutes. By far the majority of classical recordings from the acoustic era are of operatic arias, and these show the following general tendencies:

(1) The operatic excerpts are routinely cut to two-and-a-half minutes, suggesting that producers preferred to sacrifice sections of the aria rather than hurry the performers.
(2) Tempos are not obviously fast (except for certain moments of high emotional expression which tend to be performed less indulgently than today), and *parlando* and recitative sections tend to be taken at what we now regard as natural tempos.
(3) By modern standards, the tenutos at main cadences seem grossly and unnecessarily exaggerated, indicating no immediate concerns about the clock.

As we listen to Caruso's recordings or to Verdi's original Otello, Francesco Tamagno, singing choice moments from the opera in 1903, we experience performances that are wonderfully paced dramatically, with no hint, at least to modern ears, of either constraint or hurrying.[13]

There are reminiscences by musicians who speak of the discomforts of the early recording studios and the limitations of the three-minute 'take', but these usually date from many years after the event and do not override the evidence of the recordings themselves. In a useful discussion of this question,

John Steane compares durations of pre-war recordings with contemporary live performances by the same artists, finding that the recordings tended to take less time.[14] However, stage business usually requires extra time in a live performance, and his argument is by no means conclusive.

We shall probably never know whether certain fast tempos were caused by the side-length, but we do know that many of them were not. Robert Philip cites a number of instances where side-length could not have influenced tempo.[15] To these I would add the case of two early recordings of the slow movement of Beethoven's last quartet, Op. 135, which respectively are almost the fastest and certainly the slowest on record today. Beethoven marked the movement 'Lento assai, cantante e tranquillo' (see Example 14.1 below). The Flonzaley Quartet, recording in 1927, interpret this as a flowing ♪ = 58, assuming, in effect, a dotted-crotchet beat. In striking contrast, the Busch Quartet start at ♪ = 32. The Busch's 1934 recording occupies three sides instead of the usual two, but the Flonzaley's occupies only one-and-a-half sides, the remaining half side being blank. In other words, they had all the time they needed to linger over the movement, yet they actually accelerate towards the final cadence.[16]

José Bowen has made a careful analysis of tempo in the recordings of selected symphonic works, only to conclude that tempo has changed very little over a period of eighty years.[17] In fact, Bowen's method conceals changes that might have occurred over shorter periods of time. Figure 14.1 presents the tempos in bars 4–6 from thirty-five recordings of Beethoven's Lento assai, and it shows that although attitudes to tempos have followed certain tendencies over the years, these are hardly reducible to a simple formula.[18] Furthermore, the recordings that buck the trend may sometimes be the most interesting.

Much useful work on timing can be done with nothing more sophisticated than a stop-watch. Formal acoustic analysis exposes a fascinating world of rubato and tempo change, even in recent performances which seem to maintain a strict pulse. Figure 14.2 is a plot of the timing of each quaver beat of Example 14.1, as played by the Flonzaley Quartet and the Lindsays:[19] the higher the step, the shorter the beat (and thus the faster the tempo). It shows that the implicit *subito piano* in bars 7 and 8 is articulated by both ensembles by a marked prolongation of the third quaver beat, while the Flonzaleys hurry the fourth beat of bar 9, a mannerism that might sound careless or wayward today. Yet it is justified by the musical syntax, for the root-position tonic chord does not achieve closure. Interestingly, the Flonzaleys articulate the change of gear in Beethoven's theme between bars 3–6 and 7–9 far more explicitly than the Lindsays, who preserve a quiet, rather ominous calm throughout the section.

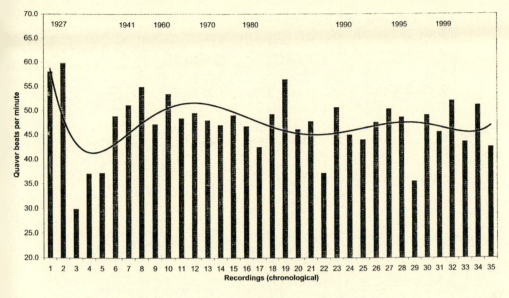

Quartets

1 Flonzaley (1927)	19 Orford (1985)
2 Léner (1927)	20 Vermeer (1985)
3 Busch (1934)	21 Guarneri (1987)
4 Toscanini (NBCO, 1938)	22 Lindsays (1987)
5 Budapest (1941)	23 Emerson (1988)
6 Loewenguth (1947)	24 Alban Berg (live, 1989)
7 Hungarian (1953)	25 Hagen (1990)
8 Hollywood (1957)	26 Medici (1991)
9 Fine Arts (c. 1960)	27 New Budapest (1991)
10 Janáček (1963)	28 Tokyo (1991)
11 Italiano (1968)	29 Bernstein (VPO, 1992)
12 Juilliard (1969)	30 Cleveland (1995)
13 Amadeus (1970)	31 Juilliard (1996)
14 Végh (1973)	32 Vanbrugh (1996)
15 La Salle (1976)	33 Alexander (1997)
16 Talich (1977)	34 Leipziger (1998)
17 Amadeus (1982)	35 Mosaïques (live, 1998)
18 Melos (1984)	

Figure 14.1 Initial tempos in thirty-five recordings of Beethoven, String Quartet in F major Op. 135, iii (Lento assai), bars 4–6, in chronological order; the wavy line plots approximate trends.

A question that is rarely asked is whether performances recorded on LP or CD have been affected by questions of timing: a cynic might assume that producers oblige their performers to hurry so that the music fits onto one side or one CD. I know of no evidence of this, but one example of a CD recording directly affecting the composition itself is Steve Reich's *Drumming*. This work originally ran for some three hours, yet is reduced to 58 minutes for the CD recorded by the composer's ensemble.[20] Whether the choice

Example 14.1 Beethoven, String Quartet in F major Op. 135, iii (Lento assai), bars 1–12

of using one CD rather than two was motivated by economic or artistic considerations, the result is an altogether new musical experience.

Case study 2: vibrato

Many aspects of playing technique are virtually unaffected by any recording technology, and one of these is vibrato.[21] For instruments and voices, vibrato is achieved by a combination of periodic fluctuations of amplitude, frequency and timbre. The earliest vocal recordings show that the modern style of continuous vibrato was already established among Italian singers at the turn of the century, but that many Northern European and American singers were still using an intermittent or very shallow vibrato up to the 1920s. Yet even the Italians in the early 1900s rarely indulged in the wide, slow undulations routinely heard in present-day opera houses. The voice of Caruso is characterised by a fast, continuous vibrato and a controlled but prominent use of portamento, as shown in Figure 14.3. This represents the c$\sharp^{1}$, f$\sharp$ and b of the well-known passage from *Tosca* reproduced

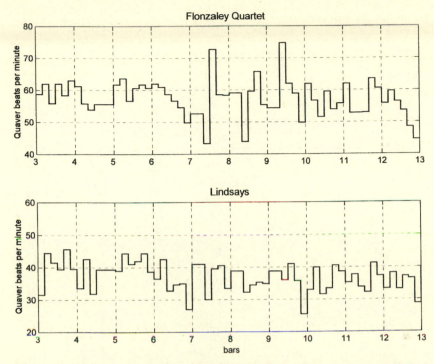

Figure 14.2 Timings in Beethoven, String Quartet in F major Op. 135, iii (Lento assai), bars 3–12, as recorded by the Flonzaley Quartet (1927) and the Lindsays (1987), measured in quaver beats per minute (i.e. metronomic values); the higher the step, the shorter the beat.

Example 14.2 Puccini, 'E lucevan le stelle', *Tosca*, Act 3, bars 20–1 (based on Ricordi vocal score, p. 290)

in Example 14.2. Each wavy line in the figure corresponds to one harmonic of the sounding note.[22]

There is an enormous amount of detail to be read from Figure 14.3. It is possible to make very precise measurements of the duration of each note, its timbral colour (which harmonics are strong or absent), modes of attack, and release and portamento. The affective falling away from the $c\sharp^1$ is clearly visible on the graph and measurable to about a major third. The main energy of the $c\sharp^1$ is focused on the second harmonic, $c\sharp^2$ (c. 550 Hz), the fundamental $c\sharp^1$ being almost entirely absent.[23] Figure 14.3 also shows the singer's

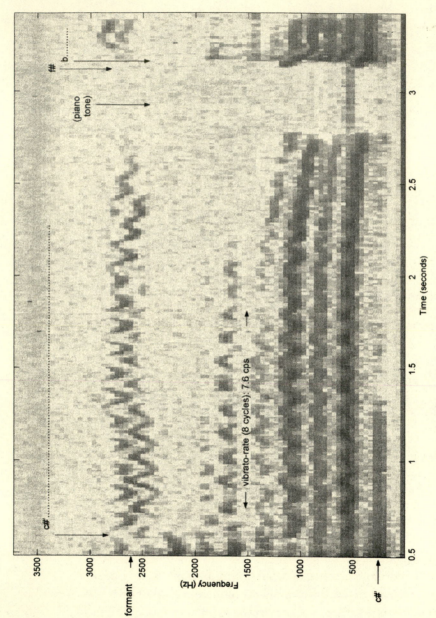

Figure 14.3 Spectogram of the boxed passage in Example 14.2. The wavy lines show each harmonic of the vocal tone; the faint straight lines represent piano tones. The tone is cut off at the tenth harmonic, c. 2770 Hz, which is $e\sharp^4$, two octaves above the top of the treble staff.

formant, that is, the 'buzz' that can be heard in all well-trained male voices. This lies in a frequency band around 2,600 Hz ($\approx$ d$\sharp^4$), where the wide, overlapping waves, caused by the vibrato, ensure that the formant is an almost continuous band of high sound. Finally, by counting the peaks of the wavy lines and measuring start- and end-points, it is easy to determine the vibrato rate as about 7.6 cycles per second (cps), as indicated between the two arrows.[24]

The earliest recordings of violinists came just in time to capture the end of a playing tradition that was to change dramatically in the twenty years from 1910 to 1930. Joachim's single set of records, made in 1904, illustrate a selective and highly undemonstrative use of vibrato, which is not part of the basic tone.[25] As regards woodwinds, recordings show that, before about 1930, vibrato was never employed except by certain flautists in the French tradition. Léon Goossens gives a graphic account of his attempts to introduce vibrato in the 1920s. Although he 'suffered a great deal of abuse and jibing from other players', his efforts were rewarded by Thomas Beecham, who selected him as first oboist for the new London Philharmonic Orchestra in 1932.[26] The first clarinettist in the same orchestra, Reginald Kell, quickly followed suit, and the effects of this revolution can be heard in many pre-war orchestral recordings. But some of the earliest orchestral recordings, such as Artur Nikisch and the Berlin Philharmonic in a remarkable rendition of Beethoven's Fifth Symphony from 1913, demonstrate just what a good woodwind section can achieve without vibrato.[27] Many recordings even from the 1950s demonstrate that much less vibrato was used than would become fashionable in the next decades.

No less fascinating is the use of vibrato on other instruments, such as the trumpet or bassoon. Of special interest is the history of vibrato on the French horn. In the first half of the century, Eastern European orchestras used it routinely and very expressively. Recordings of Czech and Soviet orchestras provide striking examples for the curious listener, and for the very brave horn player.[28]

Although vibrato is generally unaltered by the recording process, it may well be affected by the producer. Elisabeth Schwarzkopf testifies that her husband, Walter Legge (the doyen of post-war producers, and notorious for exacting the highest standards from his performers), was not afraid to complain when he heard the hated 'wobble'.[29] Legge produced most of the major EMI/HMV recordings of the 1950s, including many wonderful LPs of the Philharmonia, an orchestra he had founded specifically as a recording ensemble.

Interpretation of recordings

Recordings clearly reveal a wealth of information about changing performance practices through the twentieth century, of which I have barely scratched the surface. The larger question is how individual factors such as intonation, vibrato, timbre, balance, synchrony and mode of attack, accentuation, ornamentation[30] and, not least, structural control combine to generate the holistic listening experience offered by the recording itself. The best accounts of recordings at this level remain those of certain critics, who have developed a sophisticated language for dealing with the listening experience. Much critical work is spoilt by the childish game of trying to discover the 'definitive' recording or the 'best buy'. Comparing recordings is in fact an excellent method of revealing and celebrating the wonderful diversity of interpretations and personae revealed by the archive of recordings. And if, for the musicologist, the language of criticism is too imprecise, it can be supplemented and supported by acoustic analysis, as I have tried to show. Yet there is no music until the sounds of performance are interpreted, and the critic's language at least provides a basis for discussion of why a particular recording is musically so moving, or exciting, or magical, or just plain dull.[31]

There are many recordings in which the composer has been involved in the production or the performance. Sometimes, the composer has recorded the same work more than once, and these recordings make for fascinating comparisons. The inevitable differences between them suggest that a composer's single interpretation or 'approved' recording should never be taken as definitive. This is illustrated by the two recordings of Elgar's Violin Concerto conducted by the composer. The earlier one, made in 1916, is a heavily abridged and rescored version, which, although Elgar's own, hardly offers the modern listener a satisfying experience of the work itself. Yet the solo violin playing is fascinating. The soloist is Marie Hall, an English violinist respected on both sides of the Atlantic, and her recording reveals a most exquisite violin tone and a remarkable sensitivity of phrasing. It is interesting to compare her playing with the famous 1932 recording by the young Yehudi Menuhin.[32] Menuhin's technique is essentially modern: the 'spun' tone depends on a tight, continuous vibrato; the playing is forward and virtuosic; and each phrase is expressed in a rhetorical manner which perhaps betrays Menuhin's youth, yet is not substantially different from a modern violinist's approach.

Hall's more lyrical approach is arguably closer to the spirit of Elgar's score. Her playing is suffused with that poignancy and sense of loss that seems proper to Elgar's music, as indeed to so much English art and literature of the early twentieth century. And although Elgar expressed unqualified delight at

Menuhin's playing, he could not have imagined such playing when he wrote the work in 1910, for the modern style did not then exist. His ideal of violin performance, and even of the work itself, must therefore have changed as playing styles developed in the 1920s. Even so, Hall shows that such changes are not necessarily beneficial, and that playing Elgar's Concerto does not have to be the high-octane affair it often is today.

The wider influence of recordings

The influence of recording on our wider musical practices is only beginning to be recognised.[33] Has music come to be conceived as more abstract, disembodied and ideal as a result of the invisibility of its performers on records, or have recording methods merely responded to current ideologies of what music ought to be? One thing is clear: we need to resist the facile option of assuming that a given recording presents 'the work itself' in any authoritative sense. Post-war works are particularly vulnerable to this tendency. When they are known from a single recording and are rarely performed live, it is easy to assume that the idiosyncrasies or even the incompetencies of the recorded performance are what the work is, that the recording is 'how the work goes'. Multiple recordings allow us to explore the work as a many-faceted object, or even as something not materially determined until it is read or performed.[34]

Hindemith once claimed that every performance is a corruption of the work, but recordings demonstrate the importance of the performer's voice as a complement to the composer's. It is through the performer's persona – and perhaps the producer's as well – that 'the work itself' comes alive and acquires particular musical meanings. Each recording is a unique artistic creation achieved by a synthesis of composition, performance and particular recording methods. Little wonder, then, that recorded music has played such a central role in our musical culture over the last hundred years. With the advent of new formats such as very high digital sampling and internet broadcasting, we can look forward to an equally exciting and influential future for classical music recording in the coming decades.

Notes

1 See Nicholas Cook, *Music: A Very Short Introduction* (Oxford: Oxford University Press, 1998), 13.

2 See Edward T. Cone, *The Composer's Voice* (Berkeley: University of California Press, 1974). On performance 'as a species of acting' see Joel Lester, 'Performance and analysis: interaction and interpretation', in John Rink (ed.), *The Practice of*

Performance: Studies in Musical Interpretation (Cambridge: Cambridge University Press, 1995), 213; see also chapters 7 and 11 in this volume.

3 For two recent examples, see Ronald Woodley, 'Strategies of irony in Prokofiev's Violin Sonata in F minor Op. 80', in Rink, *Practice of Performance*, 170, and Peter Johnson, 'Performance and the listening experience: Bach's "Erbarme dich"', in Nicholas Cook, Peter Johnson and Hans Zender (eds.), *Theory into Practice: Composition, Performance and the Listening Experience* (Leuven: Leuven University Press, 1999), 55–101.

4 For a general history of recording, see Michael Chanan, *Repeated Takes: A Short History of Recording and its Effects on Music* (London: Verso, 1995).

5 See Ronald Gelatt, *The Fabulous Phonograph: 1877–1977* (London: Collier Macmillan, 1977), 236.

6 See Joseph Horowitz, *Understanding Toscanini: A Social History of American Concert Life* (London: Faber and Faber, 1987) for a fine critical discussion of the tapes of three complete operas recorded at Salzburg in 1937.

7 For discussion, see John Culshaw, *Ring Resounding: The Recording of 'Der Ring des Nibelungen'* (London: Secker & Warburg, 1967).

8 See Roger Nichols's editorial notes in the Peters Urtext edition of *Miroirs* (1991).

9 Culshaw, *Ring Resounding*, 55.

10 CD transcript on EMI CHS 7 61038 2.

11 For a technical discussion of asynchrony, see Carl E. Seashore, *Psychology of Music* (New York: Dover, [1938] 1967), 248–53.

12 The most important early pianists can be heard in the series *Great Pianists of the 20th Century*. Rachmaninoff's recordings are on RCA 09026 61265.

13 Tamagno's complete recordings are in the Pearl Opal collection, CD 9846.

14 John Steane, *The Grand Tradition: Seventy Years of Singing on Record, 1900–1970*, 2nd edn (London: Duckworth, 1993), 10.

15 Robert Philip, *Early Recordings and Musical Style: Changing Tastes in Instrumental Performance, 1900–1950* (Cambridge: Cambridge University Press, 1992), 35–6.

16 The Flonzaley's recording is on Biddulph LAB 089-90, the Busch's on EMI CHS 65306-2.

17 José A. Bowen, 'Finding the music in musicology: performance history and musical works', in Nicholas Cook and Mark Everist (eds.), *Rethinking Music* (Oxford: Oxford University Press, 1999), 435.

18 The curved trend-line in Figure 14.1 (a sixth-order polynomial) is an attempt to track averages over shorter periods.

19 'The Lindsays' is the official title of this quartet. The timings come from ASV CD DCS 403.

20 Nonesuch CD, 979 170-2.

21 The terms 'vibrato' and 'tremolo' have variously been used to refer to aspects of what I am collectively calling vibrato: see Seashore, *Psychology of Music*, 33.

22 Figure 14.3 is from the CD transcript *Enrico Caruso, The Puccini Recordings (1902–1916)*, Vocal Archives, VA 1216, track 10 at 1' 46".

23 That the fundamental does not need to be present is proved by psychoacoustic tests. For a similar case in a violin tone, see Seashore, *Psychology of Music*, 98. Johnson, 'Performance' provides a more detailed discussion of my methods.

24 Except for some soubrettes, few operatic singers today have a vibrato faster than 5 cps; more mature voices typically oscillate at a rate of 2 or 3 cps. The conclusions reached about vibrato in John Steane's fine critical analysis of twentieth-century singing can be verified by the methods I have illustrated; for example see Steane, *Grand Tradition*, 135.

25 Pearl's *Great Virtuosi of the Golden Age*, vol. I (GEMM CD 9101) includes tracks from Joachim, Ysaÿe, Elman and Sarasate. Joachim was seventy-two at the time of his recording, having been born in 1831.

26 Léon Goossens and Edwin Roxburgh, *Yehudi Menuhin Music Guides: Oboe*, 2nd edn (London: Macdonald, 1980), 87.

27 A CD transcript is on DG 453 804-2GCB6. The second movement is especially interesting in this respect.

28 A beautiful example of Czech orchestral horn playing is in the slow movement of the 1938 recording of Dvořák's Cello Concerto with Pablo Casals and George Szell, remastered on EMI CDH 7 63498 2. This recording is said to have been a favourite of Fred Gaisberg, who was the leading producer for HMV from the first Caruso recordings of 1902 to his retirement in 1939.

29 Elisabeth Schwarzkopf, *On and Off the Record: A Memoir of Walter Legge* (London: Faber and Faber, 1982), 19.

30 For a fine study of ornamentation on record, see Will Crutchfield's 'Vocal ornamentation in Verdi: the phonographic evidence', *19th-Century Music*, 7 (1983), 3–54.

31 I discuss this question in Johnson, 'Performance', 97ff.

32 Hall's recording is on Pearl GEMM CDS 9951/5, Menuhin's on EMI CDC 5 55221-2.

33 Two books that begin to grapple with this question are Chanan, *Repeated Takes*, and Evan Eisenberg, *The Recording Angel: Music, Records and Culture from Aristotle to Frank Zappa* (London: Picador, 1987).

34 See Lester, 'Performance and analysis', 214.

Further reading

Chanan, Michael, *Repeated Takes: A Short History of Recording and its Effects on Music* (London: Verso, 1995)

Cook, Nicholas, Peter Johnson and Hans Zender (eds.), *Theory into Practice: Composition, Performance and the Listening Experience* (Leuven: Leuven University Press, 1999)

Day, Timothy, *A Century of Recorded Music* (New Haven: Yale University Press, 2000)

Eisenberg, Evan, *The Recording Angel: Music, Records and Culture from Aristotle to Frank Zappa* (London: Picador, 1987)

Horowitz, Joseph, *Understanding Toscanini: A Social History of American Concert Life* (London: Faber and Faber, 1987)

Philip, Robert, *Early Recordings and Musical Style: Changing Tastes in Instrumental Performance, 1900–1950* (Cambridge: Cambridge University Press, 1992)

15   The criticism of musical performance

RAYMOND MONELLE

Considered as a serious form of writing, the concert notice is a relatively new thing. Until quite recently there was a prejudice against it; it was
beneath the attention of sophisticated persons. One could write about music
theory, about styles and fashions and influence, about new compositions.
But there was something degraded and sneaky about criticising concerts and
performers. Even a distinguished critic like William J. Henderson declared:
'We are confronted by the demand of the interpretative artist. Of this any
one who places the function of criticism upon a high plane would wish to
say very little. The consideration of the performer is the least important
office of real criticism.'[1] The great musical writer Ernest Newman argued
in a 1931 newspaper review that repeat performances of well-known works
gave the critic nothing to do:

The Promenade Concerts, though rich in delights for the plain music-lover, still
present the minimum of pretext to the critic to air his views, for the programmes
are mostly given up to works of the most familiar kind. There has been during the
past week a Wagner night, a Beethoven night, a Brahms night, and a Tchaikovski
night; and as none of these composers has written much lately, there have been no
new works for the critic to exercise his infallible judgement upon.[2]

Perhaps because of this prejudice, the story of performance criticism
is rather different from that of general music criticism. Most histories of
criticism concentrate on the judging of *compositions*, especially new ones,
and the standard anthologies of critics like Eduard Hanslick and Bernard
Shaw naturally give most space to those masterworks that were new in their
day. Strange to say, the narrative of this familiar aspect of musical life, the
performance review, has still to be written.

Yet today, this kind of writing dominates music criticism. How has this
change come about? Clearly, the sharp decline in the performance of contemporary music has led critics to concentrate on performing artists; in
the eighteenth century, much of the music heard was fresh from the composer's pen. Furthermore, instrumentalists were often also composers; they

performed their own works, and critics naturally concentrated on the works, rather than the performances. But as the canon of classic works solidified – largely with the help of music critics – multiple performances of canonic works revealed the extent to which the performer contributes to the experience of music. At first (this is especially evident in the writings of Shaw) it was acceptable to make remarks, even unfavourable ones, about music already accepted into the canon, but in modern times, when most works performed are canonic, critics are not expected to praise Handel or grumble about Brahms, as Shaw did. They are meant to concentrate on the performer.

The very earliest music criticism in specialised periodicals like Johann Mattheson's *Critica musica* (Hamburg, 1722–5) or Lorenz Mizler's *Neu eröffnete musikalische Bibliothek* (Leipzig, 1736–54) contains very little assessment of performance. One sometimes comes across general assessments of a performer's style, but seldom are actual concert or opera reviews published. But towards the end of the eighteenth century, reports of opera productions might provide shrewd descriptions of the singers; for instance the Berlin *Litteratur- und Theater-Zeitung* of 1781 includes many reports of operas. In that year it reported a visit to Berlin of the bass Ludwig Fischer, the first Osmin in Mozart's *Die Entführung* (1782):

Herr Fischer, Imperial and Royal Singer, stayed here for a few days; he twice played the messenger in *Zémire et Azor* [by Grétry], and on one occasion between the acts sang two arias by Holzbauer from the grand opera *Günther von Schwarzburg*. Every connoisseur wondered at the purity and range of his voice, and the whole public was enchanted by his altogether pleasing performance and the great facility of his throat . . . [3]

This is primitive criticism, neither showing nor demanding any sophisticated knowledge of music or singing.

The first journal of really wide influence was the Leipzig weekly *Allgemeine musikalische Zeitung* (*AmZ*),[4] which first appeared in 1798. The editor, Friedrich Rochlitz, quickly realised that readers wanted more than the general articles and reviews of new works that had characterised previous publications. Early issues occasionally contained 'correspondence' from the German musical centres, Berlin, Vienna, Dresden and so on, sometimes (but not always) with comments on actual concerts. By 1800 these had crystallised into regular *Nachrichten* (news), in which the concert and operatic life of the German cities was described, often with detailed accounts of performers, especially singers. The following 1802 review of a concert which featured the cellist Nikolaus Kraft, a member of the Schuppanzigh Quartet, shows experience of many players and an understanding of the instrument, as well as a strong view of what constitutes good playing:

He is a very notable violoncellist; his tone is not of that dull and nasal type which one so often gets to hear on this instrument, but powerful, manly, full (fat, as musicians say); his playing is swift, assured, precise, delicate and pure (apart from a few details in the most distant registers, which were not entirely successful); he knows admirably how to handle his bow . . . [5]

This is an actual review of a concert, rather than a general essay on an artist's style such as had been common in the previous century.

This journal eventually came to print some of the most detailed and judicious reviews of performance ever published, demanding of its readership a professional knowledge of instruments, technique and style, as we see from an *AmZ* review from 28 April 1830 of a fine violinist, Heinrich Wilhelm Ernst:

Herr Ernst, still a young man, possesses all the resources which, combined with the iron of his obviously exceptional diligence, might set him in a few years on the way to becoming one of the greatest living artists; for he has unusual facility in passagework, leaps, double stops and the like, together with a powerful, pure tone and nimble bow-control; his performance in an Adagio, if not entirely to be praised, is not to be despised. But it is to be regretted that Herr Ernst, without knowing it, is on a false artistic track, in that he seems to be just an imitator, and wants to play *à la Paganini.*[6]

This is not a review for the ordinary reader. The *AmZ* clearly expected its readers to possess some inside knowledge of instrumental technique. The true craft of popular music journalism had yet to be discovered.

The publication of musical commentary in daily newspapers, as opposed to weeklies or monthlies, began after the turn of the nineteenth century, probably with J. C. F. Rellstab's reviews (1808–13) in the Berlin *Vossische Zeitung*. In London and Paris the newspaper review – the main focus of modern criticism – grew out of the theatre notice. In fact, Julien-Louis Géoffroy (1743–1814), who wrote drama criticism for the Paris *Journal des débats*, made a parade of his ignorance of music, though he frequently reviewed operas.

In the early years of the nineteenth century *The Times* sometimes carried reviews of the shows at the main London theatres, including operas. At first these were written by a theatre critic, Barron Field, or by the manager of the paper, T. M. Alsager. Later, in 1843, a real music critic was appointed, Charles Lamb Kenney. For a time, however, this made no great difference; the reviews, still unsigned, continued to comment on the audiences and the ladies' dresses, and there was very little criticism of music apart from opera. When a concert review did appear, the comments were brief and generalised – as in the following account of a performance at the Birmingham Festival on 19 September 1843, conducted by William Knyvett, with the contralto Maria Hawes and Knyvett's wife Deborah Travis singing: 'Mrs Knyvett gave "Pious orgies" [from Handel's *Judas Maccabaeus*] with great accuracy and purity of style. Her performance of Handel's music remains as perfect as ever. The beautiful air "Jehovah crown'd" was assigned to Miss Hawes, who sang it with power but, perhaps, in some passages, too much laboured energy.'[7] It was not yet considered that *The Times*'s readers were ready for more detailed or sensitive musical comment.

At the same time, a development was taking place in Paris which would determine the future of the performance notice. In 1827 François-Joseph Fétis, librarian of the Paris Conservatoire and afterwards director of the Conservatoire in Brussels, founded the weekly *Revue musicale*, a serious and responsible journal which included concert reviews among its general articles on music. Most of each issue was written by the indefatigable Fétis, who took his duties very seriously, writing in a heavy, uncompromising style. The poet Heinrich Heine, who himself wrote music criticism for the Augsburg *Allgemeine musikalische Zeitung*, commented: 'I know of nothing more uninspiring than a criticism by M. Fétis . . . composed in a particular slang and sprinkled with technical terms of which the ordinary educated reader is ignorant.'[8] A measure of Fétis's prosy style may be got from a concert review in the very first issue (February 1827):

The concert began with the first movement of that symphony of Haydn of which the opening is in D minor, the allegro in D major [No. 104]. A missed entry in the bassoons in the introduction marred its effect. The first part of the allegro was well executed, but in the second, so lively and vigorous, the orchestra lacked warmth and verve. Several fluctuations of tempo prevented the violins from playing together, and the basses, being too few in number, lacked energy in the moment of explosion [the tutti at bar 32?].

In opposition to this worthy publication, the publisher Maurice Schlesinger set up the *Gazette musicale de Paris* in 1834. So successful was the rival that the *Revue musicale* soon amalgamated with it. The writers for the *Gazette*, who included prominent figures like Berlioz, Liszt, Wagner, Castil-Blaze and Joseph d'Ortigue, affected a new, witty style derived from the drama critic's *feuilleton*, eschewing technical language in favour of impressionism, ridicule, cultured reference and personal opinion. Most articles were now signed by their authors. This was true journalism, but its best exemplars were reserved for general articles and reviews of new works.

The ordinary concert reviews in the *Gazette* were increasingly written by the playwright, composer and violinist Henri Blanchard (who became contributing editor in 1836), rather than these celebrities. The bravura of the *Gazette*'s famous *feuilletons* did not quite penetrate to Blanchard's bread-and-butter reviews; nevertheless he developed an authentic style of music journalism, evocative, non-technical and breezy. It is perhaps from the reviews of Blanchard and his successor Adolphe Botte that the modern craft of concert reviewing developed. On 5 December 1847, Blanchard described a concert at the Salle Herz at which a Mozart quartet – apparently K. 589 in B♭ major – was performed:

The execution . . . was perfect. The elder M. Tilmant [the leader] does not take too literally (and he does well) the phrase 'chamber music' which seems to be applied exclusively to intimate music performed in a small space. His broad, orchestral manner gives a kind of symphonic amplitude to a quartet that some of our violinists make pretty, small-scale and niggardly. It is desirable, in order to make it sound passionate and expressive – the characteristic signs of modern musical performance – that in certain melodic closes there be flexible treatment of that precision, that strictness of beat, which in the end gives a kind of mechanical aridity to the musical thought and sometimes deprives it of the inspiration and poetry that must have animated the composer when he wrote it.

The *Gazette musicale* was widely read and from early on began to influence musical life and make or break careers. To quote Heine again: 'The most celebrated artists lay submissively at Schlesinger's feet, crawling and wagging their tails, to get good criticism in his magazine.'[9] One of the contributors was Ludwig Rellstab, son of the critic of the *Vossische Zeitung*, who knew a little about the reactions of performers to his criticisms: his Berlin article of 1826 on the singer Henrietta Sontag had got him into trouble with the authorities, and he was imprisoned for three months in the fortress of Spandau, the first music-critical martyr.[10]

In London, also, the power of the musical press became apparent. In 1846 *The Times* appointed its first professionally trained music critic, J. W. Davison. This idiosyncratic writer soon began to acquire enormous power over the music profession.[11] He comes across in his reviews as an indulgent and generous critic, praising even those artists whose deficiencies he was bound also to record. Thus, his review of *Lucia di Lammermoor* at the Royal Italian Opera, Covent Garden, in 1847, with Fanny Tacchinardi-Persiani and Lorenzo Salvi, is a characteristic combination of high discernment and an unwillingness to say anything unfavourable about anyone:

That excessively neat and delicate execution of a profusion of ornament, that distinctness given to every note in the most rapid passages, the varity [*sic*] of colouring – the facility with which all was done, were the same as ever. Persiani's singing has over and over been compared to playing of a delicate instrument by a finished artist . . . In the second act, there might perhaps be observed some of those slight faults of intonation which were formerly known in the otherwise perfect singer, but the defect was only transient . . .

The debut of Salvi as Edgardo was perhaps the most interesting event of the evening, and his success must have answered the expectations of his warmest admirers. His voice is a pure tenor of extended compass, not remarkable for volume, but perfectly equal in every part, and possessed of the greatest flexibility. This organ he manages with the skill of a consummate artist, introducing into it the nicest varieties of light and shade, and making it eloquent with dramatic expression. Perhaps his greatest skill as a vocalist is shown in his piano passages, so completely is the voice subdued, without detriment to the value of the notes.[12]

The style and beauties of both singers are excellently portrayed – though perhaps unreliably. An ugly rumour had spread that Davison accepted bribes, and on this occasion Persiani's husband Giuseppe, who was manager of the theatre, might have influenced Davison's judgement. At any rate, when Francis Hueffer succeeded Davison in 1879, it was alleged that he 'had to engage a four-wheeled cab to carry back to distinguished musicians the presents which were brought to his door'.[13] The currying of favour with critics is an activity which has always dogged the musical world: though crude bribery has perhaps disappeared from the scene, critics may be not above accepting party invitations and free accommodation even today.

The pedantic and over-serious critic of the Fétis stamp had no future in a world where everyone was reading about music. Criticism had become a literary form. But some great critics still adopted an oracular tone and a lofty decorum. One was Eduard Hanslick, professor of music history and aesthetics at the University of Vienna. Hanslick wrote concert reviews from 1855, and in 1864 he began contributing to the *Neue freie Presse*, a daily newspaper that was read not only in Austria but also throughout Germany. Hanslick's piece normally appeared on the front page. Nowadays he is chiefly remembered for his hostility to Wagner and for his aesthetic pamphlet of 1854, *Vom Musikalisch-Schönen* (On the Musically Beautiful). But in his day he dominated European music criticism. His writings combined profound knowledge with a grave but easy style, relying on evocative description rather than technical analysis. He wrote clearly, precisely, elegantly, with sharp discernment and high aesthetic standards; but he is always good to read. When the pianist Rafael Joseffy gave a recital in 1874, Hanslick found that the poetic essence of the music was lost in a desire for technical perfection:

The poetic treasure . . . remained generally obscured. Does he lack the secret resonance of the spirit, or is it the pure pleasure of virtuosity which thus constrains him? He played Schumann's *Traumeswirren,* one of the composer's most gracious little poems, as if it were an *étude* whose objective was the utmost velocity and the ultimate degree of *pianissimo* – almost in the manner of a musical clock. Even the wonderful middle movement, that characteristically veiled, misty centre of the dream, was over-exposed to morning sunlight. It was the same with Schumann's wonderful Novellette in D, opus 21, no. 4; we saw the ballroom but not the touching love story enacted there.[14]

Such sensitivity to the poetic magic of music is unexpected, perhaps, from the notorious proponent of aesthetic formalism.

It is quite another case with Hanslick's younger contemporary Bernard Shaw, who wrote music criticism between 1876 and 1894 for *The Hornet, The Star* (in which he called himself 'Corno di Bassetto') and finally *The World,* a weekly magazine. Shaw combined a real genius for music criticism with a monstrous irresponsibility. He was vulgar, insulting, hilarious, capricious and unjust, and the standard of his performance reviews was sometimes lamentable. He liked to pretend musical ignorance, but in fact his knowledge of repertoire was extensive and he understood music-making well, especially singing, since his mother was a singer. In place of the air of learning that underpins Hanslick's writings, there is a suggestion of the *vox populi*; Shaw speaks of the price of the programmes, an engine breakdown on the railway, a visit to the dentist as though these were as important as the concert.

His prejudices are notorious. He disliked Brahms and Bruch, worshipped Wagner, was mean about Mendelssohn and admired Hermann Goetz. But his reviews of performances are sometimes maddening. Again and again, Shaw writes several thousand words on an oratorio or a set of concerts without saying more than that the performances were execrable, or excellent, mixed in with much commentary on the backwardness of the French or the plague of lady violinists. He always, invariably, has an axe to grind. He criticises a concert of Joachim with no other object than to tell us that we should not listen to Bruch's Violin Concerto. He discusses the singing of Adelina Patti only to prove that Wagner, sung properly, does not exhaust the voice.

Shaw's extraordinary brilliance and wit, then, are only marginally relevant to a study of performance criticism. Actually, he could write acutely and perceptively on performance when it took his fancy. In the following extract from a review of Beethoven's Ninth Symphony, conducted by George Henschel, he shows a deep knowledge of the work and a superb sympathy for Beethoven's style, but he cannot resist ridicule in his closing words:

As to Mr Henschel and his performance of the Ninth Symphony last Thursday, when I say that he quite understood the nature of the work, and was not for a moment in danger of the old fundamental error of treating it as mere musical arabesque, I imply that the performance was a success . . . Our minds were soon set at ease as to Mr Henschel's grasp of the situation by the vigour and decision with which we got the first subject, especially those two final bars with which Beethoven so powerfully clinches it . . .

Mr Henschel, like Ibsen's Master Builder, and like all good conductors, has a troll in him; and this troll occasionally takes to rampaging and filibustering, at which seasons Mr Henschel will not only tolerate, and even relish, rough and blatant attacks on imposing passages, but will overdrive his band . . . Now Beethoven must have known well that this was one of the common faults of the qualities he required in a conductor; and it seems clear to me that it was his dread lest any vulgar urgency or excitement should mar the grandeur of his symphonic masterpiece that led him to give the *tempo* of the first movement not merely as *allegro*, but as '*allegro*, but not too much so – rather majestically' . . .

Later on, Mr Henschel rather astonished some of us by the apparently very slow tempo he adopted for the *allegro assai*, in which the basses give out the theme of the Ode to Joy. We are so accustomed to hear this played exactly twice too fast, as if the minims and crotchets were quavers and semiquavers, and treated as a Haydn *allegro* instead of as an expressive melody, that some of the older listeners felt a little indignant with Mr Henschel for not taking the usual wrong course . . .

[During the slow movement, a lady in the chorus became faint, leading to] the proffering of fans and smelling-bottles, the commotion among gallant tenors and basses at the back, and the final desperate rally of the patient, and her triumphant postponement of her collapse to the top of the steep ladder at the other side of the door. During all which the band might have been playing Pop Goes the Weasel with no more fear of detection than if we had all been a St John's Ambulance class . . . [15]

Shaw's successor as Britain's leading music critic was Ernest Newman, the pen name of William Roberts, who wrote for the *Manchester Guardian*, the *Birmingham Daily Post*, the *Observer* and finally the *Sunday Times* during a long career from 1905 to 1958. Where Shaw was an *enfant terrible*, Newman was humane and august. Even his pseudonym was an expression of his beliefs; he saw himself as a new kind of critic, serious and judicious. However, Newman's masterpieces were his learned essays on general subjects; his actual performance reviewing was commonplace.

Much more personal and witty were the reviews of Virgil Thomson in the *New York Herald Tribune*. Thomson was an eminent composer, of course; as a critic, he was heir to a distinguished tradition of American musical writing which had included magnificent critics like Henry T. Finck, who wrote for the *The Nation* and the New York *Evening Post* between 1881 and 1924; the cultivated William J. Henderson,[16] writing for the *New York Times* and the *Sun* between 1887 and 1937; and Thomson's contemporary Olin Downes, whose pieces for the *New York Times* influenced music history (for example, he helped to establish Sibelius as a canonic figure).

George Szell's approach to Beethoven's Fifth led Thomson to examine the moral content of this symphony:

An energizing moral result is more valuable than any misreading of the composer's specific thought is dangerous. Besides, the piece will recover from its present military service just as easily as it has from its past metaphysical and political associations . . .

In order to throw the symphony into a key of direct action, Mr Szell has been obliged to emphasize the assertiveness of the masculine material and to sort of slip over the significance of its tender and gentle passages. He made the strings play loud and rough, with that fierce impact that the Philharmonic strings achieve so admirably . . . With the appearance of the trombones, at the beginning of the last movement, the horns appeared as hopelessly outclassed in the weight-throwing contest as the woodwinds had been from the beginning. The whole disequilibrium made Beethoven sound no end authoritative and didactic as a composer, which he certainly was, but hopelessly incompetent as an orchestrator, which he was not. And it is exactly the musical ineffectiveness of the orchestral contrasts that proved, in spite of the moral impressiveness of the rendering, that violence was being done to the spirit of the work, whatever one may consider this to be.[17]

Such a combination of performance criticism with a profound insight into the moral content of the work itself is rare indeed.

In Germany, criticism remained in the hands of eminent practising musicians and music professors. Their style was dignified, authoritative and weighty rather than witty or elegant. Heinrich Ehrlich, who wrote for the *Berliner Tageblatt* from 1878 to 1898, was a distinguished pianist. His counterpart in Hamburg, Max Loewengard, was a professor of music theory. The most notable of this group was the musicologist Alfred Einstein, who produced criticism for the *Berliner Tageblatt* until 1933, as well as revising Köchel's catalogue of Mozart and publishing a definitive book on the Italian madrigal.

In more recent times, music criticism has become less oracular, less *ex cathedra*. Nowadays, critics with heavy axes to grind are not really acceptable; one is expected to concentrate on the performer, not on one's pet theories about the music itself. However, two tendencies have blighted the art of music journalism. First, the lavish space allotted to the music critic has contracted; only a few journals, like the *New Yorker*, have continued to reserve thousands of words – such as Shaw or Hanslick could command – for musical writing. Modern critics, competing for space with pop music, film, radio and record reviews and above all with advertisements, must often express their views in 500 words or less.

Second, the ease of transport has tended to centralise music reviewing to leading cities. If an orchestra gives the same concert in several centres, or an opera company tours an opera to different theatres, a national newspaper like *The Times* will naturally review it only once. This has caused the decline of great provincial newspapers, or their removal to the capital. A similar process has been observed in other countries, notably the United States.

But in any case, the accepted journalistic style has changed. The quirky, dignified, gentlemanly writing of Ernest Newman has given way to a kind of laconic crispness, clever rather than learned, bantering rather than witty, streetwise rather than authoritative. Instead of the majestic sweep of a long review article, the best critics aim now for the memorable one-liner. Commenting on a performance by the guitarist Carlos Bonell of an eleventh-century Mozarabic chant, that admirable stylist Hilary Finch found the music 'turning in tiny pentatonic circles, plucked out just below the sound-hole in a coppery voice which seemed to come from beyond time itself'.[18]

Perhaps the most important change of emphasis in modern criticism is the discovery of the 'interpretation'. Where earlier critics wished to praise or condemn, or at least to assess the performer's realisation of the composer's 'intentions', contemporary writers have acknowledged that the performer adds his or her personality and thoughts to the work. Thus, there may be many different renderings of the same piece, all worthy in their own ways. Joan Chissell, reviewing a Mahler series for *The Times*, noticed that Otto Klemperer and Jascha Horenstein approached the composer differently:

[Mahler's First Symphony] is youthful Mahler, and Mr Horenstein made it sound young. With the repeat in the first movement, the performance lasted an hour, but time sped by because rhythms were so buoyant and textures so translucent. Whereas Dr Klemperer in the seventh last week stood back objectively and for the most part left detail to look after itself, Mr Horenstein did just the reverse; everything was very precisely phrased and coloured, yet always without the slightest trace of emotional inflation.[19]

There is no suggestion that Horenstein, or Klemperer, had got closer to the 'real' spirit of Mahler; merely that their personalities were different. This attitude has been encouraged by the availability of recordings, which permit the objective comparison of different interpretations. Andrew Porter, when drafting a later review of Mahler's Ninth Symphony, went out and bought a record of Bruno Walter's rendering in order to compare it with the version he had just heard conducted by Pierre Boulez. He was surprised to find that Boulez's tempos were very similar to Walter's, though the impression was quite different.[20]

Finally, critics acknowledge different styles of performance of canonic works; no longer is one style right, another wrong. In August 1999, a reviewer in the *Independent* adjudged Alfred Brendel a 'Classical' pianist, implying that there are other kinds of pianist whose playing might, on another occasion, be just as good:

Classical music, and classical performance, are not really a question of what you do, more of what you don't do. Alfred Brendel is, perhaps, the world's leading Classical pianist. He does not join a short breathless delay to every important note. He does not insert an emotional swell into the middle of every phrase. He does not play fast passages too fast, or slow passages too slow. And when the score says you have to repeat a section, he repeats it.

The result is narrative rather than expressive. You find yourself following an enthralling story rather than being emotionally lifted up. Everything is delivered with the utmost refinement, and he never once plays a cliché, even when the composer writes one.[21]

Critics are sometimes cursed by performers and their supporters for being irresponsible, striving for mere effect, taking lightly the devoted work of serious artists. Most musical writers would repudiate these charges. They are honest people, and usually write from the heart. Naturally, they must engage the interest of their readers; music criticism cannot be written in the same style as financial reports or boxing commentaries, though most of us have learned some useful lessons from sports writers.[22] Critics are also sometimes accused, by dissenters from their views, of reporting just 'one person's opinion'. But that, of course, is the sole and proper mission of music criticism. As Shaw knew, one's most resolute enemies will still buy the newspaper in order to read one's words and curse one afresh.

Notes

1 *Musical Quarterly*, 1/1 (1915), 75.
2 *The Sunday Times*, 30 August 1931.
3 *Litteratur- und Theater-Zeitung*, 4/1 (1781), 52; all translations are mine except where otherwise indicated.
4 A. B. Marx founded a Berlin magazine of the same name in 1824.
5 *AmZ*, 28 April 1802, 498–9.
6 *AmZ*, 28 April 1830, 270. Ernst, who was later praised by Berlioz, Joachim and Mendelssohn, was performing in Stuttgart.

7   *The Times*, 20 September 1843.
8   Quoted from Max Graf, *Composer and Critic: 200 Years of Musical Criticism* (London: Chapman & Hall, 1947), 217.
9   Quoted from ibid., 218.
10 See ibid., 173–4.
11 By 1851 *The Times*'s circulation had reached 40,000; see ibid., 260.
12 *The Times*, 14 April 1847.
13 *The History of The Times. Part 2: The Tradition Established, 1841–1884* (London: Office of The Times, 1939), 445.
14 Quoted from Henry Pleasants (trans. and ed.), *Eduard Hanslick, Music Criticism 1846–99* (Harmondsworth: Penguin, 1950), 123–4.
15 *The World*, 8 March 1893; quoted from Bernard Shaw, *G.B.S. on Music*, with a foreword by Alec Robertson (Harmondsworth: Penguin, 1962), 118–20. The review might contain a sly dig at Hanslick, who had described music as an 'arabesque'.
16 Henderson's high-and-mighty view of performance criticism was quoted at the beginning of this chapter.
17 *New York Herald Tribune*, 18 March 1945; quoted from Virgil Thomson, *The Art of Judging Music* (New York: Greenwood Press, 1969), 140–1.
18 *The Times*, 28 December 1999.
19 *The Times*, 9 October 1968.
20 Andrew Porter, *Music of Three Seasons, 1974–1977* (London: Chatto & Windus, 1979), 427–8; the review was published in *The New Yorker*, 8 November 1976.
21 *The Independent*, 30 August 1999.
22 Ernest Newman wrote about sport as well as music, and Neville Cardus had two careers, writing on music and cricket.

Further reading

Cone, Edward T., 'The pianist as critic', in John Rink (ed.), *The Practice of Performance: Studies in Musical Interpretation* (Cambridge: Cambridge University Press, 1995), 241–53

Haskell, Harry, *The Attentive Listener: Three Centuries of Music Criticism* (London: Faber, 1995)

Newman, Ernest, *A Musical Critic's Holiday* (London: Cassell, 1925)

Price, Kingsley (ed.), *On Criticizing Music: Five Philosophical Perspectives (The Alvin and Fanny Blaustein Thalheimer Lectures, 1978–1979)* (Baltimore: Johns Hopkins University Press, 1981)

Thompson, Oscar, *Practical Musical Criticism* (New York: Da Capo Press, [1934] 1979)

16   Performers on performance

JONATHAN DUNSBY

How the performer feels

'I can attest to the fact that in all the days of my long life, I have never heard a single singer pronounce this happy truth: Today I feel well.' This comment of an international authority on singing may seem amusing, but it also entails a number of important indications about what performers think about performance. There is, for instance, an undoubted connection between performance and the performer's physical and mental well-being. Making music has many well-documented therapeutic effects, but it is always a physically taxing activity, if also often highly invigorating. Western music makes considerable mental demands, for example of the memory and the ability to concentrate. It also requires control of the emotions – or so it seems, in that one would be surprised to see a tear trickling down a violinist's cheek at a particularly moving moment in a performance, despite the importance of facial expression in the overall effect of an observed performance. As one writer put it when discussing the sense in which a performance is a simulation, 'performers at work may have their minds on any manner of things. In the spirit of professional entertainment, someone performing sensitively might simultaneously be bored to distraction and hankering after a restful career in real estate.'[1] Second, in the particular source from which the opening quotation is taken, the context is a discussion of what a singer should feel, and this represents a whole class of writings and other evidence by performers across the ages that performance has a 'goal' of some kind and is not a casual activity – not one that is, as it were, as good on a bad day as it is on a good day. Performing requires an exceptionally high degree of training and skill, right up to a level that was called 'almost superhuman' by one of the last century's leading conductors.[2] Third, since the quotation is in fact not from the recent past or even the last two centuries, but from 1757,[3] we learn that things may not change so much over the long term. Mozart's piano playing was written about in the 1780s almost as if he were an international competition winner of the past few years,[4] and ancient Greek mythology described Orpheus and his magic powers as a lyre player in much the same way as the 'reality' of mass communication in the early twenty-first century re-animates the quasi-divine presence of a Frank Sinatra or a Freddie Mercury – or, in the realm of instrumental performance, a Jimi Hendrix on guitar or a Stephane Grappelli on violin.

Performing music is such a positive activity, engaging so many kinds of human attention and human reflexes, that what we might call 'just playing' (and 'just singing') could seem to be mostly what performers think it is about. Yet clearly a surplus is needed to go beyond mere execution, and this is where a distinction must be made between those performers who are more inclined to the intuitive approach, and those who feel that some kind of thorough cognitive underpinning yields better results. Hans Keller – who was not only a remarkable commentator on music, but himself a fine player, and teacher of some of the best Western string players of the later decades of the last century – wrote of 'the unthinking player who prides himself [sic] on "just being a player", and who has never thought, but only felt music – who, in fact, feels thought to be the foe of feeling, whereas in musical reality, there is no feeling that cannot be articulately thought'.[5] He is telling us here that 'how the performer feels' is an inadequate premise for the study and practice that we are considering in this volume. If nothing else, it must be remembered that musical 'feeling' for the performer is an amalgam of emotion and intelligence, of response and control, of empathy and command, of the autonomic and proprioceptive (to use more technical physiological terms). To put this point at its simplest but also its most profound, and in a way that we can all somehow grasp, 'feeling' is an amalgam of being and doing.

It is plain that commentary on performance, worthwhile commentary, is likely to be extremely difficult. Writing about *pieces* of music, about such ineffable and mercurial phenomena, becomes at least doubly elusive when anyone is writing about the *performance* of pieces of music, about phenomena that, however much we may record them through technology, are like, say, a football match – in some way essentially over forever, once they are over. However, it is in the nature of human beings to want to understand and record what they are doing. There is no ungraspable distance between a cave drawing from 20,000 years ago of a wild animal that was once hunted – all the desperate and indeed lurid immediacy of what went on never to be recovered – and a newspaper report from one hundred years ago of a memorable interpretation of a recently composed Puccini aria. Similarly, just as prehistoric hunting practices essential for survival were passed on and codified, so some among the generations of musicians have grasped the nettle, faced the fact that there is such a thing as the *practice* of Western music, asked themselves how it is performed and have tried to express this.

How the performer feels about the music

José Bowen writes of the '*illusion* that there is such a thing as a neutral (or natural) performance style'.[6] If there is such a thing as this illusion, and if Bowen is not simply erecting a straw man to bolster his argument, I believe it is an illusion principally of the listener; but even then perhaps 'illusion' is not often the right idea. To give a concrete case, although I shall perhaps never be entirely comfortable with John Eliot Gardiner's modern, 'authentic' Beethoven symphony recordings compared with Herbert von Karajan's interpretations with the Berlin Philharmonic (the musical gold standard of the 1960s), I never once believed that Decca was enshrining something 'neutral' or 'natural' in its post-World War II recordings, before the age of 'authenticity'. All the evidence points to the fact that performers are and always have been aware, although perhaps not fully, that their work takes place in a cultural context. They know who taught and influenced them. They know that as they become older they are less open to influence in the sense of real change in how they do their work. They know that their 'world' of music-making can become increasingly irrelevant to new generations, but, conversely, that in old age they may have a special role in keeping an almost-lost style of performance alive.

If Bowen typifies the view of a scholar making a forensic examination after the event, rather than that of a performer who for an ulterior artistic purpose may need to have faith in some starting point without going too far into its credibility, he is nevertheless right to imply that performers do always display an attitude towards their music. Let us consider three questions that may be taken to represent a substantial cross-section of the relatively modern attitudes of performers towards their music. Why did Glenn Gould play Bach on the piano? What did Dietrich Fischer-Dieskau think he was doing other than 'just' singing Schubert's lieder with the right notes in the right order? And what is a conductor supposed to make of the musical score?

In Gould's case, we must bear in mind that not only was this master pianist by common consent one of the greatest interpreters of the twentieth century, devoted (almost pathologically, some have insinuated) to the enhanced quality of recorded sound, where the best elements of different performances can be spliced together into a performance at a transcendental level that can never, or hardly ever, be expected on any one, live occasion; but he was also a musical philosopher who was convinced that music exists in an ideal state never to be fully realised. This was obvious to him at a practical level. In an essay on 'The Prospects of Recording' (1966), he wrote: 'the determination of the value of a work of art according to the information available about it is a most delinquent form of aesthetic appraisal'.[7] Gould took the view that Bach did not have a particular claim to knowing how to write his music down or how to bring it to life in sound beyond his own immediate circumstances. It suffices that Bach was a genius of musical invention, and we should not expect the Cantor of the eighteenth century also to be an accurate futurist able to conjure up in his imagination the Steinway grand piano of the nineteenth and twentieth centuries. Gould was completely clear that Bach could no more anticipate the future (despite composing himself into it) than we can recover the past (despite our need to assimilate it). Had Gould lived into the authenticity debates of musical scholarship and, in due course, musical commerce beyond 1982, he might well have dampened down some of the historical and philosophical hubris surrounding significant contributions from non-practitioners.[8]

In this context, then, not only did Gould believe it right to play Bach on the piano, but an artistic duty. In a detailed essay on Gould's approach, Jean-Jacques Nattiez expresses the core of this aspect of issues of authenticity:

> Technology ought to free the interpreter, in choosing how to perform, from the tyranny of chronology, and the player has every right to freedom of interpretation, even to having more than one conception of the same work. For [Gould], Bach scores are nothing other than 'an excuse to build up an infinite variety of pertinent performance systems' . . . The same goes for the listener, who is encouraged not only to hear in a disk something different than Gould himself would have predicted . . . but for whom he hoped for a future period where technology would allow any listener to participate in the final make-up of the recording. Today, 'dial twiddling is in its limited way an interpretative act' . . . and tomorrow the listener should be able to choose from sixteen takes of the same passage . . . and splice together different kinds of interpretative solutions.[9]

There is a certain amount of thinking to unpack here. Since for Gould music exists in an ideal state – a platonic form, in fact – it is not an overstatement for Nattiez to refer to the 'tyranny' of chronology. By way of illustration, here are two apparently similar statements:

(1) Bach died in 1750 and could never have read these words.

(2) Bach wrote keyboard music for the eighteenth-century harpsichord which could never be properly performed on the piano in the twentieth century.

The first statement is self-evidently true, according to all we know of empirical reality. The second statement might be true but is certainly not the same kind of statement as the first. If whether it is true or not comes down to the word 'properly', we nevertheless see that there is a contingency in the second statement that does not apply to the first. Performing, as Gould teaches us so radically, floats free of time (and indeed place and all the other contingencies of the origins of the musical work). Yet Gould is not saying that the performer can do anything and get away with it. Far from this, he carefully – and this is to be found in different ways throughout his writings – ties the performer to the composition, here with the word 'pertinent'. Without going too much further in the argument, we can see that the listener, in Gould's technological brave new world, has a similar responsibility. We cannot even usefully guess what Gould would have made of the possibility, which now exists, of the listener deciding to listen to one of his recordings at a much faster tempo than issued but at the original pitch (a technology that was only in its infancy in the early 1980s). Maybe he would have thought this went beyond the 'pertinent'; but we shall never know, as the tyranny of chronology dictates.

From these challenging thoughts it is perhaps a little comforting to turn to our second subject, Dietrich Fischer-Dieskau, on singing the notes. He is clear from the outset that there is more to performing than getting the notes in the right order, if the perceived compositional value is to be conveyed: 'viewing . . . the time-span of German romantic song, one sees highlighted, as the essential point of departure for any conceivable future development, the need to express human feeling, to communicate, and to renounce mere sound-play'.[10] His commitment to such renunciation is undoubted, as can be heard in his vast legacy of recordings, but the technical is never far from his mind. Witness this careful reflection about Wolf:

the difficulties to which Wolf exposed both performer and listener were new and manifold. *Technical accuracy* was demanded to a degree that disconcerted his contemporaries. Until Wolf, no one had required performances with such a wide range of aural effects. The declamatory shape of the song seemed unsurpassable; Wolf, without demur, did away with *bel canto* and coloratura.[11]

More generally, Fischer-Dieskau feels that 'the interpreter as a kind of builder of bridges to the new that is to come . . . is left with the glorious task of preserving, by means of immaculate performance, the existing creations of the masters'.[12] Again, however, there is something to be contemplated beyond the apparent frankness of what is stated:

Though we arrive at a perfect mastery of the instrument to be played, the work, its spirit threatens to elude us. It is not easy for us to discern the principles of organization which have provided the work with its spiritual substance. We can only strive to hear the music in our own minds in the same spirit in which it presented itself to its creator . . . Music and poetry have a common domain, from which they draw inspiration and in which they operate: the landscape of the soul.

Together, they have the power to lend intellectual form to what is sensed and felt, to transmute both into a language that no other art can express.[13]

Here we see coming together many of the points raised above. Not only is the general argument supported, but in particular we are told about the performer lending 'intellectual form to what is sensed and felt', which as indicated seems to be a given of Western music. There is some confirmation too here of Gould's commitment to what German scholars of the twentieth century called the *Werk-Konzept* (the musical work as a concept) – in other words, to the idea that pieces of music exist in some kind of Gouldian 'ideal' state that the great performer must somehow capture, as Fischer-Dieskau puts it, 'in the same spirit in which it presented itself to its creator'. Fischer-Dieskau was clearly much more committed to the possibility that there is a historically pertinent *Werk* to be rediscovered, but it is instructive to see the affinities between two transcendent performers who, viewed locally at the time, were so different: the one, Gould, committed to not appearing live and to 'inauthentic' performance, the other soaking up the adulation of real audiences worldwide at the service of that holy grail, the 'spirit' in which this or that song 'presented itself to its creator'. There is an underlying match between these geniuses of the voice and the piano from recent times, who are vastly catalogued in the recent history of recorded music. What Jeremy Siepmann has written of Gould would be a legacy Fischer-Dieskau might have adopted of himself:

Regarded as questions rather than statements, let alone answers, many of [Gould's] most individual and searching performances are among the most illuminating on record. He has driven me time and again to go back to the score and learn from it afresh – not in emulation of Gould, whose most extreme mannerisms remain both inimitable and undesirable – but in search of renewed contact with the spirit and the endless fascination of the music itself. One can ask no more of any musician. In his best performances, and to a degree not matched by any other player, Gould induces a sense of consuming joy and wonder, and a jubilant awareness of the privilege it is to be alive.[14]

On the other hand, because his interpretations are shorn of experimenta-tion and appear to represent a mainstream standard, Fischer-Dieskau offered to audiences and to fellow specialists alike an acute feeling of 'authenticity' in its common sense, of a rekindling of the composer's so-called intentions ('so-called' because we can never really return to an earlier time, or for that matter ever really know what someone else is thinking). 'He understands what the *composer* felt', wrote another notable artist, the accompanist Gerald Moore, 'and is able to *reveal and express* it so piercingly that it goes to the heart.'[15] Yet where there is a lack of experimentation, there must be a tendency towards recycling rather than reinvention in what performers feel about the canonical repertoire, even a tendency towards 'cultural stasis'.[16]

This hint of a sour note will remain as we look at what conductors feel about music, at least in the opinion of our principal informant Gunther Schuller, who had a long and internationally successful career as a player, conductor and composer. Schuller tells us that 'the idea that a musical artist, a conductor, ought to serve the music – rather than the music serving the musician – is occasionally given lip service, but is rarely put into practice'.[17] He goes on to observe that conductors not only have often been less competent in certain aspects of their art, but have also taken the wrong attitude to the music. They should not be interpreting it at all, but rather their performances should be 'realizations' – and Schuller cites Ravel as his authority for demanding this. To give a concrete example, one might study his discussion of the opening of Beethoven's Fifth Symphony, an account intense in its detail, and sweeping in its condemnation of most of the ninety recordings surveyed which wrongly, he argues, place the accented first bar of each four-bar phrase consistently a bar late.[18] No one would blame Schuller for finding it remarkable, even irritating, that a point elaborated by the master-theorist Heinrich Schenker in 1925 was still being ignored nearly seventy years later by the conductor Normal Del Mar,[19] and had been ignored in thousands of performances in between. This is a particular case of a general point that Schuller finds confirmed in his study of recordings of eight major works of the symphonic repertoire:

The average audience, even many music professionals and 'experts', has little or no idea what, say a Brahms score really contains, what it really says. As a result, if the orchestra plays a performance technically well . . . an audience is likely to assume (how can it do otherwise?) that what they are hearing corresponds to what the composer wrote, especially if they have gotten some emotional charge from the performance. (As I have explained many times . . . the emotional charge an audience may get from a given performance may not be one intended by the composer, and may be quite extraneous to the music, may indeed be a substitution by the conductor.) The audience, the average listener, is left only with the ability to measure a performance by a sense of whether it was 'exciting' or 'not exciting' . . . What is the answer to these problems? . . . higher industry standards, more artistic integrity and honesty in the field; a more discriminating . . . better educated, more culturally literate audience and critical fraternity – goals and dreams of which we have fallen severely short in recent times.[20]

One thing can be said about how this performer viewed performance: he was not complacent! It should be added that this is not in any sense a call for some kind of de-humanising of a 'realization'. Schuller would certainly empathise with the pianist and noted writer and lecturer Alfred Brendel that 'to understand the composer's intentions means to *translate* them into one's own understanding'.[21]

How performers say performers should feel about the music

The views discussed above are necessarily somewhat generalised, but even so the informed reader may have suspected that some music-analytical focus would be inevitable in this overview of our topic. Certainly, two emblematic examples will enable us to encounter the possibility of a stringent need for and reliance upon an analytical approach to musical performance. First – and to some a little surprisingly perhaps, since this performer is the arch-romantic (in the popular mind at least) Sergei Rachmaninoff – is a comment on the crucial shaping of any piece of music at the point of climax:

This culmination, depending on the actual piece, may be at the end or in the middle, it may be loud or soft; but the performer must know how to approach it with *absolute calculation*, absolute precision, because if it slips by, then the whole construction crumbles, the piece becomes disjointed and scrappy and does not convey to the listener what must be conveyed.[22]

What exactly might Rachmaninoff mean by 'absolute calculation'? Presumably it will be represented by a different psychological state for different performers (very possibly related to what scientists call the bipolar balance of the human brain, which is a highly individual matter). Yet, to return to the *Werk-Konzept* mentioned above, Rachmaninoff is asserting that there is a musical structure in each piece, which exists independently from any particular performer. The performer has to identify the structure, assimilate it and control it well enough in real time to represent and, ideally, accurately convey it. Whatever the typical view of Rachmaninoff, who was after all one of the most 'inspired' and inspiring musicians of the early twentieth century, his commitment to structure should come as no real surprise from a performer of such consistent excellence who composed large-scale, extremely complex and in many ways modernistic music.[23] 'Calculation' is not, then, a startling concept in this context, but a memorable assertion of the control that musical structure must exert on the performer, and this implies that structural analysis in some form simply must be part of the performer's work, however hidden from the public gaze, however invisible in the final product. Indeed, the public may be surprised to find that performance itself typically occupies a rather small part of performers' attention. Actual performance is the tip of an iceberg of performers' practice and rehearsal, which in countless different ways is the 'analytical' level of music-making, the time when everything is put in place mentally and physically for the on-stage 'calculation' that has but one opportunity to be right. Otherwise, one is 'just playing'.[24]

Performers, then, are on a scale from being dimly aware of the analytical level (Keller's literally 'unthinking' player, mentioned above, is maybe rare, although this is not to minimise the general validity of his point) to finding it a constant and conscious issue, as is surely the case at the highest echelons of music-making and as has always been so in Western music. Theorists, however, are exceptionally well primed to be aware of the analytical level and to have figured out precisely what they think about it. It is not only Schenker's background as one of the most famous piano accompanists of the late nineteenth century, but also his development of a powerful theory about the structure of Western masterpieces that gave him the confidence to believe that 'performers on performance' should always acknowledge the priority of understanding over doing. 'Once the content of [a] piece is completely understood', he writes in an essay of 1925 on the Largo from Bach's Third Sonata for Solo Violin, 'performance poses no problems.'[25] He goes on to point out that there is a watertight correspondence between, for example, the 'primary dynamic shading' of the underlying structural events of a piece (those which articulate, as it were, its 'plot') and 'inner shadings' of the musical surface: 'Beyond all these shadings, still further, more delicate nuances come into consideration . . . But they must all be integrated into the primary dynamic scheme and the inner shadings of a higher structural order.'[26] He is also careful to remind us elsewhere, however, that a 'higher structural order' is not an excuse for the performer to neglect the tiniest details of a score, any more than 'the trail-map spares the climber the necessity of negotiating every path, stone and morass'. The detail, he says, 'must mean the same thing to the performer as to the composer'.[27]

Impressions

Closing remarks should also offer prospects. The voices from the past, which have been insinuated into the reader's future thoughts here, are making some clear demands. They ask for commitment and humility, which ought to go without saying. They also do not obscure some fundamental questions, to which answers are required so that one may get on with the urgent job of recreating the music of the past in the future, but which are never going to be somehow 'solved' for all time. Presumably it will never be clear what a piece of music actually, finally, decisively 'is'. Even to ask this is probably not the most intelligent and useful possible question. What a piece of music can best 'be' is a noumenal, memorable, consciousness-altering experience for the listener. This is what such as Mozart and Murray Perahia, to put one of the earliest piano virtuosos alongside one of the most recent, and Schuller and Del Mar, recent conductors whose thinking could hardly be more different, all offered in their daily work.[28] Yet the performers who do tell us about performance tend to record their views, as we have seen, at the thin end of the wedge, naturally preferring to concentrate on the fleeting goal, the product, rather than on the journey, the substantial process by which they arrive at the goal. If Orpheus did tame wild beasts with his lyre – and who are we to say otherwise? – he must have known exactly what he was doing as a performer.

Notes

1 Stan Godlovitch, *Musical Performance: A Philosophical Study* (London and New York: Routledge, 1998), 127.

2 Hermann Scherchen, *Handbook of Conducting*, trans. M. D. Calvocoressi (London: Oxford University Press, 1933), 3.

3 Johann Friedrich Agricola, *Anleitung zur Singekunst* (Berlin: Winter, 1757); quoted from Julianne C. Baird (trans. and ed.), *An Introduction to the Art of Singing by Johann Friedrich Agricola* (Cambridge: Cambridge University Press, 1995), 218. Agricola's work was an annotated translation into German of Pier Francesco Tosi's *Opinioni de' cantori antichi e moderni* of 1723, which had already appeared in English in 1742 (London: J. Wilcox).

4 See for example Michael Kelly's reminiscence of Mozart's playing in Louis Biancolli (ed.), *The Mozart Handbook* (New York: Grosset & Dunlap, 1962), 134.

5 Hans Keller, *The Great Haydn Quartets: Their Interpretation* (London: Dent, 1986), 15.

6 José A. Bowen, 'Finding the music in musicology: performance history and musical works', in Nicholas Cook and Mark Everist (eds.), *Rethinking Music* (Oxford: Oxford University Press, 1999), 445; my emphasis. For more on the idea of 'illusion' in performance studies see Jonathan Dunsby, *Performing Music: Shared Concerns* (Oxford: Clarendon Press, 1995).

7 Glenn Gould, 'The prospects of recording', in Tim Page (ed.), *The Glenn Gould Reader* (New York: Knopf, 1984), 341.

8 An outstanding historical contribution to this debate was Richard Taruskin's 'The pastness of the present and the presence of the past', first published in Nicholas Kenyon (ed.), *Authenticity and Early Music* (Oxford and New York: Oxford University Press, 1988), 137–207. In the philosophy of music a landmark publication was Peter Kivy's *Authenticities: Philosophical Reflections on Music Performance*

(Ithaca and London: Cornell University Press, 1995). For a remarkable psycho-biography of Gould, see Peter Ostwald's *Glenn Gould: The Ecstasy and Tragedy of Genius* (New York: Norton, 1997).

9 Jean-Jacques Nattiez, 'Gould Hors-Temps', in *Le combat de Chronos et d'Orphée: essais* (Paris: Bourgois, 1993), 46–7; my translation.

10 Dietrich Fischer-Dieskau, *The Fischer-Dieskau Book of Lieder: The Texts of Over 750 Songs in German Chosen and Introduced* (London: Gollancz, 1976), 11.

11 Ibid., 20.

12 Ibid., 27.

13 Ibid., 27–8.

14 Jeremy Siepmann, 'Glenn Gould and the interpreter's prerogative', *The Musical Times*, 131/1 (January 1990), 27.

15 Gerald Moore, *Am I too Loud? Memoirs of an Accompanist* (London: Hamish Hamilton, 1962), 178; my emphasis.

16 This notion is discussed extensively in Leonard Meyer's *Music, the Arts, and Ideas* (Chicago: University of Chicago Press, 1967).

17 Gunther Schuller, *The Compleat Conductor* (New York: Oxford University Press, 1997), 4.

18 Ibid., 109–24.

19 Norman Del Mar, *Conducting Beethoven* (Oxford: Oxford University Press, 1992).

20 Schuller, *Compleat Conductor*, 538–43.

21 Alfred Brendel, *Musical Thoughts and Afterthoughts* (London: Robson, 1976), 25; my emphasis.

22 Geoffrey Norris, *Rachmaninoff* (London: Dent, 1993), 78; my emphasis. This quotation is also discussed briefly in Dunsby, *Performing Music*, 93–4. Cf. Fanny Waterman's comments, quoted on page 108 above.

23 The Symphonic Dances and the Fourth Piano Concerto are examples of Rachmaninoff's compositional modernism, not, clearly, by the standards of a Schoenberg or a Stravinsky, yet it is now obvious that Rachmaninoff was anything but a 'conservative' composer. Even Arnold Whittall enquiring into the essential history of twentieth-century modernism allows Rachmaninoff's music the accolade of being 'entirely persuasive in its revitalization of traditional essences' (*Musical Composition in the Twentieth Century* (Oxford: Oxford University Press, 1999), 37).

24 Although this important truism does not perhaps need to be referenced, as a matter of record – and oral history – it was said in passing by pianist and conductor Murray Perahia at a rehearsal in London with the Academy of St Martin's in the Fields, April 2000. Similar views are developed in chapter 3 in this volume.

25 'The Largo of Bach's Sonata No. 3 for Solo Violin [BWV 1005]', trans. John Rothgeb, in Heinrich Schenker, *The Masterwork in Music: A Yearbook, vol. 1 (1925)*, ed. William Drabkin (Cambridge: Cambridge University Press, 1994), 37. The generic title of Schenker's volumes of brilliant, mature essays is *Das*

Meisterwerk in der Musik, and this author believes that the correct translation of 'Meisterwerk' in this context is 'masterpiece'. Cf. chapter 9's discussion of the importance of mental preparation.

26 Schenker, *Masterwork,* 38.

27 'Further consideration of the Urlinie: I', trans. John Rothgeb, in ibid., 109.

28 Two of these performers were also composers – although it is self-evidently a strange gambit to write that Mozart was 'also' a composer.

Further reading

Brendel, Alfred, *Musical Thoughts and Afterthoughts* (London: Robson, 1976)

Dunsby, Jonathan, 'Performance', in Stanley Sadie and John Tyrrell (eds.), *The New Grove Dictionary of Music and Musicians,* 2nd edn, 29 vols. (London: Macmillan, 2001), XIX:346–9

Dunsby, Jonathan, *Performing Music: Shared Concerns* (Oxford: Clarendon Press, 1995)

Moore, Gerald, *Am I too Loud? Memoirs of an Accompanist* (London: Hamish Hamilton, 1962)

Page, Tim (ed.), *The Glenn Gould Reader* (New York: Knopf, 1984)

Schenker, Heinrich, *The Art of Performance,* ed. Heribert Esser, trans. Irene Schreier Scott (New York and Oxford: Oxford University Press, 2000)

Index